New Ministries:
The Global Context

New Ministries:
The Global Context

WILLIAM R. BURROWS

ORBIS BOOKS

Maryknoll, New York 10545

The Catholic Foreign Mission Society of America (Maryknoll) recruits and trains people for overseas missionary service. Through Orbis Books Maryknoll aims to foster the international dialogue that is essential to mission. The books published, however, reflect the opinions of their authors and are not meant to represent the official position of the society.

Copyright © 1980 by Orbis Books, Maryknoll, N.Y. 10545

All rights reserved

Manufactured in the United States of America

Library of Congress Cataloging in Publication Data

Burrows, William R
  New ministries.

  Bibliography: p.
  1. Church. 2. Church renewal—Catholic Church.
3. Pastoral theology—Catholic Church. I. Title.
BX1746.B87   262'.14   80-17261
  ISBN 0-88344-329-5 (pbk.)

Contents

Preface

In a maturation so gradual as to have almost escaped detection from the outside, the missions founded in Africa, Oceania, and parts of Asia in the nineteenth-century missionary expansion movement of the Christian Church are on the point of becoming mature, local churches. Only one thing seems lacking. And that lack makes the present moment of passage a precarious one. This book means to address the crisis of dependency in Third World ministries by attempting to deal with a two-pronged question which gets to the heart of the major shortcoming in the young churches:

What model of local church fellowship and ordained ministry is most suited to help these young churches become both fully Christian and vitally relevant to their respective cultural contexts?

The moment is freighted with both danger and opportunity. Many of these churches could become, within a generation, self-ministering and self-reliant members of the World Church, if the opportunity is taken to encourage them to decide their answers to the question above. Or, if the true nature of the crisis is not understood and dealt with, they could remain caught in the web of dependency unwittingly woven by the good intentions of the Euro-American churches.

There is truth in the claim that there is, indeed, "a crisis of dependency in Third World ministries."[1] Our task here is to heighten our awareness of the complex and convoluted web of dependency built into north-south ecclesial relations. We will be arguing that the health of the World Church depends upon a recognition of the full scope of that dependency crisis, and a consequent action to overcome it by furthering true ecclesial independence in the midst of authentic communion and unity.

What follows, then, is an attempt to conceptualize the insight and articulate the stroke which will cut the Gordian knot inhibiting church growth in the Third World: dependence upon the Euro-American model of church fellowship and ordained ministry. The goal is to help identify steps which will unleash the creativity of Third World Christians, a spiritual energy often held in check by the need to express itself in foreign modes of thought and action.

The nineteenth-century missionary movement, which today is coming to a conclusion of sorts, was a success in bringing many people and nations to embrace faith in Jesus Christ. But it had presuppositions which need unearthing if we are to grasp the issue which today makes the passage of the young churches from dependence to independence so precarious.

ix

The most basic of those presuppositions, and the one germane to our present study, is the policy that the church in the Third World must adopt the structures of the church in Europe and North America.

James Bergquist and P. Kambar Manickam have traced out the way in which that presupposition operates in terms of what they call the *Missionary Standard Model*.[2] At the risk of oversimplification, let us take the Missionary Standard Model as a technical term describing the almost universal evangelization pattern utilized by Euro-American churches in the nineteenth-century missionary movement. The center of that model is an ordained clergyman who directs a mission "station," the basic unit in the organization of the conversion process. The source of inspiration for the model is the standard rural, European parish, either Protestant or Catholic; it is this parish structure which is modified for missionary purposes. Part One of this study revolves around an analysis of the socio-political and religious situation in the Third World, and attempts to show why the utility of the Missionary Standard Model is to be seriously questioned.

If the church needs a new shape in order to accomplish its mission, what is keeping us from debating the question and drawing the practical conclusions? It is argued in our study that presuppositions about the nature of the ordained ministry have predetermined the outcome of the discussion of either ecclesiological or Christological matters. In Part Two of the study, therefore, we examine the history of the development of the present shape of the hierarchical form of the ordained ministry in order to show that it is legitimate, even mandatory, to give the young churches the freedom to create models which reflect the requirements of their respective historical and cultural contexts, even when this would lead to their departing from patterns which previous generations of Christians have considered obligatory.

Thirdly, there is a need to suggest, at least tentatively and in outline, what sort of ecclesial and ministry models might help in the passage from the status of a dependent mission to that of a self-reliant local church. Part Three of the study makes suggestions regarding this issue. Because we deal with the church in cultures so widely differing from one another, our suggestions must be confined to the sorts of things which will free local Christians *themselves* to make the necessary changes. Here we do not want to be in the position of being one more group of outsiders telling local Christians what to do.

Though I write as a Roman Catholic, I have attempted to do so ecumenically. The good householder is one who knows how to bring both new and old wares out of his storehouse (Matt. 13:52). That we have tried to do here. One of the strengths of Catholicism, one underused today, is the richness of its history and traditions. What is required is the courage to open the storehouse and see that history gives us the warrants for bold experimentation today. It may be more necessary than ever before that

Catholics realize that part of the storehouse of Christian traditions is that which wears the label, "Protestant." Catholics must develop a willingness to treat their experience not as something alien, but as part of the common heritage of one church imperfectly united.

Our focus in this book is on ordained ministry. Many, however, feel that this topic is merely an "in-house" issue, and that to discuss it takes attention away from more important problems: social justice, or articulating the meaning of Christian faith in the contemporary world. Perhaps our choice of focus needs an apology. I have come to see the relationship of ordained ministers and the church they serve as rather like that of chickens and eggs. Chickens, of course, produce eggs; and eggs produce chickens. It is an endless cycle of reproduction and evolutionary adaptation.

In this process biological species and social groups face new situations and must learn from them if they are to survive. They pass on the benefit of such experience in their genes and in their libraries. The church, in a similar manner, is shaped by its historical environment. The clergy is the corps of men and women whom the church selects to guide it in the process of negotiating the slippery slide of history. It is clear that the church shapes its clergy. But does the clergy in turn not shape the church? And is it not true that today the ordained ministers have the major voice in determining how the church will react to its environment?

A major strand in the argument is based on a judgment that the balance has been struck too heavily on the side of giving decision-making power to the ordained corps. Serious enough in Europe and North America, this problem becomes extremely critical in churches where this corps of office-bearers is of a different culture than the laity. Moreover, serious attention must be given to the question of whether the present clergyman model of the ordained ministry does not inexorably force young churches into dependence upon parent churches long after that relationship could and should have ended.

We are, then, speaking of institutional change and reform. But such matters are often greeted with a not-too-polite yawn in the years of disillusionment that have followed the initial enthusiasm for reform which welled up in the reign of Pope John XXIII. Even the robust personality of Pope John Paul II has been unable to overcome that ennui. Indeed, one senses that the second John Paul may force the church to turn back from any major changes. His concept of ministry, though informed by acute sensitivity to the deeper problems that afflict the human spirit, seems Tridentine in desiring acceptance of the traditions of the last four hundred years. We shall be arguing that an adoption of the more pluriform spirit of the church's first four hundred years is more apt for the Third World.

Reluctantly, one might fairly conclude that the shape of the ordained ministry is one of those lesser issues which simply have to be faced at the same time as one addresses matters of greater intrinsic importance. For the manner in which the greater issues will be confronted depends, in large measure, upon the "basic Christian communities"[3] which, in a most significant sense, *are* the church. And the health, even the existence, of these communities in the World Church depends upon breaking the log-jam created by the present shape of ordained ministry.

One of the most serious issues facing the church today may be the isolation of the ordained ministers from a solidarity with the laity which would allow them to stand in their midst as persons with credentials to speak authoritatively. Just as the problems of each culture and historical epoch differ, so will the manner in which leadership will be exercised; so, too, must indigenous culture, history, and sociology affect the shape of the church's corps of ordained ministers.

Although we will be speaking mostly of "in-house" issues, such matters are not peripheral to the crises of our times. It is hoped that an explication of the history and theology of ordained ministry may help in creating a willingness to loosen up structures which have been frozen tight for several centuries.

Ordained ministry has a relationship to the local church as complex as that of the chicken to the egg. If we are to create effective local communities, the shape of that ministry must be able both to be discussed and to be altered.

*   *   *   *   *

Every book has its history, and this one's begins in 1972 when I arrived in Papua New Guinea from studies in theology at Rome's Gregorian University. My assignment, after a period of time to gain experience with Melanesian culture and mission methods in the field, was to teach systematic theology at Holy Spirit Seminary, the major seminary of the Catholic Church for Papua New Guinea and the Solomon Islands.

Anomalies in the seminary's operation and a sense that we would never accomplish our goal — providing indigenous replacements for some 520 expatriate priests —within any foreseeable time, led me to formulate my ideas in the following manner: (1) It was clear that foreign missionaries had ceased to be first-contact evangelists and had become *foreign pastors* mainly because there were no indigenous priests available to take their positions in the Missionary Standard Model. (2) *Were we in the seminary doing the church a real favor by uncritically accepting the Missionary Standard Model?* Or were we, perhaps, in a position where some radical questions had to be asked, by us, about that model and its presuppositions?

Everything we were doing in the seminary rested on the dubious presumption that the Missionary Standard Model was valid. The more I grappled with that presumption, the more I was driven to seek a theological and practical solution to the dilemmas it presented. The Roman

Catholic policy of training men to replace foreign pastors presently manning the Missionary Standard Model required both celibacy and a high level of education. It guaranteed, as well, long-term dependence upon Europe and America for both personnel and money, long after the Melanesian church should have been mature enough to stand on its own as one part of the world communion of local churches.

A second and more important issue touched the very life of faith. Everyone felt the need of a theology contextualized for the Melanesian scene. Yet only when Melanesians truly controlled the shape of their own church would they be able to carry out this task. Even well-intending foreigners were often wet blankets on such developments.

The chance to reflect systematically on these issues was presented when I was invited to prepare and deliver a series of lectures on ministry for the Association of Clerical Religious Superiors in Goroka in 1975. Encouraged by these men, and stimulated to go further because of their questions, I published the results of my initial studies in Papua New Guinea.

My confreres and friends in the Society of the Divine Word, especially Arnold Steffen, Nicholas de Groot, Kees van der Geest, Martin Neuhauser, Raymond Kalisz, and Patrick Murphy, gave me support and sustained my belief that the questions with which I was grappling were vital. Father Murphy died an untimely death in a road accident before this manuscript was completed. The topic of the rights and shape of the local church was dear to his heart and the center of his fruitful ministry. To him I owe much, both for friendship and for help in identifying and isolating crucial issues. John Beverley, Mary Smith, Wendy Flannery, Denise Coghlan, Patricia Carroll, and Mary MacDonald were loyal friends who cheerfully suffered through my endless monologues as a project steadily became a full-blown preoccupation and perhaps an obsession.

Most of all, I owe an unpayable debt to my students at Holy Spirit Seminary. They taught me a good deal more than I ever taught them. They, more than anyone else, helped me re-evaluate some of my most precious presuppositions about the meaning of Christianity and the church.

My friends, Morea and Loi Vele and their families in Gaire and Porebada, did more than they will ever know to help me participate in and appreciate the riches of the Melanesian way of life. Their families were members of the United Church of Christ. I had no official responsibilities in their villages; they made me wear no mask. I came to appreciate their unique and Melanesian form of Christian faith. Countless fishing expeditions to the glorious world of color in the outer reefs, joining with Loi's father, Heau, and the men of Gaire, put me in a world where I had to learn from them. It was one of the most significant experiences of my life.

Ill health forced me to return to the United States in 1977. I was already in the midst of expanding this manuscript when I began studies in theology at the University of Chicago Divinity School. There the lectures of

Professors David Tracy, Langdon Gilkey, Martin Marty, and Brian Gerrish sharpened my theological focus. These men helped me become more aware that religion is a perception of an invisible inner dimension penetrating the everyday world and to see Christianity not as a timeless religion but as intrinsically conditioned by history even as it has a mission to shape history. Professor Anne Carr, Associate Dean of the Divinity School, helped me identify and root out male biases in my ways of thinking about ministry, and to reflect on the Christological issues which lie at the heart of the doctrine of ministry.

A brief word on style and substance may be appropriate. I envision this book as a conversation with men and women to whom the future shape of the church in the Third World is a vital question. Many aspects of the conversation have ramifications for the churches of Europe and North America. But rather than focus on these, I have tried to center this book on questions most pertinent to the Third Church. I hope that some "mission in reverse" will occur as the experiences of young churches illuminate some of the problems facing the parent churches.

Footnotes have been kept to a minimum. They are utilized to explain terms or concepts which may be unfamiliar to some readers, or to give credit to an author from whom I have borrowed directly. Most of what is found on these pages is the result of my reflection on the thought of others. Countless conversations cannot be reproduced. The bibliography lists books and articles that I have found helpful and stimulating in pondering the topics of this study.

Much of the matter contained here will be controversial and controverted. I offer these reflections, not as a final word, but as a chapter in a debate which deserves a major place in church life as the faith community in the Third World struggles to become a more effective minister of God to a troubled humanity.

PART ONE

The Church's Ministry in
a New Global Context

1

The Church in a Global Village

The church is in the world as God's servant to minister to human needs, not to be served but to perform service in God's name. Few would argue with this, or with the theological principle that specifies the nature of the service which the church properly calls its own. Most would accept the notion that the service flows from the fact that the church is the community of those who believe in Jesus Christ as the revelation of God's concern for humankind's salvation. Jesus is the one in whom salvation's liberation has occurred and who reveals the shape of the world to come. In a mysterious manner, moreover, the church and Christ are one—he its head, and it his body in the world.

The church cannot be explained in other than theological terms. Though social, political, and economic factors are important, it is the theological dimension that makes the church Christ's body and not just another philanthropic organization. It is important to stress this in these opening remarks, for in what follows we will be reflecting more on secular issues than on theological ones, attempting to show how the secular issues constitute contextual factors which have an intrinsic bearing on how the more specifically religious mission of the church is carried out.

Today the theological statements made in the first paragraph are susceptible to the most varied interpretations, not out of a willful desire for bifurcation, but because people read the contextual dimension in different manners. Here I spell out my interpretation of the church's position in the global village in order to provide a foundation for later chapters where I will set out more concretely the sort of changes necessary in the structure of the ordained ministry if the church is to minister to the needs of humankind in many different contexts.

The Fundamental Contextuality of the Church

A context is the entire body of factors that surround and comprise a given situation. Contextual thinking is a mode of reflection that tries to take these various factors into consideration.

Aside from concrete social, material, and historical contexts, there exist only abstract principles. One of the problems in thinking about the church has been the tendency to consider it universally and abstractly, without coming to grips with the contextual factors that alone give flesh to its mission in concrete historical and cultural situations. To decontextualize anything is to rob it of what makes it either interesting or important, and any attempt to deal with the church from universalist perspectives makes it difficult to come to grips with important contextual factors which *intrinsically* affect the church's mission.

The aim, then, is to unfold the fundamental contextuality of the church in order to understand better why it is so vitally important to give priority to the development of local churches which are fully involved in the particularity of their own people's total cultural situation. Jesus himself makes this necessary. We are increasingly aware that he is a man understandable only in first-century Jewish terms. His message and the way he understood himself were in terms of his Jewishness in his own century. True, he transcended that context in what may be called a "wineskin-breaking ministry" (Matt. 9:17), but that transcendence of his own cultural heritage is misunderstood if abstracted from his particular life in a particular place and time. The scandal of Christianity is the claim that a matter of universal importance has been revealed in an embarrassingly particular man.

A brief analysis of sin and salvation points up the need to think concretely rather than abstractly about the nature of the church's mission and ministry. Salvation is offered by God as a way for human beings to transcend their personal and social limitations. Ultimately salvation is an offering of a spiritual "replacement" for what men and women "displace" in the act of conversion. But we shall be misunderstanding that act of transcendence if we think that the spiritual can be abstracted from the concreteness of sin as it is embedded in our personal and social situation. We are not taken out of the world, but aided to live in the world in a new manner.

Jesus is said to save us from "sin." Understood correctly, sin is a limit factor in human existence, estranging us from the ground of our being, from our truest selves. Before it is a transgression of any actual law or commandment, sin is the basic estrangement of the human being from his or her own self. Sin is larger than individual human acts of infidelity. Unfortunately, though, certain developments in theology have tended to make us identify sin with personal falls, and virtue with personal accomplishments. Such a view is an impoverishment of the notion even if there is a certain truth expressed by it.

It is important to realize that the root concept of sin sees humanity "wandering in the dark" and "missing the mark." The concept of sin makes sense only in the light of a certain goal or target in life which it is our vocation to arrive at, our fate always to fall short of. Sin wears a contextual face that differs from one people and culture to another, even if its most basic dimensions are defined in terms such as egoism, narrowness of heart and mind, selfishness, concupiscence, or the lust for power.

From a New Testament point of view, Jesus reveals the goal or mark for true human living, and in so doing unmasks sinful existence as a manner of life that is too narrow and self-preoccupied. His teaching on the presence of the reign of God in the ordinary affairs of daily life is meant to rescue human beings from too narrow a concept of the meaning of their lives, and propel them out into a world of transcendent values which are, paradoxically, to be found in the midst of the most ordinary matters: friendship, nature, offering fellowship, serving, responding to the demands of love, and political activity.

The meaning of life is more than eating, drinking, prestige, and personal well-being. In fact, it is in abandoning anxious concern for such things that the Christian is to find true freedom and fulfillment and to discover the power of God transforming the narrow self. This is a power and love that does not embrace the human being in the abstract but as a person, so personal that even the hairs of our heads are numbered. God does not love the human race as a global reality; God loves *individuals*. And the race is loved, as it were, on the rebound. As has been said, if Jesus' teaching is to be rejected, let it be rejected because it seems too good to be true. The mysterious, cosmic force that has brought forth life, says Jesus, cares for each person and is not to be known as deistic power or impersonal *mana* but as Father. We are loved not because we have a human nature, but because God loves the particular resonances of each person's self, the mysterious inner music that only *I* can make.

That is the positive side. Negatively, though, the teaching of Jesus cuts through sham and pretense to unmask the alienation and division that is the human's lot, the innate leaning a person has to be less than he or she ought to be. At an equally important level, it unmasks the propensity of society as a whole to close in on itself and its values of self-interest: the oppression of the human spirit in the name of the group, the exploitation of many for the benefit of a few, the demand for blind service to state and tribe. All these conditions make it impossible for many ever to come to a positive appreciation of themselves because they count for so little in the eyes of the powers who deem themselves important.

The church's mission is essentially a contextual ministry because the concreteness of sin and alienation differ radically from one cultural and historical epoch to another. What is universal is evil, but evil is not a univocal concept which has the same concrete meaning in every place and time. Rather, evil and sin are alienation and deprivations of goodness in concrete contextual situations. Estrangement wears one face in New York City, another in the slums of New Delhi, still another in the relatively affluent subsistence of a Papua New Guinea village. Here the Latin American theologies of liberation are instructive. Their proponents are acutely aware of the concreteness of sin, and the necessarily contextual response which the church must make to the ought-not-to-be situations of particular peoples in particular places.

Ours is not fundamentally a study in soteriology (the meaning of salvation) nor in ecclesiology (the meaning of the church). We are examining ways in which the ordained ministry of the church can be better put to the service of contextually relevant local churches. In this issue, though, ordained ministry makes no sense if it is not a reflection of much more basic soteriological and ecclesiological insights into the concrete nature of the church's mission. One of the persistent defects of the classical theologies of ministry and priesthood, as they have been applied in modern situations, is precisely the inability to come to grips with matters such as the ones we have discussed in nonwestern contexts. It can be argued, probably rightly, that the present malaise of the church in its Euro-American homelands springs from a similar inability to come to grips with the peculiarly modern forms of estrangement and sin.

The theory of ministry we are moving toward is broader and deeper than a theology of "priesthood," though priestly ministry is, we will argue, *one* essential component of ordained ministry. Ultimately the church exists only insofar as Christ is incarnated in actual communities which are in touch with the problems of concrete liberation. The ordained ministry is one of the means God uses to help local churches to do this. The Church Universal is a figment of the imagination except as a communion of local churches, but these local communities will differ as the concreteness of salvation differs from place to place. It is meaningless to propound beautiful theories of ministry and church if there is no local church wherein these theologies come to act.

In the following four sections we will examine some of the global vectors that shape the new contextuality of church life. In later chapters we will articulate a theology of the local church in the light of principles and insights now being established. Theology must learn to engage in what Shoki Coe has termed a "double-wrestle:" (1) wrestling with the *text*—the message received from tradition; and (2) wrestling with the *context*—the message of the contemporary situation.[1] Only in this way will one be in touch with the concreteness of life that gives flesh to the church's universal mission as God's servant. What it means to be "of service" to the world or to be the "body of Christ" in the world is revealed only in this double-wrestle.

Global Political Vectors Affecting the Third Church

Though global politics is a complicated business, to take some sort of stand on the morality found in its complexity is necessary. If my premise is accepted, that the church's concrete mission is fundamentally contextual, the attempt to take seriously the world of politics is important.

Vatican II's Pastoral Constitution on the Church in the Modern World is a plea for contextual thinking, even if the term itself never appears there. That document signaled the church's desire to take seriously the obligation to read critically the "signs of the times" in order to learn from these signs and to interpret them in the light of the gospel.[2] We are light years away from the heady days of the 1960s when many thought that this would be an easy task. Speakers who today begin with a call for the church to be "relevant" to the modern world elicit a groan of pain more often than a cheer of enthusiasm. Part of the disenchantment lies in the refusal of a stubborn world to follow the beckoning of theological wands.

Viewed in the broadest political terms, the church since the sixteenth century has ridden the wave of European superiority in military, economic, and technological power. Though it is not diplomatic to raise the point, it seems only honest to admit that the spread of Christianity in the modern missionary movement was at least partially due to the weight of European power and cultural prestige. The colonizers used the missions to "civilize the natives" in order to make them more amenable to the plans of the occupying powers. Many people took on Christianity just as much for the sake of adjusting to the new realities as for spiritual reasons. It was a way of gaining power over the colonial regime, and expressed their hope of a path to a materially better way of life. The direction of events was from a dominating north to a submitting south.

Though colonialism was neither an unmixed blessing nor a curse, it was undoubtedly the salient factor in north-south relationships for at least four centuries. However, there is little to be gained by arguing about whether colonialism was mostly good or mostly bad, for colonialism, at least in its classic form, is mostly ended. That classic form has been replaced by an even more dangerous indirect colonialism. It is this neo-colonialism, together with strong feelings against historical colonial relationships, which today constitutes a strong challenge to the Christian churches.

The departure of the colonial powers has been termed a *first liberation*. Although political independence was thus gained, that first liberation has often painfully exposed the fact that the new nations were not automatically bettered by the departure of the masters. The Latin American experience is instructively paradigmatic. The Spaniards and the Portuguese have been gone for well over a century, yet the South American nations have attained neither stability nor a tolerable standard of social justice and human development. Enthusiasm for independence has been replaced by cynicism as one government follows another without, in most instances, changing the situation for the better.

The first liberation of a people merely injects a nation into a more complicated world scene, which is often more violent than just. One family of nations controls the means of production of sophisticated goods and possesses the technology needed for further development, while the emerging nations are caught up in a whirlpool of power blocs jockeying for positions of influence, and are the recipients of the most confusing and contradictory advice on how to develop themselves. But one need not think only of macroeconomics and geopolitics.

Closer to the heart of many nations' problems lies the difficulty of creating unity between previously warring tribes and races. As well, there are the elites who owe their positions to the system established in the colonial era or to earlier class stratifications. They benefit from an unjust order, and would much prefer keeping the existing state of affairs rather than a reform, for they profit enormously from the jobs and cash which the system confers on them.

Tibor Mende is most instructive in the even-handed manner in which he assesses the complexity of economic development.[3] It will not do a whit of good to blame capitalism for all the ills of the underdeveloped world when the governments of the underdeveloped nations are unwilling to require the reform and discipline necessary to harness their most important resource: their people. Aid will never help if an infrastructure that favors self-reliance is not present. And this is a matter of an often-absent political will within the poor nations. But if self-reliance were to become the pillar of development policy, it is precisely against the privileges of the internal, national elites that political will would have to exercise itself no less than against external, international neocolonialism. Because of a reluctance to marshal this sort of power, a north-south name-calling match goes on with everyone blaming everyone else for the lack of authentic development.

Fundamental changes are required, not the least of which must take place inside the developing nations. Some would feel that these changes can be evolutionary in nature, not revolutionary, but this distinction may be illusory. Evolution, in popular imagination, is thought desirable, but in reality old manners of acting become costly and inefficient. Old habits are unable to cope with new demands. Species wither and die. Evolution is a painful affair, probably no less painful and bloody than revolution. One either adapts to changed circumstances or dies. That choice seems to be the issue facing the underdeveloped world no less than the industrialized nations.

Nation-states are born in the hurrahs of enthusiasm. They mature through painful trials. There is no other path. Greed, dishonesty, exploitation, manipulation, persistent tribalism, and racism all take their toll and become the forces pushing the human family to more comprehensive solutions of its problems. Today, then, we must speak of a *second liberation*. Ways must be found for nations to harness the energies of their peoples in the pursuit of humane development and the creation of an order of justice which will reflect the values of traditional cultures, but which at the same time will be adequate to push affairs beyond slogans. Without an authentic second liberation, the cycle of decline and misery will only pull nations and their peoples ever deeper into despair.

Freire is right when he sees the first step as one of "conscientizing" the masses, making them aware of their potential to determine their own destiny.[4] Too much talk about development is merely an exercise of the elite planning for others rather than a genuine participation with the downtrodden in a mutual effort to discern solutions. Without participation by all segments of society in critical self-awareness, there can be only a succession of changes at the top rungs of society while the masses remain sunk in passivity and despair.

What does all this mean for the churches? We are all accustomed to hearing the reiteration of the statistics of underdevelopment. In the industrialized nations of the north, this engenders a nagging sense of guilt which never leads to effective action. For the downtrodden themselves, such oratory may have a dangerous narcotic effect. For the repetition of a litany of sins committed against them easily leads to a tendency to blame others for their plight. "If international capitalism is responsible, of what use is it to work to improve things?"

What is too often not adverted to is the *guilt by association* which the Christian churches suffer. The church is seen by many to spring from the same northern hemisphere nations which are judged guilty of the wrongs done to the southern hemisphere. Colonialism and its aftermath are inseparably associated with the church. The specialist knows that the matter is more complex. The ordinary man or woman, though, is not an intellectual, and the churches' guilt by association could have an increasingly significant effect on how the church will be perceived.

Communism and socialism are often seen as prime movements of the future. Tillich has gone so far as to call the possibility of making the socialist decision the *kairos* of our day.[5] True, both socialism and communism are western ideologies, but they have a double advantage: first, of not having been tried before, and, second, of seeming more in tune with traditional communal values. Thus, if one wants to make a break with the colonial, capitalist past, they provide a ready-made model for reform. If and when that happens, the church is placed in an ambiguous position, for the missions are often perceived as a part of the legacy left over from colonialism and as rooted in northern-hemisphere, capitalist societies.

Moreover, and I do not think this is merely my own experience, most Euro-American missionary priests and bishops are capitalist in their orientation. When one goes further and realizes just how strong is expatriate influence, especially in Catholic missions, the church becomes a highly visible target for those who condemn the laissez-faire attitude that is the general mission position on political and economic issues. The church is made to seem unsympathetic to the aspirations of the socialism and communism of the "progressive" segments of the new nations. This is to be deplored.

In reality, to attempt to settle the problem by a socialist versus capitalist confrontation is probably too simplistic a means of solution. But these are the terms in which most progressives in the Third World have come to understand their nations' plights. At the very least, there is a growing social and psychological climate which is unfavorable to a church which seems to be firmly lined up with the capitalist powers. The Catholic Church, especially, because of its institutional cohesion and prominence, projects an image of siding with stable regimes, of being suspicious of socialism, and of preferring familiar evils of known corruption to the unknown demons unleashed by disrupting the status quo. This is a difficult matter to face.

On the one hand, there is no justification for jumping on every revolutionary band wagon just because it is the fashion to do so. Nor is there any justification for throwing the weight of the church in an uncritical manner behind any political force. Yet, when one considers the tensions involved, one is left with the impression that for a church favoring the status quo the most significant political vector of our times—socialism—is poised like a dagger aimed at the heart of the church's continued existence. Caution seems to be the preferred element in meeting the problem, but caution favors the status quo; and it is the status quo that is under attack.

At this point, little more can be said than to observe the following. Given the volatile nature of politics in the Third World, it would be a mistake for the church to *seem* to favor the capitalist system. In addition, whatever can be done to speed up the transfer of authority to nationals must be done. Expatriates should be in positions where they function under the supervision of nationals. Steps must be taken to reduce even the appearance of outside control. These points, however, will never be enough, for they are merely a passive reaction which will at best lessen the danger of injury.

More in keeping with the inner nature of the church is the exploration of ways to develop among the laity awareness of their responsibilities in working for social justice and human development. The church is not the hierarchy. Even though calls for the church to engage in social development work are often calls for the *hierarchy* to do so, this entire dynamic runs the risk of an updated but still pernicious form of Caesaro-papism. If there is any lesson to be learned from European church history it is that the involvement of the hierarchy in political questions is not an infallible means of promoting social justice. Fortunately or unfortunately, bishops, priests, popes, and cardinals have no special grace for reforming the state.

Just at the time when the renewed appreciation of the laity ought to make us aware of their role in the transformation of the secular order, a new species of clericalism seems intent on catapulting the hierarchy into politics. One cannot both contemplate a cake and eat it too. Either one accepts a basic community model of the church and recognizes many ministries, most of them lay, or one does not. Among many progressive Christians today there exists an acceptance of the basic community model along with a desire that the hierarchy be the force behind social reform.

It remains that the church must develop in such a way that it is seen to be clearly on the side of the Third World as a force for conscientization. To remain attached to the northern hemisphere is to be hitched to the dominant power in today's world. However, that does not mean that the church is on the side of social justice.

It would be well to remind ourselves that the present preponderance of power in the hands of the northern hemisphere nations cannot realistically expect to long endure. Scarcely nine thousand years ago people everywhere lived in relative equality in egalitarian societies. Then, in the Ancient Near East, a chain of events led to the foundation of cities and great empires. Eventually the rise of scientific thought and the political will to use technology and translate it into military and economic power led to the rise of the West and the shape of today's world. The European races gave birth to a new world order with themselves at the center. Today analysts realize that we stand on the brink of a new ordering of world power. Hints are seen in the power of the Arab oil cartels. India and Latin America are awakening. China is fully aware of its power. The African continent is a checkerboard, but the pattern is clearly one of a much more sophisticated awareness of the power and importance of its nations.

If concern for justice alone is insufficient, then an attentive reading of global political and economic vectors ought to influence the church to give more autonomy to the young churches.

Movement Toward Creating Home-Grown Institutions

Most of the underdeveloped nations of the southern hemisphere and elsewhere owe both their entry into the modern world and the shape of their governmental structures and institutions to the ministrations of their former colonial masters. In some cases there has been a happy blending of old and new. More often, however, the institutions are mired in frustration. This is only another way of saying that in the colonial era the traffic of influence was from north to south. Because of a dissatisfaction with the way governments, schools, health services, the law, and the churches operate, there is in progress a growing search for paths to develop home-grown ways of operating these institutions. No one seems able to envisage a single solution, but it is generally observed that the institutional forms left over from the colonial era are inadequate to meet present needs. The matter is made even more complicated by the evident fact that traditional cultures have been substantially eroded, and there is often little that can easily serve as a model for creating indigenous institutions.

The uneasiness felt toward imported institutions and the prevailing impression that they must be altered carry with them an important set of consequences for the churches. To date the churches have allowed only the most superficial alteration in structures, offices, and habits of exercis-

ing authority. This state of affairs has resulted from the common belief
that the basic church structures were divinely willed. Insensible to the fact
that many present-day practices are of merely human invention, church
leaders have elevated them to the rank of eternal truth.

Although Mao Tse-tung's successes in China may not have endured
long beyond his own death, he remains a paradigmatic figure who has
captured the imagination of Third World intellectuals. His greatest success was in contextualizing a western ideology and making it work in Asia.
The same is true for the strong attraction exercised by Nyerere in Tanzania and Castro in Cuba. The mysterious process whereby popularity
and acclaim are bestowed by the multitudes on a few tells much about the
deepest aspirations of people. The influence of these three men comes
precisely from their having been able substantially to modify western
techniques and ideology for their own purposes, and to put them to work
for their people. Whether in the long run they prove fully successful is less
important than the fact that they are *believed* to be successful.

What people believe makes them act. And today Third World peoples
believe that home-grown institutions are important. Except for incurable
romantics, there are few who believe today that traditional cultures alone
can provide the models necessary for the technology and politics needed
to shape a viable nation able to guide its own destiny in the contemporary
world. There are even fewer people who believe that substantial modifica-
tions are unnecessary if the colonial era's legacy is to be at all relevant
today.

If a church does not allow its adherents to modify its shape significantly
in the process of becoming a home-grown church, it will be like a seed
falling on thin soil. The seed may sprout and grow, but when the sun
comes up hot on the morrow (whether it be in a year, a decade, or several
generations later), the church will wither and die since its root system has
not gone down deep into the subconscious soil of a people's worldview.
Unless the mission becomes a church deeply rooted in native soil, it will
never weather the heat and the drought that will inevitably befall a young
church in a young nation. In that event, many Christians will be ashamed
to be part of a western cult in the midst of nationalistic revivals, and will
simply cease to belong to the church.

Decentralization of the church could be a first step in helping an
indigenous church to emerge. At the same time there are needed strong
national and regional episcopal conferences organized to give effective
leadership. Yet it is a fact that in the Catholic Church, Rome has kept the
juridical status of such bodies vague. While *seeming* to give the indigenous
church great powers, curial congregations have acted in such a way that
local bishops believe that, in fact, they have little *real* authority to allow for
significant modification of structures. The result is that, fearing repri-
mands if they exceed their authority, bishops forget that they themselves,

not the curial congregations, have responsibility for guiding the creation of a local church.

It would seem fair to say that the Roman congregations need to be restructured to give assistance to episcopal conferences, not to regulate them. The complaint is heard that bishops do not exercise the authority that they already clearly possess. This is probably true, but a large share of the blame must fall on those who have confused the entire question of whether or not it is the local church which really should run its own affairs. It would appear that detailed directions are still assumed to come from the top down.

To study how a human individual comes to maturity may be apt here. Maturity is not gained by a parent's waiting until a child shows perfect judgment before granting him or her freedom. At a certain point the child simply begins to act independently and to learn through painful experience. In the same way local churches could begin to act with some independence and gradually learn to shoulder ultimate responsibility for their decisions. Generally, however, quite the opposite happens. Many episcopal conferences function for only one week in the year, when the bishops are able to get together. Jealous of their individual independence, bishops fear to create meaningful secretariates with the authority to carry out conference policies. The lack of professionalism in some bishops' conferences may be just the reason that Rome is reluctant to clarify their powers and extend their authority.

That the curial congregations are professional cannot be denied. Complaints about such congregations should be limited to charges against the thrust of their activities, not about the seriousness and professionalism with which they approach matters brought to their attention. There is solid reason for saying that if local churches are to develop, they can learn a good deal from the professionalism of the curia.

It may well be that some expressions of dissatisfaction will be heard if bishops attempt to make their churches more home-grown in shape and style. Such expressions are nothing new in the history of the church, nor are they necessarily opposed to a spirit of charity. The Council of Jerusalem, recounted in Acts 15, shows that even at that early time in the history of the church, the central authority of the church, residing in the Jerusalem Christian Sanhedrin, had to face the issue of local initiative in controversial matters, and had to overcome hard feelings. It did so, not by paternalistically preventing disagreements from occurring, but by facing the disagreements fairly and squarely. This early incident, when central authority had to alter its views in favor of innovation in younger churches, might be taken as a canonical warrant for similar actions today!

The problem of tight control by the church's central organs of authority should not, however, be allowed to cloud the main issue. Even in Protestant churches where there are no strong centralizing tendencies, the same issue is acutely felt. There is a deep need for the young churches to modify substantially the Missionary Standard Model bequeathed them in the colonial era. Today that modification is taking place in only the most superficial matters. Yet without a home-grown shape the sort of fellowship necessary to secure a deepening of gospel inculturation will not take place.

Traditional Cultures and Secularization

A third vector affecting the future of the young churches no less than their parent churches is the impact of secularization or modernization on traditional cultures. In planning for the future it is important to realize that the young churches exist in lands where cultural stability is not to be taken for granted.

Recent sociological literature has tended to show the falsity of the notion that the best way to understand cultural changes is under the rubric "secularization." Peter Berger,[6] David Martin,[7] and Peter Glasner[8] have shown that secularization has been a term used as a catchall phrase, and that it may not be helpful for understanding what is actually happening. Nevertheless, the term has become almost universal. We will utilize it here in the sense given it by Bishop Lesslie Newbigin,[9] a missionary bishop of the Indian missions, who is familiar with the inroads that secularization and modernization are making in the Third World. His views may be summarized as follows. Secularization is:

1. A social process taking place throughout the entire world . . . leading to fundamental changes in the dynamics of all cultures and religions;

2. A process in which traditional mystical-supernatural-religious elements, which before held a culture together in a meaningful and coherent belief system, lose their hold on and ability to influence human functioning in the traditional manner;

3. A process in which technology, the idea of "progress" (variously understood), business-thinking, and critical, empirical, and scientific approaches gradually replace traditional epistemologies;

4. A process which has the *positive effect* of making possible transcultural dialogue, the achieving of a higher world order of unity, and the overcoming of former inadequacies, along with the *negative effect* of breaking down traditional cultural values and leading to disorientation.

This loose description is equally applicable to both the European and the American world as well as to the Third World. Its influence on the industrialized nations has been widely discussed. It is our task to consider it and its effects on the Third World.

To deal with the young churches and their members realistically, one must realize that even the remotest islands of the Pacific have to a great

extent been affected by secularization. Christian missions have themselves
been one of the principal bearers of the movement that now threatens to
swamp both traditional Christianity and indigenous religion. Christianity
has within it the seeds of a power that will inevitably weaken the animistic
beliefs of most traditional religions. Africans and Pacific Islanders, along
with tribal Indians and Buddhists, formerly lived in a world of ancestral,
natural, and regulative spirits. Their world was populated by spirit beings
who operated in direct and indirect ways to influence life; but today the
impact of education and modernization have tended to undercut those
beliefs. While traditional religion is still for the most part alive and well, it
exists in a truncated and syncretistic form that would hardly be recognizable by people who lived by these beliefs two hundred years ago. Today
traditional beliefs are blended with Christian and secular ideas in an
uneasy union. The liveliest forms of local religion in Africa and Melanesia,
for example, are the spirit religions and the "millenarism" which an-
thropologists also term "adjustment movements" (the Cargo Cults).[10]
These adjustment movements can be considered as halfway
stations between traditional and fully modern existence, breathing
spaces where men and women can contemplate the path to a new way
of life that has both a fascinating irresistibility and a fearful dimension to it.

Adjustment movements may persist for a longer or a shorter period, but
eventually they are doomed to failure as last-gasp attempts to understand
the new world in terms of an old epistemology. They are responses to both
Christian teaching and secularization. In them the soul of a people is
revealed much better than in the proper liturgies of the mainline
churches. This should be said positively even if one is pessimistic about
their staying power. They are the cry of the human spirit for life; they are a
perception that the heart of the universe is not inert matter but living
spirit, a living earth that sustains and gives life. As such they are a healthy
antidote to the rationalistic and overly doctrinal approaches of orthodox
Christianity, and the even less life-giving encroachment of science,
technology, and business.

There is another important aspect of the spirit churches and the adjustment movements. As schemes for social and economic development
are proposed by governments and international agencies only to fade
away with the slightest of practical results, it becomes clearer that the
inertia of "primitive" peoples will not be overcome until development
planning finds a rationale which will show itself to be life-giving and not
life-suffocating. What westerners may term "poverty and ignorance," the
rural masses may well consider a well-rounded and humane life, better
than that enjoyed by either the well-fed citizens of the northern hemisphere or their own educated and city-loving elites.

But even if the masses are fearful of and react against the impact of
modernization, it remains a fact that they are deeply affected by what they

resist. Change takes place even against one's will. In this entire context, Bishop Newbigin argues that we must note the positive, theological significance in the secularization movement. It is, he maintains, one of the elements in the historical process being utilized by God to nudge the world toward the coming Kingdom of God. The withering of traditional cultural values weakens racial and ethnocentric thinking. The disappearance of such patterns of thought and the creation of new, cross-cultural lines of communication can be considered a this-worldly manifestation of the kingdom.[11]

This positive element in secularization overcomes as well the secular/sacred duality that has bedevilled Christianity for generations as complex events have made faith in both Protestantism and Catholicism a private matter. For grace is present whenever people are reconciled to one another; and secular forces often bring about that reconciliation between once warring tribes and races more effectively than the preaching of the churches. This is just one example of how secularization can be interpreted as one part of the process God uses to bring about the at-one-ment of a broken and fragmented world.

There is grave danger that Euro-American peoples will believe that the impact of secularization is another example of the superiority of their culture and ideas over those of the underdeveloped world. The truth, when perceived from a Third World perspective, is somewhat more complex. While the citizens of the Third World may, indeed, be attracted to the material benefits which the secularization process may confer upon them, countless millions of these people refuse to be impressed by what secularization and modernity do to human spirits. Here they sense grave danger. "Why," I have heard Papua New Guineans ask, "are Europeans so sad faced and unable to enjoy life?"

This evaluation of the spiritual ravages with which technology seems to be accompanied in practice may well explain why the impoverished and hungry masses of Asia, for example, have not thronged with enthusiasm to the promises of modernity and have not given whole-hearted allegiance to modern nation-states. One should attend to a "silent language" spoken by many citizens of the Third World, a language which, unfortunately, few in the industrialized world seem capable of hearing.

Primitive peoples often speak a silent language of passivity and suspicion when they contemplate the international organizations coming to them with a myriad of plans for rescuing them from the developed nations' definition of poverty and ignorance. The inarticulateness of these peoples is often mistaken for a lack of intelligence. In reality, however, they know secrets too precious to tell, and their sullen silence is a very important, if often unrecognized, chapter in north-south dialogue. It is the hard-of-hearing do-gooder who needs to be open to the silent language of rejection given by these people to so many well-intended schemes for progress.

The silence of the masses is a phenomenon not often adverted to or analyzed. Yet we have a key to understanding that silent language when the success of small schemes is studied. Such development projects are usually the result of a long-term dialogue between a people and a single person who comes to live among them, learns their language, and respects them. The people soon recognize that this person can be trusted not to destroy their souls, and so they follow his or her advice. Secular change will be accepted only when deeper spiritual values are treated respectfully.

Despite the sullen reception often given large development schemes, secularization and modernization are still reshaping traditional societies at a great rate whether the people like it or not. Values are relativized. Radio and film make the masses aware that the values of their own clans are not universal; they see that other people have different values and survive, even flourish. So the process of modernization goes on, silently chipping away at the ethnocentric foundations of all cultures.

Christianity itself bears universalist and transcultural myth-destroying seeds that engender this process of relativizing even if it has never been free of its own brand of pernicious ethnocentrism. For the very image of God which the Judeo-Christian tradition proffers is that of a transcendent figure who, paradoxically, cannot be imagined. This is the fundamental genius of Judeo-Christian faith: God is a figure who cannot be domesticated and remain God. This entire paradox catapults the believer into a freeing transcendence which is the core of secularization itself. The world comes to be seen as having in itself a value that does not stem from an animistic sacralization of matter. Neither do people have to follow blindly the patterns of life laid down by their ancestors. For God is personal, rational, and loving, and has given freedom to human beings to shape the world. God's plan is not foreordained regarding the minutiae of life, but a conferral of intelligence and responsibility on men and women. The Christian religious dimension enters when one realizes the religious dimension of ordinary existence. Human beings become God-like precisely in accepting responsibility for acting intelligently in their world.

When the ministry of the church takes place in the context of a global village, in which we find secularization freeing humankind from a passive acceptance of fate, the task of the church is one of helping people to realize the transcendent stakes at play in commitment to the world. The search for justice and authentic human development breaks through sacralized, given patterns of what "must be" to help us realize that we have the possibility of shaping worlds that never have been and yet might be. Such is the intrinsic dimension of morality: freedom of choice and responsibility to enhance and to transform humanity.

The Christian church's mission in the context of cultural changes and relativization of values is to help the people who are guiding the entire process to remain aware of the transcendent, theological significance of what is essentially an inner-worldly, secular event. Awareness of this transcendent significance will be revealed more surely by deeds than by words, and this focuses attention on the concrete forms which Christian communities can and should assume if they are to be an intrinsic part of the change.

The Changing Shape of Ecclesial Life

If secularization weakens the hold of both traditional Christian and non-Christian religious interpretations of reality, what does this entire flux mean for ecclesial life in the Third World?

That secularization has led to a decline in the influence of the churches in the western world is easily seen. And despite the fact that many theologians have greeted this with positive reactions, there remains the anxiety which the decline in public religious observance has caused church leaders and the ordinary faithful. In the Third World the pattern is hardly clearer than in Europe and America. Indifference to Christianity is possible in a way that indifference to traditional religion never was. For, on the one hand, traditional religious belief was a part of one's blood and soil; the question of individual commitment to it was scarcely raised. And, on the other hand, numerous people became Christian because it seemed a better way of gaining the same this-worldly security promised by traditional religion. When Christianity failed to deliver its expected results, the stage was set for syncretism. The vitality of syncretistic movements is well documented everywhere and seems to show that the "quantity" of religious emotion has not been diminished by modernity even if a certain malaise about religious truth has set in. It may only be because the sociologists of religion who report these phenomena enjoy the discomfort they cause the mainline churches that they do so in such detail and with such relish. It is nonetheless apparent that the religious scene in the Third World is disconcertingly pluriform. Adjustment movements, spirit churches, and secularization represent profound challenges to the mainline churches' attempt to proclaim themselves as *the* vehicle of God's providence.

Traditional explanations of life and means of controlling spiritual powers have lost their coherence and dominion, but it is not apparent that the mainline Christian churches have offered anything equally satisfying. Ancestors, who yesterday were revered for having taught a valuable way of life, may today be feared when a taboo is transgressed, but they are no longer objects of veneration as they formerly were. Nor are the expatriate missionaries any longer considered the purveyors of absolute "truth."

It seems more honest to deal with the entire complexity of the present religious situation by saying that something is being born, but we have little idea of what it will resemble when it comes to maturity. In the main, though, both Protestant and Catholic Christianity have presented themselves as means of spiritual salvation. First adhered to with enthusiasm, today they are seen as having only a tangential relationship to the more concrete problems of life. If the future continues the same basic configurations of interest, what can be expected? Will Christianity be eventually relegated to the peripheries of life? Nothing could be further from the intent of Christ. The following models make no claim to be all-encompassing, but they do represent some possible futures for Third Church Christianity, and are based upon present today conditions.

CONTINUATION OF PRESENT MODELS?

If the church continues its present mode of operation, especially if it presents itself as a community offering primarily a spiritual salvation beyond this world, can we expect anything but a continued alienation of the urban elites who will shape their nations' political, economic, and social futures? It would seem that rural Christianity might persist as at present, a major influence on peoples' lives, but it would not be a force for conscientizing these people and putting them into the mainstream of decision making for the future.

Though the churches until now have been eminently successful in their work in the Third World, largely because of their heavy involvement in education and health programs, the day seems to be coming when secularization will crowd out anything more than a nominal presence of the church in these areas. Increasingly, in most Third World nations, education is dominated by persons for whom the churches' religious concerns are marginal in importance, yet present models of church activity are heavily weighted in the direction of educating youth and are centered on the rural populace. Indeed, the church finds it difficult to get into touch, not just with the educated elites, but with the simple workers who throng to the cities. But it is in the cities that the future of these nations seems to be unfolding. Thus, to continue with present models would seem to be an option for marginality.

NEW METHODS FOR URBAN AREAS?

It might seem possible to develop new methods for making contact with urban Christians while maintaining the present models in the countryside. At first blush this is an attractive option, but when one looks more closely, it appears to be merely a stopgap measure. To provide the number of fully trained clergy necessary to make contact and establish urban communities would utterly deprive the rural areas of necessary ministers. These rural areas are already struggling merely to keep open the mission stations begun in the era of postwar mission expansion.

This difficulty has become apparent in Papua New Guinea where the Society of the Divine Word declared the urban areas to be areas of primary concern and has tried to provide priests for the urban apostolate among migrants. However, these attempts immediately run into a two-pronged dilemma. Most of the missionaries are plagued with a feeling of inadequacy when asked about going to the rapidly-growing cities. Secondly, the rural bishops, hard pressed to keep their parishes staffed, feel that they cannot spare the "key men" who are asked to leave for the cities. As well, there is the problem that also plagues the European and American world: how does one explain teachings of the gospel to urbanites? Given the present organization of the church, it will be difficult to develop new methods for ministering to the urban masses.

TURN TO A "BASIC COMMUNITY" STRATEGY?

More and more one hears that the strategy of the church should be one of identifying basic communities which already exist, and then of developing forms of ministry which will allow these already existing communities to become the model and locus of the church. As will be apparent in later chapters, this is the option I feel is most realistic. Here it will suffice to note that such a move would entail a substantial modification of church structure, particularly since it will soon be clear to anyone who tries to implement such a strategy that it involves challenging the entire clerical structure of the ordained ministry and the stranglehold it has on the meaning of "church." In rural areas it will involve shifting from utilizing large central stations to making local villages the basic unit in church life. In this plan, one runs immediately into the question of who will be entrusted with sacramental ordination and ecclesial authority. Large numbers of part-time leaders will be required. And the present church structure and ordination policies make it difficult either to find or empower such men and women.

The question of identifying basic communities and creating forms of ministry to help them become true local churches is the subject matter of the rest of this book. But the attempt to reshape the church to respond to such needs in Third World conditions runs quickly into presuppositions about what form the church is allowed to take. It will be argued that we have allowed Euro-American presuppositions to stifle creative thinking and practical response. This strong statement is made not to impugn the motives or denigrate the hard work of missionaries, but to invite critical response and dialogue.

What do we mean when we speak of "basic community" and say that such groupings should become the "local church?" The term, as it rises out of the Latin American and Filipino attempts to find more natural ways to live the Christian life, means: (1) identifying meaningful sociological units where face-to-face relationships either exist, as in a rural hamlet or an urban compound, or where such units would answer felt needs for community, for example, among professionals who, though not geographically united by dwelling close together, are united by their special vocational concerns; (2) attempting to use these groupings as the basic model of church to replace the traditional "parish" with the full-time, fully trained clergyman at its center; (3) doing this in such a way that these basic communities become centers for liturgical worship, formation, and the praxis which would flow out from the group into society-at-large as a response to the gospel message.

The upshot of a basic community approach would be a restructuring of the local church at the grassroots in order both to help people to under-stand better the meaning of the gospel and to offer them the empower-ment of the Spirit to transform their daily lives. One problem with the current large parish or mission-station model of the church is that religion easily becomes peripheral—a matter of Sunday church-going. Now that was never the intention of the church in using the current parish model. It is just a fact that social changes (both in the Euro-American homelands of the church and in the areas we loosely call "missions") have brought us to a point where our institutional shape may be too rigid to deal adequately with formation needs, worship styles, and praxis.

What I am attempting to develop in the rest of the book is an approach to ordained ministry which will be faithful to theological tradition yet flexible enough to help in the identification and creation of such local churches. There will be corresponding needs for change at the diocesan level of church life as well as at national and international levels. The key to it all, though, is a shift to a basic community model of the local church.

2

A Dependency Crisis in the Third Church

Dependence vs. Interdependence in the Church

A healthy world order would be marked by interdependence among nations and institutions, all blended with self-reliant independence. Peoples and nations, even in a just world, will necessarily depend upon one another, for not even the largest nation-states are completely self-sufficient. But today there is a power balance which allows a few countries to dominate international affairs. They are, of course, the nations bordering the North Atlantic and Japan.

Not all these nations' power is directly political. We are increasingly aware that giant transnational corporations follow a law of their own, and may be even more important than the nation-states they spring from and paradoxically transcend. Perhaps the most significant economic and political current of our time is the agonizing search for ways to reduce this sort of dominance in order to create a world order in which freely chosen, interdependent collaboration between equals can make the globe we live on contribute more to humane life.

While we may be willing to face the fact that political and economic powers have been used unwisely to create dependence in the secular realms of business and politics, what may be new is the realization that this same pattern is part and parcel of the younger churches' relationships with the Euro-American parent churches. The pages that follow will provide reflections on this dependency pattern.

Fr. Walbert Bühlmann, O.F.M.Cap., introduced the term "Third Church" in his widely acclaimed book on the World Church in its new global context.[1] Bühlmann's *The Coming of the Third Church*, together with writings of Adrian Hastings, Choan-Seng Song, Leonardo Mercado, Kosuke Koyama, and Charles Nyamiti underlie our entire argument. For Bühlmann, the "First Church" is the Church of both ancient and modern Orthodox Eastern Christianity. In terms of world development, the First Church was eclipsed by the "Second Church"—Latin, Roman, and Catholic—when western Europe rose to predominance and the First Church was confined by the rise of Islam. In terms of world Christianity, the Second Church (and its Protestant offspring) became *the* Church.

In the colonial era northern Europe became the power center of the world and, in the sixteenth century, exporter of the first modern missionary movement. In that first missionary movement, Catholicism entered

India, China, Japan, the Philippines, and Latin America. In the nineteenth century, with an equal impetus from Protestantism, a second effort was mounted in Japan, India, and China, and a huge first-contact effort was begun in Africa and Oceania. The Third Church has been the result: a church which in 1960 comprised 48.5 percent of the world's Catholics, and which in the year 2000 can be expected to make up 70 percent of Catholic Christianity.

Bühlmann's thesis is twofold. First, changes in the international political order will make domination of the Third Church by the Second Church increasingly intolerable. Second, the very nature of the church makes this political intolerability assume theological dimensions. The Christian church, by reason of its very essence, is supposed to incarnate a living Christ and not merely to purvey doctrine and philosophy. It is not simply an international religious organization. Moreover, in its incarnational vocation the church has an obligation to reflect on the deeper implications of the new global context, and to do whatever is necessary to make its structures and modes of operation fit the nature of its call. It is not sufficient to plant a Second Church model in the Third World.

Our discussion revolves around the shape of the ordained ministry in the Third Church, and its primary referent will be world Catholicism. However, our study is also ecumenical since, with only slight differences, the same forces are at work in the Protestant churches. While we concentrate on the Third Church, I do not mean to exclude the Second Church from the reader's attention. It is only too evident that the ordained ministry, indeed the very shape of the church itself, presents a problem for the Euro-American churches as well. But the urgency of the crisis is much more acutely felt in the Third Church. The question is whether the way the church has structured its ordained ministry does not necessarily entail a continuation of an unhealthy dependence of the Third Church on the Second, long after that relationship should have shifted to self-reliant interdependence.

When the sixteenth-century missionary movement began, there was no thought but that the shape of the church in its new homes would be that of the Latin Christianity that had sent the missionaries. Though Matteo Ricci in China and Roberto de Nobili in India challenged that assumption, their initiatives were finally rejected. The same is true of nineteenth-century missionary activity. If numerical success is a gauge of intrinsic success, it is clear that missionary movements failed in areas where people adhered to "higher" religions and succeeded in areas where people had "primitive"*

---

*The word "primitive" has often been used with the meaning of "crude." In our opinion it is a word that deserves rehabilitation to designate cultures which still retain a close relationship to the origins of human life and where modern, critical, scientific thought has not supplanted traditional, mythic consciousness, as it has *to some degree* in the highly technological northern industrial nations.

beliefs and were more insecure in the face of the colonial incursion. Today, though, the somnolence of these once primitive peoples is fast coming to an end. Education, politics, religious ferment, the World Wars, technology, and economic factors have caused intense dislocation. True, the bulk of the rural populace still pursues traditional ways, but former beliefs and practices are under assault and are losing ground. Will such cultural changes also bring to an end the current widespread influence of the Christian churches? Religious indifference was impossible in traditional cultures; it is increasingly a live option today for many bewildered peoples.

The colonial era gave the churches positions of immense influence in Africa and Oceania. To a large extent, in fact, it may be said that people embraced Christianity as much for the motive of attaining modernization and a better way to cope with the new political realities of colonialism as for purely "religious" reasons. When it is discovered that a better material way of life is possible without Christianity, will many be likely to abandon the church? Will the desire of such people to direct their own destinies engender a widespread hostility (already evident among many of the educated elite) that will be wary of a church that seems to be the last visible vestige of colonial domination?

This is a delicate, though not a subtle, matter. In facing it, some of the Second Church's most cherished presuppositions about the meaning of being Christian will be challenged. An honest contextualizing and inculturating of the gospel, along with the challenge of developing forms of fellowship which will bring together local believers in vital, basic communities of faith, will demand far-reaching changes in mission policies. It is not enough to give a notional assent to the need to adapt liturgical and institutional forms in external matters. More important is the need to find ways of life in community which allow and encourage nonwestern Christians to express what their encounter with Christ means to them.

The ordained ministry in the Third Church is one of the key factors that will help or hinder the process of a local church's coming to a self-conscious, mature independence. The relationship of clergy to church is, we have said, like that of the chicken to the egg. Which produces which? The only answer is that each creates the other. Is the present shape of ordained ministry in the church likely to further inculturation or hinder it? Will it aid the local church to become self-reliant in an interdependent communion of local churches, or keep Third World local churches dependent? It is our argument that the clergyman model of ordained ministry may well be a negative influence, perhaps *the* major way in which cultural imperialism remains alive in the church.

To those used to thinking of missionaries and their efforts with awe-filled reverence for their sacrifices, this may be a hard truth to swallow. The hard work and dedication of generations of missionaries are not here being demeaned. Third Church members will, in fact, be among the first to sing the praises of their missionaries and laud what they have done to help them towards a more humane way of life. But even the best-intended gift may endanger the independence of the receiver if both partners in the exchange are not careful to give and receive in a way that will help the recipient to become self-reliant.

The entire issue makes sense only in terms of the modern shift in attitudes toward two important dimensions of human existence: history and culture. Modern historical consciousness entails an awareness of the basic relativity of any social body or theoretical position. Put in the barest way possible, the problem of theology and church today is that we have become *theoretically* aware of historical relativity and the complexity of historical process, but have not yet been able to draw the *practical conclusions*. There is a sense in which the European past of the church is still being made absolute and normative for nonwestern peoples. The a-historical person sees ferment in society and church as the lamented disintegration of divinely willed and sanctioned ways of life. The historically conscious person, on the other hand, realizes that such shifts have always been a part of church life, and that today we witness only a speeding up of a process which formerly was so gradual as to be almost invisible.

The problem for the churches today is one in which historical relativity is linked to a new appreciation of cultural relativity. The contemporary world is one in which nonwestern perceptions of the nature of reality and the meaning of human life greatly diverge from both Roman Catholic and Protestant orthodoxy's understanding of the world. Such ideas should force us back into church history to ascertain how western Christianity developed. We would discover, for example, how ancient Teutonic and Celtic myths and worldviews were allowed to influence the gospel message. We would realize that such cultural elements have always had a profound influence on Christian self-understanding. Western church leaders would be led to allow other cultures to have their moment in a similar situation today. None of this is new to theoretical missiology. What would be new in the present context would be to allow the young churches the same freedom which the parent churches once enjoyed. It is a matter of letting happen on the practical plane what we have long given theoretical assent to.

Cultural relativity is not a new fact. The human race has always been characterized by a plethora of different cultures. What is new today is a different perception of the meaning of cultural relativity and the existence of cultural imperialism. What is to be faced is the fact that a church which has long thought of itself in terms of universal values stands accused of imposing its own relative cultural perspectives on the young churches.

As Christian self-understanding developed in the encounter which was played out between the Hebraic-Greek-Roman thought worlds and the world of the northern peoples who have become the major purveyors of Christianity to the modern world, certain understandings of normative cultural values developed. In the encounter with the primitive cultures of Africa and Oceania since the nineteenth century there has been predominant until recently a conviction of the superiority of European cultural values. This conviction of superiority led the missions to establish schools where the languages of instruction were European and the curriculum largely western in content and orientation. However, in the interests of honesty, it must be admitted that many Third World peoples shared the assumption of European cultural superiority. It is not very useful to accuse anyone of moral fault. The issues are far too complex and intertwined for that to be helpful.

What is important to realize, though, is the fact that the shape of the missions today emerges from an era when it was presumed that to become fully developed, local churches would have to resemble their Euro-American parents. Western canons of acceptability and what would count for "culture" were rooted in Greco-Roman standards and norms. It was the demand that the converts adhere to those canons that led to the failure of the church in the highly developed and self-confident cultures of China, India, and Japan. Thinking members of these cultures and religions quickly realized that their own canons of acceptability were equal and often superior to European norms. The reason for the poor results of Christian mission among the higher classes of Asia can be attributed to the refusal of the church officially, at the level of policy, to sustain the creative work of such men as Ricci and de Nobili.

This may seem a highly abstract and oversimplified presentation of both history and the contemporary situation. But it is important to realize that this necessarily simple reading of the facts uncovers presuppositions on the shape of local churches which still operate today. It was not uncommon even as late as 1965 to hear missionaries from Papua New Guinea and Ghana say that there would be a need for foreign priests in the "missions" for another century or more. The desk of any superior general of a mission-sending society is even today covered with requests for missionaries. Why? Because of the assumption that it will take several generations more for "natives" to master the skills necessary to administer the church, and for sufficient numbers of fully trained and (for Roman Catholicism) celibate clergymen to take over the work of the expatriate missionaries.

The present shape of the church demands a high degree of westernization and acceptance of Euro-American values before nationals will be allowed to assume positions of responsibility. Presupposed by both Protestant and Catholic Christianity is the demand that the Euro-American model be adapted to the local situation. Missing from official policy, though certainly not from its theory, is a realization that faith and Christian life must be inculturated, not just adapted to local cultures. It is to be lamented that these practical, common sense, policy blind spots insure that the Third Church will, for the foreseeable future, be dependent upon the Second.

Inculturation as a Theologial Necessity

Western civilization has assumed that there is a universally valid standard for all of humanity. The *homo universalis* of the Renaissance is the epitome of the "Universal Man" envisaged by European Christianity. That Universal Man was, first of all, elitist. He was formed by the study of classical languages and literature, had a knowledge of music, art, and poetry, was able to speak Latin, write Greek, and read Hebrew. Here the use of the masculine pronoun "he" is not a mere lapse into the world of grammatical convention, for "he" was the model, not "she."

Nowhere has this picture of the Universal Man been so completely accepted as in the *ratio studiorum* (plan of studies) devised for the Catholic priest. That plan is still basic to Catholic seminary education's self-understanding. While almost all its details have eroded with time, its thrust is still alive and well. The ideal of the Universal Man must be at least approached before a man can be considered for ordination. That ideal has had a great negative impact upon the process of inculturating Christianity in nonwestern cultures. It must be examined critically, because the sociology of knowledge today makes us keenly aware of the importance of nonconscious cultural biases in imparting a sense of the important and the real.

At present the path to "official" responsibility in the church, the sole path, is the seminary. And the seminary is not so much a community in search of ways to carry the ministry of leadership into new contexts as it is a place where universal basics are imparted in the lecture hall. Only the men who receive these basics are considered for ordination and future high responsibilities in the church. The tendency to send the best and brightest to Rome—precisely at a time when at home they would be entering manhood and learning to appropriate their native culture's deepest values—has insured that most national bishops in the Third Church have high respect for the European and Roman roots of Catholicism. But whether a man studied in Europe or in his homeland, the result would be more or less the same. The modern seminary curriculum in the Third World may be different in details from the Tridentine seminary curriculum, but the underlying spirit is identical. Seminaries in the Third World have certainly made great strides in teaching more culturally relevant material. That must be stated quite clearly. But the goal of seminary training remains the same: to prepare a man to be the equal of his fellow priests and of cultured men anywhere in the world, the standard being the western notion of the *homo universalis*.

Success in attaining that goal has not been lacking, and the very keenness of Third World governments to obtain the services of priests and ex-seminarians for demanding jobs is proof of a certain success. Seminary graduates are generally recognized as being among the most competent men that a Third World government can call on for service. It is an accomplishment that the seminaries can rightly be proud of. But is it an aid to the inculturation of the gospel message?

The thrust of seminary training toward fashioning the Universal Man aggravates the crisis of dependency by hindering inculturation and contextualization of the gospel. This does not mean that our schools should not teach men and women the processes of logical thought, and bring them into contact with the best that international scholarship has to offer. The question is this: do *all* future priests have to go through the sort of training now presupposed by general ecclesiastical law? Because of international Roman Catholic policies, a certain latitude is allowed for the adaptation of the so-called *ratio fundamentalis* (basic plan) of priestly training. But again the key word is "adaptation," and adaptation of the message does not go far enough.

It has become increasingly clear that secular university eduction alienates Third World graduates from their people. Is the same true of seminary training? In cultures where dreams and myths assume a tremendous importance when people are puzzling their way through life's questions, does a critical, highly rational approach to reality necessarily turn out the best minister? Christ will be successfully incarnated among such people only when he and his message become the stuff of dreams and visions and enter into the dilemmas of decision making in a manner difficult for most westerners to appreciate. Can the graduate of a highly rational, scientific, theological program participate meaningfully in the myth-dream world of the villager?

In the face-to-face, community-centered cultures of traditional life in areas of the world like Melanesia or Africa, virtually everything becomes grist for discussion around cooking fires or in breaks between chores such as gardening or house building. Spirit beings are thought influential in matters such as sickness or health, the fertility or barrenness of women, the success or failure of a garden. Where does Christ fit in? The real theology of these people is the one being hammered out when matters such as the cause of disease are discussed. It was a similar process which led Teutonic warriors to alter their picture of what it meant to be man. The real dynamic of inculturation is no different in Melanesia today than it was in the year 754 in a log house along the Rhine when the words and actions of St. Boniface were the subject of long discussions. Local theology arises out of such dialogues, and one should not expect it always to remain faithful to the fine dogmatic precisions of the early councils. Christ is a living person, not a doctrine.

All this is not to say that the writing of books and the academic study of theology have no place in the Third Church, nor that the process of writing local theologies should be put off till the process of inculturation is completed. Rather, the issue is this: the process is never complete because culture is not static, and the question of where Christ is with his demands and transformative power must always be asked anew on another tomorrow. The misfortune is that, because of the Euro-American tradition of theoretical scholarship, we are too apt to overlook and downplay the cooking fire and city compound as places where serious theologizing goes on. We have transported a European way of doing scientific theology to the Third Church, and in the process run the risk of short-circuiting the messy, seldom-orderly dynamic of inculturation. To think that responsibility for the church can be entrusted only to men who have examined conciliar orthodoxy, the teachings of Aquinas and Luther, and the doctrine of transubstantiation may very well be to exclude the experience of many sensitive (though formally uneducated) Christians from positions of official responsibility.

Theological dependence refers not merely to the fact that most scientific theological and pastoral books and articles are written by western writers for a western public. Theological dependence is the entire problem of the spiritual and intellectual heart of the Third Church lying in the Second. It is to the Second Church that most look to find out what it means to be Christian. This is not to doubt the existence of Asian, African, Filipino, or Oceanic thinkers who are trying to interpret their own and their people's experience in the light of Christ. But the sociology of the theological enterprise is such that it is mainly carried on in the formal setting of lecture halls with too little recognition of the inculturation dynamics set out above. In the institutional forms, which speak louder than theories of inculturation or the attitudes of talented and sensitive missionaries, local Christians are taught not to trust their own experience, but to seek answers given in other places and at other times.

Inculturational or contextual approaches see the beginnings of Christianity in a seed which was once planted. That seed is a Jewish life, death, and resurrection, the explicit word of God's love and concern for human beings revealed in Jesus Christ. From one point of view, Christ is independent of culture, but from an equally valid point of view he is not alive until he lives in transformed minds and hearts. That transformation may have a different agenda and form in Zaire than in Belgium. Certainly Tillich's famous adage bears repeating: "Religion is the substance of culture, culture is the form of religion."[2] There is an intrinsic link, then, between religion and its cultural expression, but that does not allow us *a priori* to decide that a given cultural form cannot be the vehicle of an authentic response to God. If we skip too quickly over the confused, transitional phases where Christ begins the process of transvaluing the values of every culture, there is an acute danger of de-souling the convert. The reality of the world is that nature is a process in God's hands. A static Christology can easily ignore the fact that the religious act of responding to a living Christ, *active as the principle of transformation of every relative value,* gives spiritual substance to the ebb and flow of history in its every facet.

The question of the theological nature of world process is deeply embedded in Judeo-Christian tradition, but cannot be said to have entered into what the official Church today will allow to count for theological facts. What the primitive knows intuitively, that the world is an awesome place, the dwelling place of spiritual powers, has been allowed to slip away from modern Christians as the process of secularization has led them to dichotomize the world into the spiritual and the material. A recovery of the biblical perspective would make us realize profoundly that concern for inculturating and contextualizing the gospel message is not just a side dish but the main course of the meal.

In Papua New Guinea an influential Catholic priest-politician, John Momis, and a lay lawyer-philosopher, Bernard Narakobi, have disturbed many an expatriate churchmen. When I first listened to them speak of the impossibility of splitting state from church, my judgments were not much different from those of the majority of my fellow expatriates. What finally led me to reassess my position was a not very pleasant experience. The Seminary Senate, which had an overseeing role at Holy Spirit Seminary, was concerned that the seminarians were too much drawn to politics and were misunderstanding their future role as priests. The staff was asked to explain to the seminarians a statement of the International Synod of Bishops (1971) which spelled out the official attitude on priests' involvement in politics. I was asked by the rector to go before the seminarians as the messenger of light only to be met by a rejection of both the document and my explanation that chilled me to the bone on a day when the mercury was hitting 95 degrees. How could they be so unreasonable, I wondered?

As time went on and the painful experience was sufficiently in the background to allow me to discuss it with the students, I began to realize what it was that Momis, Narakobi, and most Melanesians believed. For them it was inconceivable that religion and politics should not march hand in hand. The western notion of their separation was demonic, for it split apart the form and substance of culture. Their position was one of terror at the thought of a world where religion and politics would be related as the sacred to the profane.

To this day I do not believe that the Melanesians have sufficiently reflected on the problem of pluralism and the dilemmas arising from having a number of opposed theologies in conflict. The theory of religious toleration and the secular state has been the western response to pluralism, just as it will probably be necessary in Papua New Guinea and elsewhere if other people's rights to hold contradictory beliefs are to be maintained. This does not, though, weaken the basic truth of the position that Christian values must be inculturated and contextualized in the very form and substance of public life. To attempt to do less would be tantamount to saying that belief is merely a private matter and religion can be removed to the peripheries of life. This is something the Melanesian finds impossible to imagine. And it may be that one of the major gifts that Melanesians and others coming out of traditional religious outlooks will contribute to the parent churches is a sense of the wholeness of life.

I believe it is demonstrable that in the Second Church the split between religion and living has developed to such an extent that the church is incapable of understanding the more organic approach to inculturating and contextualizing the gospel which people such as Momis and Narakobi represent. The western history of religious wars and persecution has led the Second Church to accept as ideal a world in which the church is allowed to pursue a mainly sacral role without outside interference. Without anyone consciously wishing it, the Second Church's transplanted structures virtually assure that in the Third World, too, there will eventually be an almost total estrangement of religion from culture with the inevitable isolation of religion that will ensue.

Following the principles of the sociology of knowledge, then, we can see how presuppositions about the nature of theological education in the formation of future priests hinder the inculturation of faith. Here institutional reform is required! The pious will counter by saying that the central issue is faith, not institutional models. The disillusioned reformer of the sixties, well aware of how impervious to change are church structures, will be equally unhappy with the same assertion. But the fact stubbornly persists: the public shape of both the church and its seminaries leads to theological dependence and hinders the gospel's inculturation. This is a form of ethnocentrism quite foreign to the spirit of Christ's own teaching.

John L. McKenzie's *Theology of the Old Testament* indicates that the ethnocentrism of Judaism was an element seriously challenged by Jesus. Says McKenzie, "One must recall the gospel figure that Jesus put new wine into new flasks (Mark 2:22; Matthew 9:17; Luke 5:37–38); he shattered the categories of the Jewish religion and culture from which he emerged."[3] The root sin of the Jews, from a New Testament point of view, was their nationalistic interpretation of the Covenant. Now much of what we find in the New Testament is as much part of a polemic against the Jews as it is historical fact. Nothing said here, however, should be interpreted as a crude revival of Christian prejudices against Judaism. For the Christian Church itself has gone on to erect its own ethnocentric edifice and, in the process, to sin against its Jewish brothers and sisters precisely because it did not understand that Christ's wineskin-bursting ministry constitutes a critique against any attempt to absolutize one's own experience and history. What may be equally unpleasant to Christian ears, especially when it is used to challenge some of the assumptions of mission work, is this: missionary Christianity, like postexilic Jewry, has not been able to transcend its own ethnic and nationalistic thought-world. Observes John L. McKenzie, "It is only candid to say that Christians who have seized on an often spurious 'messianism' of the Old Testament hope for the future as a vindication of their own religious system, have as a body risen no higher."[4]

Because of the presupposition that the European experience was normative, the missions of the church have been unable to sow the gospel seed and then to allow their converts a subsequent reinterpretation of the gospel in the light of their own cultural traditions. Anthropology makes it clear that whenever a new element is introduced into a culture, that new factor will be reinterpreted in the light of a people's own thought patterns. But the Roman Catholic Church has attempted to exercise control over the process of reinterpretation by insisting upon the binding character of Second Church formulations of the meaning of the Christian fact and Euro-American patterns of fellowship and worship. In the matter of the formation of an indigenous corps of office-bearers, the standards maintained guarantee that only those who undergo a profound westernization of their thought-world will be called to responsibility. This policy has been carried out with the best of intentions. Indeed, one of Papua New Guinea's most open and talented bishops in a discussion with me on the shape of the seminary said, "We have to learn from the experience of the church. Not to give our priests the finest education possible is to let in all the problems of the ignorant medieval clergy."

This manner of acting has guaranteed the purity of classical doctrine at the price of sterility. In Melanesia today, for example, the really fresh and vital expression of religious sentiment is to be found in the Cargo Cults in a form of millenarism. In Africa, the same dynamic is found in the native spirit churches which splinter off from the mainline denominations. Millenarism and spirit churches seem to express better the soul of Christians seeking a way to express their beliefs than do the orthodox practices of organized congregational life. European history can profitably be combed for parallels to these millennial movements. But such popular religion has largely been passed over, or at most made into a series of footnotes to the "real" history of theology. The great councils and synods met popular belief head-on, and orthodox Christianity's great creeds were the result. The wrangling that went into their formulation is really not much different from the debates presently suppressed in the Third Church. The crucial difference between now and then lies in the present inability of the church to allow the Third World church to move ahead freely.

Orthodoxy in the past was arrived at in the murky ambiguity of historical process that was replete with human foibles and passions. Present ordination policies, as they reinforce the rigidity of church structures, leave no room in the Third Church today for such change to occur. It would be different indeed if the ranks of office-bearers were filled with men and women who shared the worldview of the millenarian or the spirit believer. To be sure there would be some turmoil, but the resulting conflicts might bring about a profound inculturation of the gospel more effectively than the present sterile debates over liturgical and catechetical adaptation.

In the inculturation and contextualization dynamic I am here picturing, there would be a crisis of dependency in the Third Church even if there were sufficient numbers of men completing their studies in Third World seminaries. My argument for change in policies is *not statistical, but theological*. Even if large numbers of indigenous priests were ordained every year, and even if they were all very good priests, they would be burdened with two heavy loads. First, in order to keep up the life-style in which they were formed, it would be necessary for them to be fully salaried. This would engender financial dependence because most local churches would be unable to support them in the relatively high living standards of the foreign missionaries whose places they would be taking. Should it be advocated that they need not live in the life-style of their expatriate counterparts, caution would be needed lest it seem that they were being discriminated against. As well, there would be the question of a style of life in which Catholic priests could preserve their celibacy. There is no question but that a certain amount of travel and a different pattern of socialization are necessary if they are to maintain a celibacy which many already find extremely burdensome.

A second family of difficulties, which even the best indigenous priest faces, springs from the level of education he has received. Formal schooling may render ineffective his ability to participate totally in traditional culture. An example may make this clearer. A young priest's mother dies and he returns home for a month of mortuary celebrations. What happens? His mother was a prominent woman, so every one is interested in knowing not *what* caused her death, as westerners would be, but *who* caused it. Our priest has talked with the doctor at the hospital and has been informed that she died of bone cancer and that her death was inevitable. But in the traditional cultural logic, sorcery is the only conceivable explanation of why such a young woman could have sickened and died in a few short months. Someone must have had something against her, and because she was a prominent woman the people feel they are paying the young priest and his family an honor by taking seriously the process of discerning the agent of the sorcery. Educated to think of most diseases as having natural causes, the priest is in a serious dilemma. Not to participate wholeheartedly in the sorcery-divining rites which are an intrinsic feature of the mortuary celebrations is a severe breach of etiquette against men and women who are expressing their love for the family precisely by engaging in this process. But to participate in the rites with conviction is not easy.

The point is that this sort of divining rite is an intrinsic part of traditional culture, and a genuine locus for theological thinking lies in this family of questions. Yet it becomes extremely difficult for the indigenous priest to embrace the issue with intellectual earnestness except as a theoretical one. Far different would be the state of mind of a catechist whose mother may have died in identical circumstances. Though he may have some suspicions regarding traditional sorcery explanations of the death, he *feels* himself deeply involved. Is such a person, though not so well-trained formally in academic theology, not a more likely candidate for a ministry of theological reflection around the cooking pot than the well-educated priest?

And so one sees the deeper dimensions of the dependency crisis of Third World ministry. In order to survive personally in the boundary situation to which he has been relegated by having to fill the shoes of his expatriate priestly counterpart, maintain his celibacy, and be faithful to his highly rationalized approach to life situations where tradition sees sorcery present everywhere, the indigenous priest requires a life-style quite different from that of his cousins who have remained in the village. This, in turn, hinders him from *feeling* the same way about life's problems as do his cousins. What at first appears to be merely a problem of how to educate a priest turns out to be a crucial, basic, and serious question of inculturating the gospel.

The Need for Institutional Change

The Gordian knot is the presupposition that the local church emerging out of the mission must resemble the parent church that sent the missionaries. The question we have raised is the following: *Must* the models utilized by missionaries in evangelizing continue on in the local church? Too little consideration has been given to such questions, and where they have been raised in journals, books, and conferences on missionary questions, there has not been evident an official readiness to draw practical conclusions from missiological insights. Very little in these pages is new. The theoretical insights are quite generally accepted. It is at the level of practical policy that the difficulty lies. The presupposition of mission work has been that the "mission" is at an end when Father O'Reilley or Pastor Schmidt from Kansas City or Minneapolis is replaced by Father Ngabung or Pastor Akuoko from Kavieng or Alotau. In both Catholic and Protestant policies the indigene is expected to function in the same way, more or less, as did his expatriate counterpart. To maintain that presupposition is to prolong a needless crisis in Third Church ministry.

Finally, the identity of the missionary himself is in question. Especially in Catholicism, missionaries have crossed a vocational bridge which few have reflected upon. At a certain point in the life of the missions, they ceased to be *missionaries* and became *foreign pastors*. When an Indonesian bishop requests the Superior General of the Society of the Divine Word or the Franciscans to send more missionaries, he is usually asking not for missionaries but for pastors to take care of local communities. I am not aware of any serious questioning of the theological appropriateness of these requests on the part of superiors general, though one does find such a questioning attitude more often in Protestant mission boards.

To begin with, it is a matter of defining the difference between a missionary and a foreign pastor. I would delineate the role of the missionary in the following terms: *the primary role of the missionary is evangelization and beginning the process of establishing a local church*. That may involve several generations of missionaries, but the job description would remain the same. What has tended to happen in Catholic missions is that ordination policies and presuppositions about the shape of local churches have made it necessary for foreign priests gradually to shift from a role primarily defined as evangelization in a contact situation to a position of being foreign pastors in churches which should rightfully have indigenous pastors. I would delineate the role of a pastor in the following terms: *the pastor has a role of teaching, preaching, counseling, and guiding a local community of baptized Christians*. A theological nitpicker could well object that a pastor's first work is also evangelization. I agree. But it is not evangelization in a *contact* situation. And therein lies the rub.

The missionary plants a seed. A pastor cultivates it, waters it, cares for it. The distinction is important. Because of the institutional presuppositions already discussed, Catholic priests have largely become foreign pastors in local churches set up along Euro-American lines. It is a weighty matter and would appear to have been entered into with too little critique of the bias in favor of Euro-American ecclesial structures. Because the structures of mission and local church have been confused, this situation has gone on developing with a logic of its own. Numerous discussions can be heard among missionary-pastors about adapting to traditional customs in matters such as music and art in the liturgy. Very little is heard about the basic structure of the church. There is, of course, the post-Vatican II weariness with debating about structures. And to mention the phrase "institutional change" is to invite a yawn. But it is only realistic to be aware that institutions must be reconstructed if the work of the church is to prosper. The question really is: What shape should the local church take? Have we allowed Second Church biases to work unconsciously to predetermine the answer to these questions?

I have said that the Gordian knot of church building is an intricate collection of presuppositions. One may disagree about the direction toward which my argument is tending, but I maintain that these presuppositions must be critically examined. In this problem the chicken-egg relationship of clergy to church is central. Each determines the other, but while the shape of the church enjoys logical priority, the existential reality is more complex. The subject of this chapter has been the unfolding of that complexity.

One further critical issue must be raised. We have argued that the church's structures must be changed, opened up, to enable the process of

inculturation to go ahead more naturally. A critical reader will undoubtedly have already raised a question something like the following: What
about the fact that traditional cultures are themselves going through
radical changes? Is there not a danger that inculturation could lead to a
wedding of the gospel with outmoded ways of thought and to a way of life
which formerly primitive peoples want now to abandon in favor of modernization? This question is extremely important. For it is a fact that
traditional societies are undergoing massive changes today. Furthermore,
it is doubtful that primitive societies can long survive in the world, since
the influences of modernization are everywhere making inroads on traditional patterns of life and belief.

In the entire problem created by the impact of modernity upon traditional societies, it would seem best to admit the complexity and ambiguity
of the issue. In the second place, it would seem that the very process of
modernization is one from which the church has nothing to fear, for
historical process is simply an aspect of the fact that our world is not static
but dynamic. The argument for loosening institutional structures is an
argument for allowing this very crisis into the church as one aspect of the
task of contextualizing the gospel.

Some would see the study of primitive mythologies as *the* source for
local theology. I believe the matter is more complex, and that primitive
mythologies and logics are only *one* source of an inculturated Christian
faith. It is important to study and enter into the emotions aroused by a
millenarian movement such as the Melanesian Cargo Cult if one is to
understand that most Third World peoples have spontaneously opted for
modernization. There are conservative pockets, of course, who would
prefer to return to the old ways. But by and large Third World Christians
are men and women seeking modernization and its benefits at the same
time as they are terrified by their insecurity in the face of systems they
cannot control and forces they cannot comprehend.

When one deals with the inculturation of the gospel, what is called for is
not a retreat to cultural romanticism but an attempt to bring all the pieces
of a shattered and confusing world together in a new vision of unity. And
our argument for institutional change is not an appeal for a culturally
romantic return to primitivism. Rather, it is an unfolding of both the need
for and the possibility of new structures of ministry better able to grapple
with the confusing cultural situation that today confronts humankind.
The clergyman model of ordained ministry, with its attendant sacristy
mentality, can easily mistake its own concerns for God's concerns. In so
doing, it can readily become a roadblock to authentic inculturation in the
fluid social situation that is the modern world.

3

Wineskin-Breaking Mission of Christ and His Church

The question of the shape of the ordained ministry in the church, indeed whether or not there ought even to *be* a special cadre of ordained leaders, depends on one's view of ecclesiology: the mission and ministry of the church as a whole. The present shape of the ordained ministry grew out of an ecclesiology valid for its day. Any revision of the shape of the ordained college must demonstrate that its ecclesiology is more valid for our own times.

Chapters 1 and 2 have dealt with forces at play in the contemporary world which call into question the present shape of the church. As our special interest we have considered the problem of the church's credibility in the Third World. We have argued that current forces have altered perceptions of the church, and therefore constitute a demand for serious reflection. We have spoken of socio-political and historical forces in order to bring their meaning to bear on the future of Christianity. It would be possible, as well, to reflect on what they mean for politics, economics, law, education, and health, for basic assumptions in all of these fields are challenged by our historical crisis.

No human institution is immune to the growing realization that it must change if it is to be more fully integrated into the life-ways of a people, and become a force for authentic human development. Alienation and demoralization will result if change is not accepted. As an example, we might note that one of the most attractive sides of Maoism in China has been a thorough rethinking of priorities as part of the attempt to provide basic health care for the masses. Before moving into sophisticated modern medical technology, intermediate medical technologies are being developed to respond to the most pressing needs. It would seem to be similarly necessary to rethink church structures.

The following foray into ecclesiology is not intended to be exhaustive. To document fully everything said, and to evaluate alternatives adequately would itself be a lengthy study. Here we can only outline an ecclesiology which is simultaneously rooted in tradition, yet open to both cultural relativity and socio-political dynamics.

The answers one gives to the question of the shape of ordained ministry depend on one's view of the church's nature and mission. Ordained ministry is but one service within the church and takes its shape from the nature of the church. Church models should not be determined by the notion of foreordained structures of leadership ministries though it is my contention that the present moment is one in which the latter dynamic predominates. We will examine two basic ecclesiological orientations and then offer a reflection on how Jesus' "wineskin-breaking" life and ministry make both of them too simplistic. Too seldom has modern insight into the radicalism of Jesus' life and person been utilized as a basis for understanding either the church's life or the function of the ordained minister.

In his *Models of the Church* Avery Dulles masterfully sums up Catholic ecclesiology and identifies five basic views of the church.[1] The acclaim Dulles' work has received from Protestant scholars gives one confidence that his work goes beyond mere confessionalism. He maintains that a balanced notion of the church must allow the tensions among five models (church as institution, as mystical communion, as sacrament, as herald, as servant) to interact creatively. In what follows we will to a great degree be utilizing Dulles' insights, but the more limited focus of our study leads me to speak of two basic models: church as a means of communicating grace, and as an instrument or servant for liberation. For a more adequate treatment of the entire issue I would refer the reader to Dulles. For our purposes the two theoretical models chosen will enable us to focus attention on the shape of the ordained ministry in the Third Church. Few would hold either position in an undiluted form, but they do represent ideal types and thus give promise of helping us attend to basic alternatives in reshaping the church's ordained ministry.

The Church as a Means of Communicating Grace

Certainly the most prominent Catholic view of the church is that it is the instrument established by Christ to continue his mission of communicating God's saving grace to humankind. It is a view which can include all of Dulles' five basic models. The entire life of the church in this ecclesiology is centered on the word and the sacraments of salvation: readying men and women to hear the word and receive the sacraments, building up the necessary institutions (schools, parishes, seminaries, etc.) to insure that orthodox teaching and practice are maintained, and providing the priests and ministers who are the special guardians of correct ecclesial life. Even Protestant denominations, which put a special emphasis on the general priesthood of all believers, and which would be uncomfortable with a "high church" theology of priesthood, when viewed from a *functional* perspective, share this general ecclesiology.

There are both new and old versions of this model of church. In many ways it is the model that emerges from Vatican II, updated and more biblically understood. The progressive may not like to be told that he or she views the church primarily as a means for communicating grace. That description might suggest a traditional objectifying of what is primarily an attitude of loving concern on God's part. However, in essence, most ideas of the church as God's people and as a community of faith can be reduced finally to this pattern. This view is the dominant heritage of the New Testament and patristic era to which Protestants appeal, and of the medieval era's elaboration of sacramentology to which Catholics appeal.

The point most stressed in this view of church is the fact that salvation comes from God to human beings as a gift. God has given humankind a means of getting into contact with Jesus Christ through the word and sacraments of the church. It was a renewed understanding of this dynamic and a desire to brush away elements that obscured this fact that led to the liturgical changes of Vatican Council II. Moreover, Roman Catholics are not alone in appreciation of this fact, for many Protestant denominations have utilized Roman Catholic liturgical studies, appropriating them according to their own traditions, in their attempts to obtain a renewed understanding of the importance of rite and symbol in their own worship.

Liturgical studies led to the conclusion that historical accretions had clouded the pristine vision of Christ's centrality in the church's life of worship. The Roman Catholic response has been to pare away obscuring elements. From the Protestant side there has often been an awareness that many enriching sacramental elements had been lost. The consequence has been a renewed interest in sacraments to complement the austerity of a worship based almost solely on the word. But this result has left us with problems. Basic to them all is the fact that the breathtaking shock of social change has disoriented our total living pattern, and the modern world has not been fended off by liturgical updating.

Seldom today does one find great enthusiasm for liturgical change. There is a sober realization that the problems of faith in the contemporary world will not be chased away by more changes. In this context Lonergan observes that the basic crisis is a crisis of cultural change, not of faith.[2] But faith depends upon one's worldview, and the classicist Christian worldview of a hierarchy of truths in a world disordered by sin is reeling in the face of characteristic contemporary attitudes. The discovery of evolution, cultural relativity, the riches of non-Christian religious traditions, and an historical perspective on doctrinal development have cut deeply into traditional assumptions of the mission and nature of the church. The basic view of grace in this first model of the church finds itself in difficulty as the traditional worldview disappears. With that comes a questioning of this ecclesial model.

The responses to this situation vary. On the right, it is feared that to allow modern consciousness into the church is to betray the nature of the church and to foul up the channels of grace. On the left, it is feared that the refusal to enter wholeheartedly into the modern experience and to adapt modern language is turning people off from the church's message and also fouling up the working of grace.

In all this the ordained ministry becomes the target of both right and left with a bewildered pope, bishops, and priests left to take comfort in the ever dwindling middle that seems to sympathize with them, unsure of just where truth lies in the puzzling question of where modernity is to be met. The present befuddlement and the resultant disenchantment with an ecclesiology which seems to make the believer live with one foot on earth and one foot in heaven, combined with the problems of justice and human development, have led many to feel that another basic model is called for.

The Church as an Instrument for Human Liberation

A second vision of the church's mission and ministry presents it as God's servant or instrument for human liberation from social, personal, and environmental ills which constitute the residue of sin on earth. Such is the basic view of the several liberation or political ecclesiologies currently influential in the church.

There are differences of emphasis among the people who share this vision of the church, but basically they all believe that the church has erred in giving too much attention to grace as a heavenly matter which turns attention beyond this world in a nonbiblical manner. Rooted in Old Testament theology, the liberationists share a belief that it is *this* earth and *this* humanity which are to be transformed. The world is in the grip of sin, death, and concrete powers which are incarnated in the personal dilemmas and social evils of the day. Christ is seen as the model of the authentic human response to this situation as he gives of himself to the point of death in the cause of human liberation.

The human vocation, then, is to extend Christ's liberation in principle by making it an effective liberation from whatever now oppresses humankind. The liberationist, in other words, revives and reinterprets the traditional doctrinal distinction between subjective and objective redemption, recasting it in sociological language. Objective redemption becomes liberation in principle: a new mode of being in the world has been made possible by Christ's life, death, and resurrection. Subjective redemption is effective liberation: a *possible* mode of being in the world *becomes actual* as believers avail themselves of Christ's transformative power and strive to liberate their brothers and sisters.

Juan Luis Segundo, for example, in his five-volume series on Catholic doctrine, *A Theology for Artisans of a New Humanity,* has drawn out in a masterful manner the social implications of traditional teaching on God, grace, sin, sacraments, and church.[3] Gustavo Gutiérrez in *A Theology of Liberation* has shown the importance of beginning theological reflection from the concrete conditions of human communities.[4] Both these thinkers are Latin Americans who now have a major influence on the world theological community. Though their work may be corrected in many respects, its thrust has been accepted and appreciated. Even the cautions of ecclesiastical leaders such as Pope Paul VI have been more directed to in-flight course modification than to an abortion of their mission. Andrew Greeley's critiques on the movement have been caustic, but more designed to goad non-Latin American theologians into creative reflections on the problems of their own societies than to decry the thrust of liberationism in theology.

The principle insight of the liberationist is that it is *this* world that is the object of Christian concern. Heaven and eschatological salvation are objects of hope, but only through activity here and now does the Christian enterprise make sense. The liberationists borrow heavily from a Marxist analysis of class struggle and exploitation of the masses. This characteristic often disconcerts the political conservative. Here I am not attempting to judge whether or not these are the most fruitful sociological categories for use in analyzing the human situation. Liberation theology's truth does not depend on such tools even if they seem today to be inseparably wedded.

What, though, would the liberationist's church resemble? Here we must be honest and admit that the ecclesiology has not been fully worked out. It seems a "movement" rather than a local congregation or a worldwide organization. Where sacraments and liturgy would fit in causes uneasiness to a traditionalist who would otherwise see merit in their vision. One gets the impression that the local church would resemble a cell in a political action group and that its agenda would be almost entirely set by social problems. Prayer and religious experience are not excluded, but they seem to be subordinated to the main goal — transforming society in an activist manner.

Evaluating the Two Models

The instrument of grace model guards an important lesson of human experience. Ultimately, utopianism has always proved false. History's march has a way of smashing human hopes even as men and women seem persistently driven to try to create societies which will answer every human need. The tragic side of human life is revealed in individual and social suffering, and the Christian emphasis on grace experienced in the depths of despair is not a wisdom to be lightly tossed aside. Jesus' own glorification in John's gospel is portrayed as if he were reigning in the midst of the humiliation of the cross. Modern physical sciences present contradictory pictures on the vital question of whether cosmic life can be expected to go on indefinitely. We live in a world where opposing forces are the very warp and woof of existence and where development is dialectical. The gospels know full well the fundamental ambiguity of human existence, where humans are pulled toward spiritual grandeur and at the same time weighted down with the much more evident fate of death.

That said, it remains that the church has not itself been immune to self-glorification and has often become just one more idol. Ecclesiastical leadership persistently tries to create institutions which give the impression of triumphing over the ravages of historical change. Leaders have been so confident that the church is God's sole instrument of grace that they have lost sight of shortcomings very evident to those outside the faith community. The paradox of it all is that such ecclesiologies seem not to have realized that it is only through struggling with the storms of history's trials that one experiences the reality of divine power. Ecclesiastical finery and elaborate liturgies easily become so preoccupying as to cause believers to treat the church as a refuge *from* the world rather than as a source of empowerment for life *in* the world.

This need not be so. Sacramental life and prayer can carry believers to new levels of realization of the meaning of the struggle, enabling them to experience hope that they are in the hands of a living Father. Such experiences can give the believer an effective readiness for service in the world. What has undermined confidence in the traditional model of the church, though, is the broad realization that much of church life has led to self-centeredness and a sense of spiritual privilege quite foreign to the gospel's own message.

Those adhering predominantly to the view of church as an instrument of grace see the church as having the task of reminding people of the primacy of the spiritual dimension. But when the spiritual dimension is understood in terms of personal righteousness and experience, there is an acute danger that the church may become an island in the midst of the world and not a source of empowerment for creative transformation. On the other hand, the traditionalist would seem to have strong warrant for suspicion of certain liberationist tendencies. There is no avoiding the fact that there is a high degree of individualism in Christ's teachings. Purity of heart, concern for righteousness, the experience of God as one's personal loving Father, the call for prayer, and the establishment of a faith community where one can find relief from the meaninglessness of a purely horizontal life are all part of the biblical record. There simply *are* limit experiences — death, illness, oppression, bereavement—where the individual needs to be buoyed up in the face of events which mock utopianism. The gospel speaks to such limit situations.

The danger of emphasizing individualistic aspects is one of compromising on the fact that Jesus' own teaching, in the context of first-century Judaism, also had a strong social dimension. Yoder, in his *The Politics of Jesus,* shows that, while Jesus was not a programmatic reformer, his message has roots in Jewish social teaching, and springs from the "jubilee" doctrine and what that involved in bringing ethical righteousness to bear on personal and social conduct.[5] Luke 4:18 has Jesus beginning his ministry declaring that he has come to set captives free and to bring the good news of life's significance to the downtrodden. This Lucan passage is based on Isaiah 61 and had political significance in the ministry of Jesus. A modern application might see the mission of Christ and his disciples as concretizing God's righteousness in society: restoring ruined cities (in an age when cities threaten to crush the human spirit in a deadening sprawl of increasing squalor) and making the soil bring forth produce for all humankind's delight (in an age when unchecked exploitation of resources for the benefit of too few threatens to make the earth unproductive and barren).

The liberationist is profoundly correct in bringing to our attention the oppressiveness of contemporary social structures. Also correct is the insistence that concern for personal righteousness has made Christians too private in their spirituality, unable to unmask the institutionalized violence of a world order which keeps masses of men and women subject to dehumanizing forces. Equally profound has been the ability to translate social criticism into gospel categories to help us see the this-worldly dimension of Christ's teaching. For to "carry one's cross" is not merely a matter of bearing one's personal burdens with resignation and hope. Identifying with Christ in new contexts means a willingness to suffer now in all the murky ambiguity of history. Yoder has shown that to spiritualize the Sermon on the Mount in the manner of much of traditional exegesis is to tear out of it a socio-political content that Jesus quite knowingly put into teachings which were later collected by the evangelist and inserted in the beatitudes.[6] The search for justice is not merely the private search for an experience of God's acceptance of oneself as an individual. Rather, it is also a search for an order in which God's justice is concretized both in societal structures and in individual human beings.

On the other hand, the kingdom of God is not going to be a mere result of human moral commitment to reform. The foundation of the kingdom is the Spirit of God in our midst neither as a power created by human effort nor a reality easily available to sense observation (Luke 17:21). The establishment of the kingdom will not, therefore, be easily reducible to this or that programmatic action. One sometimes has the impression that certain religio-political thinkers believe that their particular program is *the* concrete realization of the kingdom. Such narrow thinking ignores a twofold issue: first, the spiritual danger of setting oneself up as a reformer; and second, the entire issue of the mystery of God and his purposes in the world. Each of these elements deserves comment.

Paulo Freire has, I believe, shown a unique sensitivity to the spiritual plight of the would-be social reformer.[7] In his *Pedagogy of the Oppressed*, for example, he focuses on the ambiguity of the process of searching for concrete ways to overcome oppression and struggling against the powerful. Freire realizes that the reformers who lack a profound sense of their own drive for power are often unknowingly and unconsciously trapped, for unless they are careful, it often happens that they merely promote the exchange of one form of domination for another, all in the name of liberation. In such revolutions, what occurs is merely a game of musical

chairs in which the liberator seizes the former oppressors' power. For a
time there will be jubilation, but human history shows that relatively soon
there will be a need for a critique of the reform itself. If the liberator is not
extremely sensitive to his or her own fallibility, a new cycle of oppression
will ensue as the revolution struggles to defend itself against future
generations of critics who may very well have truth on their side. Programmatic reform has a way of locking in on itself, confident of its own
righteousness, and in so doing makes what is but a *means* to an end into the
end itself.

Jesus' teaching on the dilemma of self-righteousness finds expression in
the parable of the tax collector and the Pharisee (Luke 18:9–14). The tax
collector is in fact the agent of imperialist power. The Pharisee is committed to a program of putting the ethical teaching of the prophets into
practice and represents an extremely fruitful integration of religious and
moral insight. It would not be going much too far to say that the best of
pharisaism was a first-century equivalent of liberation theology. But it is
the imperialist agent who goes away justified while the good Pharisee is
condemned. There is no way to escape a profound tension at the heart of
Jesus' teaching: commitment to righteousness in society and in one's heart
is mandatory; but we are not thereby justified in judging people by their
commitment to such righteousness.

John Dominic Crossan's excellent book, *In Parables,* shows powerfully
how the logic of Jesus' teaching in the parables is a reversal of normal,
human, religious logic.[8] This leads us to the second point mentioned
above, the mysterious reversal of human expectations. Mystery is an
important theological concept. Often used to obfuscate, it nevertheless
has an important role to play in any Christian theology of history. Crossan's careful exegesis of the parables of Jesus shows that in certain "servant parables" normal religious logic has been completely upset, for in
them it is the wicked servant who is rewarded, not the wise and prudent
servant who waits for the return of the master (cf. Matt. 20: 1–13; Luke
16:1–7; 17:7–10; Matt. 18:23–38). The normal logic of the parables of the
kingdom has perceptive persons catching an insight into the surprising
advent of God's reign, and sees them respond to the event by prudent
action. Crossan's merit is in explaining the parables cited above to show
how even this prudent attempt to reorient one's life is not enough. In the
light of the reward of the wicked servant one sees that the advent of God's
kingdom "will always be precisely that for which wise and prudent readiness is impossible because it shatters also our wisdom and our prudence."[9]
This "reversal" feature of Jesus' teaching I term his "wineskin-breaking" ministry.
We will deal with it in more detail later. Here it may be enough to register
the observation that a respect for God's mysterious purposes is necessary
in any Christian political or liberation theology. *A reversal of normal human
expectation is inherent in Christian ontology precisely because Christ is the principle
of creative transformation who overturns the best-planned schemes of reformers and
works to overthrow oppressors.*

One of the most positive aspects of Freire's *Pedagogy of the Oppressed* is the sensitivity he displays in confronting the problem of the self-righteousness of the programmatic reformer.[10] His method demands a thorough reorientation of those who would struggle for the well-being of others by demanding that they first exercise themselves to become one with the downtrodden. Any other approach merely enters into the dynamic mentioned earlier: convinced of the rightness of one's own programs, one eventually becomes an oppressor in order to guarantee the revolution. Freire has identified areas of concern which are profoundly Christian.

Summing up, it may be said that, left to themselves, neither liberationist nor instrument-of-grace ecclesiologies are enough. Nor can we be satisfied with a mere harmonization of their theologies. Both must be subsumed in a higher integration that is more faithful to the living parable who is Jesus. Liberationism runs the risk of horizontalism and of not paying attention to the individual religious dimension of human experience. Instrument-of-grace ecclesiology risks isolating the church from the concrete struggles for justice that are an intrinsic dimension of Christian religious experience. Without an experience of the holy, religious living lacks power; but it remains true that one can become so fascinated with the holy as to create a sacristy mentality quite foreign to the Gospels.

When all is said and done, it would seem a fair judgment to say that the present domination of the church by the clergy heavily weights church life in the direction of the traditional instrument-of-grace model, and that the liberation motif offers a healthy corrective deserving of profound attention. The church is organized along sacral lines. The separateness of the priestly caste, their celibacy, and their cultic role witness to the church's hope for salvation in the next world. The very centrality of clergy, especially in the Roman Catholic tradition, can be evaluated only negatively. For the ordained ministry draws attention to itself, and the separation of the priest from the ordinary experiences of the faithful can only accentuate a sacristy model's orientation to "churchy" concerns. It is important to consider the mission and ministry of the church in relation to Jesus' wineskin-breaking life and teaching. He injects a radical disorientation into human consciousness in order to reorient the believer to a paradoxical and mysterious divine presence to be discerned within the ordinary experience of daily life.

The Wineskin-Breaking Dimension of the Church

Central to Jesus' proclamation of the reign of God is a motif of reversal of first-century Jewish expectations. It should be stated immediately that much of what we have in the New Testament is anti-Jewish in nature, and labors under the apologetic need to explain why Israel did not accept Jesus as Messiah. Thus the Jews, especially the Pharisaic party, emerge in the Gospels as caricatures of deficient religious attitudes. More fruitful than concentrating on their Jewishness is the realization that their inability to accept Jesus' teaching on the present and coming kingdom is best interpreted as a paradigm of a universal human failure. The paradigmatic nature of their lack of faith lies in the universal tendency to understand the kingdom in too narrow a sense. That failure is part of a general human difficulty in accepting the radical paradox of a kingdom that reverses normal human expectations of reward for righteousness and punishment for evil-doing.

The conflict between Jesus and the Pharisees as well as a large number of his parables show well the wineskin-breaking dimension of Jesus' life and ministry. His teaching on God's surprising manner of acting and judging human actions breaks through the old wineskins of religious reward/punishment psychology. God alone judges. And God's judgments follow paths which human logic cannot understand. It is our basic argument that to elevate either the church in general, or its clergy, to a privileged position betrays a lack of awareness of the reversal logic of the Gospels. Christ appears in the midst of human society — and also in the midst of his own church — as one whose judgments break through settled manners of thought and attitudes about what constitutes human righteousness. In the words of John B. Cobb, Jr., Christ is "an image of creative transformation."[11]

The human condition is one of living in an in-between time when God's rule has been established in principle, but is not yet totally effective or visible. Paul, in 1 Corinthians 14:20–28, sees us waiting for the defeat of the final enemy—death, a symbol for the powers of evil. In Romans 8 creation groans in agony trying to give birth to a final state of affairs, the arrival of the kingdom, when each creature will receive its proper fulfillment. It is in this entire context of expectation that the church, as a community of believers, hopers, and lovers, has its existence as a servant of the coming reign of God. In the present age, the believer is in a warfare with the powers of evil (Eph. 6:10–17). But evil does not exist in the abstract. Rather, it is always concretized in the estrangement and division within individual human hearts as well as in social conditions. So while the Christian lives a life of worship and praise because the faithful believe that life is ultimately in the hands of God (Eph. 1:3–10), tension exists because of human alienation from its deepest self (Gal. 5:16–26).

A difficulty in biblical theology is the problem of discerning what a given text means in the concrete present. It is important to realize that each generation is left to reinterpret the message for its own context, for mere repetition of the Bible without reinterpretation becomes sterile indeed. It seems only fair to say with the liberationist that traditional theology has interpreted the scriptures as speaking almost entirely in individualistic terms. More consonant with the thrust of the New Testament would be to interpret it in the light of the Hebrew scriptures. Then it would perhaps be apparent that the kingdom of God is a symbol for the total transformation of this world. But in the era in which the present institutional model of the church was established, it was common for the church to understand itself to be the actual kingdom of God on earth. This was the fundamental error leading to a deification of the church and ignoring its far more humble role as servant of the kingdom.

Vatican II has attempted to strike a balance. In the Constitution on the Church, the church is described as being somehow the "first fruits" of the kingdom, a hint of what is to come, a budding forth of God's reign.[12] The Christian community ought to be a gathering of men and women who have come to perceive that God is himself the "within" of things. If they are aware that the negative judgment of Jesus against the Jews was the result of their ethnocentric inability to accept his radical teaching, Christians ought to strive to be a community of people who realize that they too are forbidden to claim arrogantly to be more than a flawed servant of a mysterious God.

A lesson from Old Testament theology may be helpful. Israel was confident that it was God's elected nation. But that did not stop the prophets, according to Gerhard von Rad's *Old Testament Theology,* from proclaiming that Israel's unfaithfulness had led to a break in the Covenant which necessitated a radical new beginning.[13] Doctrines such as that of the infallibility of the pope and rigid biblicism alike have shored up a Christian ecclesiastical self-confidence which would not feel comfortable with the prophets' radical condemnation of Israel. Yet from patristic times the church has considered itself to be a New Israel, the True Israel.

Could not the church sin so radically as to be in the position of the Israel condemned by the prophets? Jesus' statement, "Know that I am with you always, yes to the end of time" (Matt. 28:20), has been made the warrant for ecclesiastical self-confidence. Would it not be fruitful, though, to interpret Jesus' promise in the light of Old Testament experience? To do so would be to realize that he will be with the faith community, but that at times it may be necessary for him to be there as a condemning judge. If the church is lacking in fidelity to Christ as he nudges it out of a northern hemisphere mentality to a recognition of the reality of the Third Church and historical and cultural relativity, what might be the Lord's judgment?

Jesus spoke of the kingdom as a tree with all sorts of birds nesting in its branches (Matt. 13:32). The church, if it is a foreshadowing of the kingdom, would be a similar tree with many families of birds finding shelter in its branches. To continue the analogy, at the risk of making it an allegory, is it being faithful to the spirit of the Gospels to demand that the later arrivals all make their nests in the same manner as did the first comers? I think not. Yet it would seem that today the policies of the worldwide institutional church promote exactly this sort of uniformity.

The common denominator of Christians is their realization that Christ, the revealer of the meaning of life, is the one to whom they give allegiance, and the one from whom comes the power to live a Christian spiritual life. The authentic common denominator, then, is not the complex of Euro-American ways of responding to the challenge of Jesus, for Christian institutions are merely the shape which fellowship takes when men and women have the experience of converting to Christ.

In the context of this chapter on the mission and ministry of the church, it must be observed that there is no theological warrant for uniformity in church structure, for the basic mission of the church lies much deeper than visible models. The mission of the church is that of the servant who has caught sight of the mysterious presence of God in the midst of the ordinary events of life and who struggles to minister to the world in the light of that insight. That ministry is not a programmatic one of righting all the world's ills, but of being a witness to the hidden God who is present in our midst. This will sound dangerously mystical to the person who believes it blasphemous to speak of God to people with empty stomachs. But it is Christ himself who said that men live not by bread alone. And while he often fed people, there is no evidence that he felt compelled to feed everyone who was hungry in the Palestine of his day.

As servant of the kingdom, Jesus was consumed by concern for people, but his life of service can be neatly categorized neither as humanitarianism nor as religious teaching. Rather, his wineskin-breaking mindset saw deeper into the human dilemma. That deeper insight into the nature of humankind's chaos goes beyond programs, while not condemning them, and ought to characterize the sort of life practiced by Christian communities today.

The mission and ministry of the church will at times be programmatic and at times unprogrammatic. In essence, I believe that one of the key problems of the modern church is the attempt of various groups to force others into their own models. The community of belief in Christ ought to be morally large enough to exist in many different types of communities. If this is to be given room to happen, the uniform Code of Canon Law will become far less important as local churches take responsibility for their own lives and work out their own institutional shapes in response to their particular experiences, needs, and cultures.

Pluriformity will necessarily be one of the key marks of a church which, like a tree with many branches, has many families of birds nesting there. Confusion may seem to mark its life, but that confusion might be divinely inspired. Confusion shakes us loose from settled states of affairs and makes us look deeper into matters than former dogmatic certainties about life enabled us to do. The key insight on the mission and ministry of the church, as it arises from the life of Christ, is this: *the person of Christ was a living parable inextricably bound up with his proclamation of the kingdom.* Jesus' person was both the medium and the message. The encounter with him was a normal human encounter in which he invited friendship and trust, but a relationship with him drew the believer into radical paradox and reversed normal human logic.

Nothing is clearer than the fact that Jesus was a first-century Jew. But nothing is clearer, also, than the fact that his message was new wine for old wineskins, and it was soon discovered that Judaism, even radically reformed, could not contain all that he said. It was necessary for his message to be put into new wineskins lest the old wineskins burst. Jesus, then, can only be called a religious radical, faithful to the traditions of his people, and yet profoundly unsettling to his contemporary co-religionists.

None of this is new. What I find odd, however, is the fact that seldom have theologians or church leaders integrated this wineskin-breaking dimension of Jesus' life and ministry into the essence of ecclesiology and Christology. Christology has largely been the attempt to understand how the divine Logos could coexist with a human nature, not a dynamic attempt to reflect on how the ministry of Christ as a concrete individual is a paradigm of divine initiative in the transformation of existence.

If one merely theorizes on the person and nature of Christ, there is the risk of becoming static in one's Christology. A way needs to be found to break out of the impasse. I believe that the wineskin-breaking analogy is an important one in this entire process, for not only did Jesus *tell* parables, he *is* one. And just as the parables he told disoriented his listeners by pointing to a surprising advent of the kingdom that would reverse normal expectations, the parable he was can only be called a radical reversal of normal human logic. To take Jesus as a paradigm of the God-human relationship is to expect the unexpected and to see that what the Christ is concerned with is the creative transformation of unsatisfactory states of affairs.

John B. Cobb, Jr.'s, *Christ in a Pluralistic Age* is monumental in its attempt to interpret classical Christology in a transformation-of-life key.[14] Cobb utilizes the so-called "process philosophy" of Whitehead and Hartshorne in a manner which allows him to integrate the insights of modern science on the fluid, dynamic, and organic nature of the world. In this "process" manner of thinking, we live in a universe where process is the reality, not static substances. Settled states of affairs enjoy only a relative permanence, for the essential characteristic of being is its enduring tendency to move beyond what it is to become something else. In this light, the Logos is not to be interpreted in the manner of a Platonic idea beyond the world of change, but is itself the divine principle of on-going, creative transformation.

What happens in the Incarnation is that this principle of divine creativity becomes present in the person whom we know as Jesus of Nazareth. His life, death, and resurrection become a paradigm of the process by which God brings novelty into existence in the midst of what first appears to be mere death. Such insights are rooted in the Hebrew concept of wisdom, and that concept is worth looking into for what it shows us regarding Jesus' wineskin-breaking life. While the Greek word Logos has the connotation of eternal and unchanging Reason dwelling in a world beyond change, this meaning is not the only one standing behind the classical Christological doctrines. St. John's prologue uses Logos to speak of what happened in the Incarnation. Christian doctrine has tended to interpret Logos in Greek thought patterns, but it is fruitful to look at the Hebrew roots, where we discover that the Hebrew has a second layer of meaning which classical Christology has not been so successful in expressing. *Hokma* (wisdom) is one of the threads that go into the Johannine tapestry. Divine wisdom is a *dynamic image* involved in the creation and working of the universe (cf. Prov. 3:19; 8:22–31). Wisdom literature certainly was influenced by Greek thought but did not have the same *static image* in the deep structure of its semantics. Rather, the Hebrew notion of history as time in God's creative hand stands behind the concept of *hokma/logos* which John has put into his prologue, and which the early councils used as a key for articulating classic Christology, even if they (in the fourth and later centuries) may have lacked awareness of the dynamic Hebrew concept behind the Greek word.

In an age when science has enabled us to understand the evolutionary nature of the universe, we also are better able to perceive that the logic of the Logos-incarnate is one of creative transformation, not merely a revelation of a static divinity giving a "secret" to eternal life. Rather than revealing to us an eternal, unchanging One, Jesus reveals a God ceaselessly involved in transforming settled states of affairs, moving momentary (though some of the "moments" may be centuries) accomplishments—cultures, civilizations, states, individuals, art, history, species—beyond themselves into novelty.

Concretely, much of what Jesus did in his earthly ministry was to incarnate the principle of creative transformation in an historical movement that bears his name: Christianity. Jesus' wineskin-breaking ministry was unsettling to his Jewish co-religionists for the same reason it must be unsettling to us. For the logic both of the parables he spoke and the parable he is reveals just how upsetting and destabilizing is his God. Today, in a world struggling for a new shape, the meaning of Jesus could well be articulated as a revelation that historical process is ultimately benevolent, that the forces of the universe are with us if we engage in fashioning a more humane world in the light of his teaching, which leads us to find life through death to our own and the world's habitual manner of acting. This is, in essence, what I understand to be the accomplishment of the theologies of process and hope, and I have tried to capsulize this in my phrase, "wineskin-breaking ministry." The church, Christ's body, has a mission to continue this ministry of Jesus, serving the world as a people who expect God's surprises to unsettle and unstick human accomplishments.

This is all rather theoretical, of course, and may leave the reader wondering if it is mere speculation. I think not. At the risk of seeming overly mystical, I would maintain that insight into the conflict of Jesus with his contemporaries, and the reversal logic of the parables, give us a key with which to interpret our present ecclesial situation in both the Second and the Third Church.[15] The signs of the times can be interpreted as nudging the church beyond its former false sense of security in a structure believed immune to the ravages of history. Our choice is not unlike that presented to Jesus' contemporaries: to accept him and his reversal of normal logic, placing our trust in a surprising God. Jesus was the servant of a surprising kingdom. Just so, the church is meant to be a servant of that same reality. The events of the times constitute a *kairos,* a favorable moment to respond to new challenges and the principal mission of the church is to help humankind gain insight into that moment.

We have said that a theology of ordained ministry makes sense only within a theology of the church. Less recognized is the fact that ecclesiology depends on a theology of the kingdom. Pointing to the present and future dimensions of that kingdom was the mission of Jesus, and this must constitute the mission and ministry of the church. The ordained ministry, as a leadership function within the church, makes sense only in terms of this entire dynamic. As our study develops I hope to make more clear what changes this will demand in ordination policies.

PART TWO

The Theology of Ordained Ministry

4

Ministries within Ministry

Ministry has come to be a churchy word, usually coupled with the sorts of things ecclesiastical leaders do: preaching, performing liturgical activities, guiding a church community. In reality it is a far broader ideal and has conceptual roots in *diakonia,* service. In this chapter we will argue that the church's basic ministry must be understood in Christological terms, for the *diakonia* of Christ is the paradigm of the church's service. This will necessarily take us into the tangled thicket of Christological doctrine, not to propound academically a theory which will advance a new speculative understanding of the significance of Jesus Christ, but to articulate what I hope is the common faith of most Christians. An attempt will be made to unfold honestly the presuppositions upon which our theology of the ordained ministry will be based. This movement is important because one of the gravest faults in the classical theory of ministry is its reductionist understanding of Christ's peculiar mode of serving humanity.

Christ's ministry cannot be easily capsulized in abstract terms. This is because one of the central aspects of his life is his paradoxical, wineskin-bursting quality that continually breaks through the human tendency to desire comfortable settled states of affairs. He broke through the categories of Judaism. It is not so generally recognized that he will also break through orthodox Christian categories. The attempt to nail down neatly, in precise and eternally valid theological terms, just what Christ did in his earthly life is doomed to failure. In the same way, it is not so easy to determine just what he is doing in the present age. One can, of course, attempt to thematize that ministry in words such as "redemption" or "forgiveness of sins." It is possible to go even further and say with Paul that his is the ultimate force at work in the universe. But such abstractions are not enough. They do not come sufficiently to grips with the concreteness of his activity, either then or now.

In this chapter I make an attempt at clarifying one aspect of Christ's ministry in order to understand ecclesiastical ministry. We are at a disadvantage, because theology done apart from a living community that is coming to terms with Christ in its own very particular circumstances is methodologically suspect. Good theology should always be joined to praxis, and praxis is always joined to concrete opportunities and demands

55

rising out of a context. My own experience in Melanesia will provide the context of the following pages. However, an attempt will be made to move from Oceania's special situation to aspects of ordained ministry of more universal significance. Departing from reflections on traditional doctrine on the personhood of Christ, we will analyze the meaning of "service" as the ministry of the church and study the implications this idea holds for the many "ministries" needed in the church in its service to God and humanity.

The Unity of Christ's Ministry of Service

"Service" is one of those words that often confuse as much as they clarify. The church, one hears often, must be of service to humankind, just as Christ was of service. While this is true, I often wonder if, when we so easily mouth such phrases, we have really plumbed the depths of Christ's service.

Ministry and service are closely related. To minister to someone is to serve his or her needs. Ministry, however, has a religious and sacral flavor to it that service is not yet burdened with. Service, therefore, seems a much more relevant concept for many moderns precisely because it avoids the churchy dimensions of ministry. Semantics is largely a matter of identifying the connotation of words. In this section we are trying to go deeper than identifying academically the semantics of word-making and using. It is to be hoped that we can discover the meaning of the image of ministry and service in New Testament and church usage in order to clarify what it is that the church ought to be offering to the world today.

In both biblical and classical theological categories, Christ's primary service to humankind *is to have redeemed us*. Salvation is one way of speaking of Jesus' ministry. Unfortunately, to speak of redemption or salvation is again to be involved with words that have the sacral and religious connotations which so many find troublesome. They have been spiritualized and made to refer to a seeming *deus ex machina* rescue of people today from the human condition. Etymologically, though, the Hebrew roots of the word "to save" are embarrassingly concrete. The escape of the *Hapiru* from Egypt was salvation, and they were not thinking of heaven. They were saved from Pharaoh's slavery. If a person or an army was in a tight spot and got out of it, that too was salvation. The basic picture conjured up by the family of words biblically expressing salvation is one of rescue or liberation from a tight spot.

In another portrayal of Christ's mission of service, he is said to have "saved humankind from sin." Recalling once again the roots of the word "sin" may be helpful. One of the primary biblical images of being in the grip of sin is that of "missing the mark" (as with an arrow or spear) or "missing the right road" (as in being lost and confused). It is easy to see—in the light of the Torah considered as a bestowal of a total "law" (illuminating the "mark" in life, the "way" to true fulfillment)—how sin came to be considered the transgression of divine commandments. But unless one sees that sin is more basically a fundamental mistakenness about the meaning of life and an incapacity to find true fulfillment, one is in danger of emasculating the rich, existential flavor of words such as "salvation."

Our argument here is that when one gets behind the biblical terminology concerned with expressing the service of Christ to humanity, there are profound symbols involved. Perhaps the most basic one is the biblical view of a confused humanity too easily settling on goals and satisfactions that rob men and women of true identity: in other words, a picture of estrangement from the authentically fulfilling ground of human existence.

We have said already that the incarnation of the Logos should be viewed in concrete and dynamic terms. Saving a person from sin has been interpreted by many as rather beside the point if you have in front of you a hungry child, an oppressed people, an unjust social structure. Let us try to imagine what salvation from sin might mean if such plights are viewed from a concrete perspective.

First of all, the state of the oppressed is one of being gripped by the power of sin, of living in a situation where it is virtually impossible for people to gain a positive appreciation of their own worth, and where it is even more difficult for them to take their destiny in hand and create a more humane life. The situation of the wealthy or of the well-fed middle class is not fundamentally different. Such groups are equally caught up on a treadmill of inability to attain the inner freedom pictured in the Gospels as the human ideal. Salvation for either rich or poor would be a discovery of a way out of the slavery in which they are caught and an empowerment to carry out an escape. Viewed dynamically, salvation would be an encounter with Christ which would enable people to escape their bondage in a total manner. To do that, the very structures of their individual and communal existence would have to be changed. It is just this sort of total change in the conditions of existence that is symbolized by human salvation.

Historically speaking, the encounter of many Third Church Christians with the Christ of the Gospels has had aspects of just such a liberation, as is well shown in Walter Freytag's mission travelogue, *Spiritual Revolution in the East*.[1] Freytag visited various Lutheran missions in pre-World War II New Guinea and in Asia, interviewing numerous converts, men and women who could remember the excitement and enthusiasm of the days of their conversion. He found that Melanesians felt freed from the constraints of the "old order" and no longer in the grip of sorcery and fear of their enemies, for the new faith had shown them that they could be brothers and sisters of all their neighbors. While the missionaries may have had a "spiritual" liberation in mind, the Melanesians conceived of their liberation primarily in concrete, sociological terms as a new freedom with the promise of a better life—which *also* included heaven. Communal to their core, they experienced Christ as offering the possibility of an even more satisfying community than their traditional clan life had made available.

The same sense of a new freedom is basic to all true conversion. The power of sin, incarnated in one's individual slavery and the limits imposed by the social structure, is displaced. A new horizon replaces it. Looking at this from a cross-cultural perspective, it should be stressed that the very nature of the boundaries imposed by sin differs from culture to culture and epoch to epoch. The Greco-Roman merchant found the gospel an answer to the riddle of life after death. The Teutonic warrior caught a glimpse of a new sort of manhood. The Latin American peasant may find Christ pointing to a dignity denied by political and social oppression. The wealthy industrialist may be offered a mode of existence which can enable him to leave behind a somewhat paradoxical enslavement of himself which his oppression of his workers brings with it. Freed from being the oppressor, his conversion enables him to forge a humane partnership with his former enemies.

Examples can be extended infinitely, but the principle is the same: salvation in Christ is not merely a private, individual, spiritual experience. The encounter with Christ is empowering; it enables one to transcend limiting situations and experience a new freedom. Matthew, the tax collector, and the woman at the well encountered Jesus and found themselves caught up in a new freedom. An encounter is paradigmatic of the nature of revelation, for the revealing is not merely a glimpse of propositional truths *about* the deity. Rather, it is a revelation of Truth itself. The person of Christ brings one into the light concerning the authentic target and goal of life and empowers one to take the practical steps that will lead to a more responsible and deeper selfhood. This, I believe, is the service of Jesus Christ, the central point of his ministry.

Christ's service to the world today is an extension of his earthly ministry, largely a matter of seemingly chance encounters with men and women, but not easily reducible to theological categories of an abstract nature. The encounter with Christ and his good news is liberating because of who he is: the Logos incarnate, the structure of whose life and existence mirrors the authentic truth about human nature and its possibilities.

The structure of Christ's ministry is the basis of ongoing Christian ecclesial service. Creeds and doctrines serve to underpin and unfold the significance of that structure of existence. The doctrine of Chalcedon, for example, forbids our dividing up the unity of the personality of Christ in any manner which would oppose the human and divine aspects of his ministry. Whatever he did was a divine act, but no less human for its transcendent depths.

This same structure must be seen to obtain in the ongoing life of

Christian ministry and service. The tendency to reductionistic theologizing on the "essentials" of Jesus' service has brought the churches to a very
non-Chalcedonian concept of ecclesial ministry. That is to say, it has
created an impoverishment of the concept of ministry by reducing it to the
services provided by the ordained leadership. What is to be recovered is a
sense of the fundamental unity of the ministry of both Jesus and his
community.

The Ministry of the Church

The church's ministry is its service to humanity. Nor may we legitimately
divide that service into divine and human, essential and accidental dimensions. Paul's doctrine of the church as the body of Christ is his attempt to
expound and explain his experience of the on-going activity of the Spirit
making Christ present in the church. The Chalcedonian doctrine of the
unity of the personality of Christ, I believe, can be read ecclesiologically to
mean that the church's *total* life is that of the body of Christ.

One of the weakest elements in the current theological emphasis on the
church as the people of God is its inability to reflect the depths of meaning
contained in the Pauline doctrine. The church *is* God's people, but it is so
as the body of Christ, not as an association of persons with a privileged
position in the economy of salvation. Centuries of thinking of the church
as having means of salvation denied to nonmembers can be understood
historically; it even has strong biblical warrants. But the paradigmatic
nature of Christ's own suffering servanthood seems more apt in portray-
ing the basic function of the Christian church.

The church's primary service is that of *being* the community that is
Christ's body in the world. Most people think of service as *something done*
for others, not as *being someone*. But being someone is precisely the Christian community's nature. And because this mystical element makes the
church a complex body with more than a merely moral personality with a
commission to perform specified activities, the service of the church's
manifold members is analogous to the service of Christ himself.

Though it is tempting to pick out this or that aspect of Christ's life of
ministry and to identify it as "essential," it is a temptation to be resisted. In
this matter I do not mean to sound obscurant, or to seem to refuse to use
hard logic to clarify theological principles. But the most rigorous theological logic will bring us ever back to the fact that the service of both Christ
and his church must be rethought and recast in personal categories which
leave room for the surprises which spring from the uncontrollableness of
human encounters with God, other persons and social contexts.

The wineskin-bursting side of Jesus' character, incarnating the dynamic
Logos, urges us to move beyond *every* settled state of affairs into novelty. It
is just this personal surprise dimension that proves difficult for

theology because theology desires to cast the truth of the moment in bronze tablets lasting to eternity. In reality, the church must be perpetually prepared to melt those tablets down and to reframe its understanding of its mission. Not to do so leads inevitably to theological reductionism.

Reductionism takes many forms. In the context of our discussion of the ordained ministry, we will consider only one of these forms, that to which reducing Christ's service to a priestly act of self-immolation in sacrifice has led. The idea of sacrifice is foreign to most modern minds, but it is central to both scriptural and later theological thinking. The common image of Christ portrays him as offering satisfaction to the Father for the sins of humanity. The work of the church becomes that of sacramentally representing this activity for the faithful. The liturgy is the place where contact is made with the Risen One's act of atonement. The most important service of the ordained minister is that of performing the sacred rites in which the graces flowing from Christ's once-for-all, but eternally-available, action are met and received.

Though the reformed churches would be uncomfortable with the Catholic theology of ordained priesthood here presented, it is beyond argument that this concept of its primary service is dominant in most of the church's history. Moreover, it has been this sacral picture of the ordained ministry which has shaped the church's understanding of ordained ministry. The minister is primarily a mediation figure, standing for the Risen One in the midst of the community. The picture of the priest as an *alter Christus* (another Christ) has crystallized this understanding. I believe this portrayal is overly reductionistic, and I will argue the point more at length in future chapters. What is important now is to see that this liturgical and ritual emphasis has had a tremendous impact on the manner in which the church has conceived its service.

Because theology has followed liturgy (*lex orandi, lex credendi,* the law of prayer is the law of belief), and because the church from a very early stage has been dominated by a priestly class, reductionist thought has understood Christ's essential service as death on the cross which gave the Father satisfaction for sins. Both Christ's and the church's services have been cast in sacral terms which, though true in themselves, are not the whole truth. I do not argue that this emphasis was false for the ages in which it was developed, but I would recommend consideration of two vital questions. Has the modern world context, with its increased understanding of the social dimension of sin as it shows itself in concrete oppression of individuals and of societies, made it necessary for us to reconsider the former theology of ecclesial ministry and the traditional position of priesthood in the church? Does classical doctrine deal adequately with a more complex and even kaleidoscopic vision of salvation as it emerges from both the Hebrew and Christian scriptures?

Concentration on the death of Christ-the-priest reigning from the cross has colored the church's understanding of the ministry both of the church as a whole and of its ministers in particular. Both ecclesiology and the theology of priesthood have been based on the notion of Christ as priest. Ordination thus became a mystical configuration of the ordinand to the priestly character of the Crucified and Risen One. It gave the ordinand the power to re-present sacramentally the sacrifice of Christ, and brought about a mystical and ontological change in the soul of the priest.

There was coherence in this theology of ordination. But when it was linked to the concept of the power of Christ ruling over the world, it inevitably led to a highly exalted, sacral-juristic conception of ecclesiastical office. There is no attempt here to attack the partial truth of this theology, only to say that it is not the whole truth; in a word, it is reductionistic, and obscures a more organic and complex whole.

There would be few today who would maintain that the sacramental re-presentation of Christ's sacrificial act is the essential work of the church. But it is no less a fact that the structural shape of church office is built on this understanding. The church is not immune to the more general sociological law governing knowledge and the functioning of institutions. We go forward looking at a rear-vision mirror. Our present mindsets are determined by events and understandings of those events which come from past ages and which will govern our behavior unless there be a self-conscious attempt to discover and criticize unevaluated presuppositions. Though there may be a theoretical revision of such reductionist categories, practically they still reign supreme in institutional policies that prevail over subsequent theological insights. It is difficult to erase the practical residue of such sacral thinking.

The enrichment of theological thought that has sprung from the Reformation's distinctive view of Christ and church has undercut the position of Roman Catholic priestly authority figures only theoretically, and has not led to practical changes. Since the Reformation, Luther has had tremendous influence both in the families of churches founded on his revolution and among those who have opposed them. But the fact remains that what Luther and Catholicism shared regarding the role of the ordained ministry is far more significant than their relatively superficial disagreements. While bitterly arguing over churchy issues, both camps have quite ecumenically been the victims of the ravages of a theological essentialism which has reduced to sacral concerns their conception of the role of Christ and the ministry.

The post-Reformation view—both Protestant and Catholic—of the church, as a community mainly concerned with individual salvation and the sacred, enshrines the official ministers in a privileged and central position. This is not to say that these ministers are such egomaniacal types that they willfully try to retain their status after being convinced that the emphasis is wrong. Such would be an unfair accusation. Rather it is a question of a complex of modern forces, reinforced by a picture of Christ drawn with sacral brushes, having so deeply engrained itself in religious consciousness that a more wholistic picture of Christian life has been made difficult to imagine. Even if the Protestant picture of ordained ministry is not as priestly and juridically authoritarian as the Catholic view, it still remains true that functionally both reformed and Catholic ministries are quite similar. The practical picture of the service the church offers the world in both Christian families is one of sacramentally and/or homiletically re-presenting the salvific activity of Christ. The ordained minister is the primary vehicle of that work, and the shape of the church is built around it.

We have belabored this question at some length in order to make our positive point more striking. In later sections we will be more concrete about the way this question can be addressed in the dilemmas of current Third Church ministry. Here it is perhaps enough to call attention to the fact that the church's service—considering the church as a community made up of many people with many gifts—is that of continuing Christ's own ministry of encountering people and their contexts, allowing the surprise of the encounter to percolate through all the participants, and then clarifying the problems, values, and opportunities of the context in the light of the gospel. This should result in a response of praxis. As the contexts differ, and as individuals and cultures differ, so will responses. On the part of the believer the key attitude should be one of openness to both the gospel and the situation.

In advance, though, little more can be anticipated than a human condition marked by negative boundaries and positive challenges. Sin and human problems wear a contextual face whose contours must be discerned before adequate praxis can ensue. Though history and tradition may give us some preunderstanding, presuppositions alone cannot be allowed to map out ahead of time a programmed response.

This is but another way of saying that the most basic note in the church's service is its corporate personality. The Pauline doctrine that the church is Christ's body is more basic than the concrete actions of the community. The secular-sacred distinction is useful to help us understand that there are values at play which go deeper than the mere matter-of-factness of the context and the persons involved in the situation, but that secular-sacred distinction is no warrant for relegating the service of the church to the sacral realm alone. Christian existence involves a transcendence of every boundary situation, and is a way of life lived in the light of an absolute future. Although a facile spiritualizing might be tempting, this is a temptation to be avoided. And although one can say in advance, with considerable certainty, that prayer, preaching, and liturgical life will be part of the entire process of forming a community response to the demands of the context, one is not justified in raising these matters to the level of prime importance.

All this is but another way of saying that the ordained leadership's role is but one part of a community's total life. In like manner, concern for a political or social praxis is not an argument for a new Caesaro-papal alliance between altar and throne. Secular states and pluralistic societies are facts of life that cannot be waved away with clerical or theological wands, for the institutional church and organized Christianity have no special vocation to order human affairs. The entire issue is subtle, but some hint of the vocation of the church emerges from an examination of its basic sacramental nature.

The Sacramental Nature of the Church

In order to prove a particular point, the documents of the Vatican Council II, can, like scripture, be quoted by theologians and nontheologians alike. But the Vatican II teaching on the sacramentality of the church, viewed in the light of the ecumenical interest it has stirred, may be a starting point acceptable to both Protestants and Catholics. While making no pretense of giving a complete exposition of the Council's doctrine, I would like to examine the sacramental nature of the church found there, and attempt to show how even a conservative interpretation of that doctrine opens the way to a new conception of the ordained ministry's function.

The Council's teaching represents a return to the riches of biblical and patristic imagery. This is especially true in *Lumen gentium*. In *Gaudium et spes* there is a turn toward taking seriously the autonomy of the extra-ecclesiastical world. In the first article of the Constitution on the Church, in reference to the church's nature, the Council says:

> The Church is in Christ, as a sacrament or a sign and instrument of intimate union with God, as well as a sacrament and sign of the unity of the whole human race (LG 1).

For the theologian of an essentialist or reductionist bent, as a definition of the nature of the church this statement is most unsatisfactory. For, first of all, it is not very clear. Furthermore, when one reads subsequent sections of the same document, to see if the context will clarify the meaning of this definition, one is faced with further unclear, image-laden, symbolic language. Nowhere, the manualist will say, do you have something you can get your teeth into.

The Council chose symbolic language for reasons more cogent than a desire to reconcile liberal and conservative factions. The church is a mystery. Mysteries must first be dealt with in the language of myth and poetry; in religious language, in other words. This is a basic linguistic step before second-level, scientific, theological discourse can attempt to analyze and clarify the imagery. Contemporary language analysis has, in fact, restored such symbolic language to respectability after several generations of language-philosophy treated it as a poor stepchild of scientific discourse. Unquestionably, the first articles of *Lumen gentium* are poetry, and the citation quoted above is one of the few attempts to utilize more abstract and universal categories in calling the church a sacrament.

In this connection we should note first of all that the Council deals with the church as a reality intimately bound up with the presence of Jesus Christ. Pius XII's encyclical on the Mystical Body of Christ forms the background for understanding what is meant (*Mystici Corporis Christi*, June 29, 1943). In this work the Pope stressed two elements: (1) the intimate nature of Christ's constitutive presence making the church his body; and (2) the juridical principle that the visible church (not an invisible church), with an authority structure, is the community of Christ.* What is underlined is the fact that the church is not merely a voluntary association of people who trace their existence to a man named Jesus. Through his Holy Spirit, that Jesus is the Christ, the living head of his body. A mystical dimension, then, is part and parcel of the church's service, even in a secularized world.

Second, there is reference to sacrament. Commentaries on the document stress that both ancient and later understandings of sacrament are to be read into this word. The symbolism of the patristic era and the realism of Trent are telescoped. What does this mean? According to traditional sacramental doctrine, a sacrament (1) *symbolizes* a divine reality and (2) *effectively* brings about the reality signified. Water symbolizes, for example, cleansing and new life, and in baptism the rite brings about the cleansing from sin and the imparting of grace. Entailed in the term, *res et sacramentum* (reality and sign), is the notion that sacraments are effective agents which both symbolize and confer grace.

Applied to the church, this means minimally that there is more than a notional connection between Christ and the community of believers. There is no thought here that the church is a physical reproduction of Christ, for the symbolic dimension of sacramentality forbids any crude identification of the *res* and the *sacramentum*. Nonetheless, the connection here is more than a moral one, or the kind prevailing between a conventional sign (e.g., a traffic light) and the signified (e.g., a command to stop or permission to proceed). Religious symbols are ordinary realities having the ability to propel human consciousness beyond the physical elements. Humans are grasped by them, in the words of Paul Tillich, or the symbol is meaningless.[2] They become a trigger to an altered, deeper consciousness. Entering into this altered state of religious consciousness is what Lonergan means by "conversion."[3]

The Christian community or church, in the conciliar definition, is a consciousness-raising sacrament which both symbolizes and brings about

---

*It is significant that while stressing throughout the significance of the first element of Pope Pius's encyclical, the Council chose to bypass the juridical underbrush that grew up around the membership questions.

(1) the presence of Christ in a real manner, (2) humankind's unity with God, and (3) unity within the human community. These three elements deserve a brief clarification, for within them is to be found the nucleus of any ecclesiological expansion.

The presence of Christ in the community is a living presence, actively empowering human beings, leading them to participate in God's own life. It brings about unity with God by revealing and overcoming human estrangement from the divine ground of being. This in its turn creates the possibility of deeper unity within the human community, a unity founded on a recognition of brotherhood and sisterhood in which differences of culture, sex, or economic status are meaningless. There is danger, of course, of understanding all of this in a sort of *theologia gloriae* which would ignore the sinfulness of the church itself, and this has certainly been a temptation to which the church has often succumbed with the resultant explaining away of shortcomings. On the other hand, there is the tendency to spiritualize away the fact that each of the three elements is a task as well as a gift. The life and ministry of Jesus were spiritual, but not otherworldly. They were symbolic as well, but the symbol par excellence of that ministry remains the fact that new life is entered into only through profound suffering on the cross. The things Christ did and said were aimed at this world while retaining a certain parabolic reversal symbolism which forbids any exaltation of his church to a privileged status. There was a "more" to him that can be expressed only in the language of transcendence. But that transcendence was rooted in a very this-worldly life.

To leap from sacramental terminology into an other-worldly transcendence without going through the everyday ambiguities of historical existence would be to short-circuit the painful process by which the church is a sacrament of Christ's salvation. The person who reads romantic poetry may be transported into rapture. But if in that person's life there are no people to love or to be loved by, the raptures of poetic or aesthetic experience are merely mental. Unless there be the concrete struggle to make God the center of church life, to achieve unity with his designs, and to overcome societal hostilities, oppression, and estrangement, theological language about the church as a sacrament can likewise lead to a merely mental transcendence.

Theology remains notional, mental, and abstract if not joined to praxis. Documents—including scripture and those of the councils—are a poetry which can alert the believer to deeper dimensions in life, or refine experience by bringing it to full consciousness; but a concrete involvement in the pathos of life is necessary if theological definitions are to be more than notional in value. If the community's members be involved in "the Jesus-thing," the poetry of religious language and liturgical activity can lead to the inner experience of transport that transforms and empowers them to live the gospel life more deeply. But without a flesh-and-blood commitment to the tasks at hand, tasks which forge the spirit on the anvil of individual and communal life, the sacramentality of the church is meaningless.

The church, in this sacramental view of its nature, is a community that feels itself linked to Christ. An analysis of Pauline spirituality reveals the constant repetition of "in Christ" and "with Christ," phrases which reflect experience of unity with the risen Lord, and between him and his brothers and sisters in the church. An analysis of Paul's own self-appraisal shows that the central task of his life was the creation of communities in which such sentiments were generally felt. This was Paul's ministry. I believe it fair to say that such ought to be the central ministry of every ecclesial leader—the creation of a community at one with the Lord, a community which, at the same time, is attempting to bring the fruits of its ongoing transformation into the wider world.

Taken seriously, the Vatican II teaching on the sacramentality of the church means that before there are sacramental rites, there is the basic sacrament of the community's own life together. Rites, preaching, and authorities are means for realizing the more basic sacramentality of a community living out the day-to-day experiences and tasks that make up human existence. Thus, raising children, working for harmonious race relationships, helping construct just communities, counseling alcoholics, teaching catechism, working for law and order, settling public and private disputes, healing the sick, visiting the elderly, providing for the needy are sacramental in a sense just as essential as activities centering on liturgy, and governing the church. Too much concentration on these latter activities, and a belief that they are *the* ministry of the church can easily lead to a down-playing of other, equally important facets of church life.

It is a major part of my basic argument that the sacerdotalizing of the concept of ministry has been one of the most serious deformations that ever occurred in Christianity. When ordained ministry became wedded to the monastic separation from the "world," the scene was set for a fundamental myopia which would create in the modern world a sacristy mentality among the clergy and a false privatizing of Christian life. The church *is* a sacrament of salvation. Emphatically, yes! But sacrament is not a word to be surrounded with the lace of surplices, or even the rough linen of a modern designer alb. Rather, in its deepest reality, sacrament is a symbolic dimension pointing to the religious stakes of every aspect of human living. An adequate theology of the ordained ministry can be articulated only if the more basic theological meaning of Everyman's ministry is first fully grasped. To sharpen our focus on the total ministry of the church is our next task.

Specialized Ministries IN and BY the Church

Before there is administration of sacraments, there is Ministry with a capital "M." That Ministry is the service offered by the ongoing life of the community in shops, villages, farms, cities, classrooms, homes, law offices, in counseling, politics, statecraft, and recreation. As different as are the concrete sociologies of the various cultures in which such activities will be carried on, so should the forms of church structure be multiform. What one does and how one does it in an oppressive situation, such as that obtaining in South Africa, may be quite different from the manner of serving in relatively open societies such as those of Papua New Guinea or Tanzania. The key point in all this is that the specialized ministry of the ordained is not more central or basic than the specialized ministry of the lay person who works to settle a village dispute. The important point is that the church exist and act contextually.

It is, of course, all well and good to say that the community *is* the church. The existentialist rhetoric of the sixties had a refrain that went something like, "It is more important to *be* a person than what you *do*." I have always found myself rather unimpressed by this refrain. What one does is important, vitally so, in one's being. Just "being" is quite a sterile act. Eventually a person or a church is faced with a vexing problem: Just what does one do while being a person or a community?

The broadest outlines of the response to that question have already been given. First, the individual and the community live "in Christ" in faith. A transformed consciousness recognizes concrete opportunities for growth, and the obstacles which must be overcome if an integrated personal and communal life are to be had. This is brought about through discussion, prayer, study of the scriptures, and the demands of the situation, all lived through in the light of the experience of the empowering presence of the living Lord within both the individual and the face-to-face community, as it faces its own particular needs.

In a Melanesian situation, where, for example, sorcery may be believed responsible for a woman's death, discussion would become the medium through which the community would confront the reality of demonic, impersonal, magical, and material powers with the rights of legitimate self-defense, the role of revenge in the culture's value system, the command to seek reconciliation with one's enemies, and so forth. The issue is complex, and those aware of how deeply matters such as sorcery penetrate traditional cultures will not expect that a people will solve the problem by confronting a single incident. Generations may have to pass while hundreds of such incidents provide opportunities for forging Christian responses.

If we realize that the creation of humane industrial relations and just political policies and laws is a never ending challenge for sensitive, morally self-conscious discussion and activity, then we ought to be equally patient with the moral dilemmas of "primitive" peoples. But the morally sensitive Melanesian who attempts to bring the gospel to bear on the sorcery problem is providing an ecclesial service no less than the North American industrialist or union leader who tries to balance the need for better working conditions against the corporation's need to show a profit in order to provide employment. In each case one is dealing with shades of grey, seldom with blacks and whites. That is the way the human family is constructed. We are dealing with a *process* whereby communities are formed and are conscientized to see problems and opportunities for affecting changes in society. Such is the ethical dimension of Christian service. There is, moreover, the question of forming the sort of communities in which each member feels the Christian challenge of his or her own possibilities for service. To accomplish this there is the need to trace the path to adult faith.

Converts to Christianity are seldom confronted with once-for-all decisions. Rather, they are attracted to Christ through the words and deeds of the members of a community. Relatively few are knocked off life's horses by a physical intervention of a God who changes the course of their lives. Much more common is a prolonged period of reflection and dialogue with significant persons. The key to it all, I believe, is having a basic community model of church which springs from the sociology of a given culture and within which informal dialogue takes place.

Children may be brought into the community through baptism, but it is important that the focus of the community be adult-centered. Christianity is an adult affair, one part of which is concerned with child-raising. One should not expect an idyllic community of the totally committed. People will be spread all over a continuum of belief from nominal to radical faith. Some will have very clear feelings of being in Christ, and that will be the integrating element of their lives. Others, to use the words of Gandhi, will be "experimenting with truth."[4] So there should be no *a priori* demand for total commitment even if the experience of being in Christ is the basic element in Christian life.

At a time when the evangelical churches are having such an impact on the mainline denominations, and Pentecostalism exerts such a profound attraction for many, it is well to bear in mind that the path to belief is often a path with many bends and turns. Fundamental evangelicalism could well create an unrealistic model of church life with an emphasis on individual religious experience. This might in the end once again myopically restrict believers to a highly sacralized form of Christianity quite foreign to the basic model of the structure of Christ's own life and teaching. Pressuring persons might lead to conditioning without opportunity and freedom for the activity of the Spirit to percolate through the total life of the experimenters. The fact is that the church is a complex organism whose members will differ widely both in their abilities to experience the inner workings of God and in the sort of gifts they will bring to outreach ministries.

In the context of church service, viewed in the light of cultural differences, two basic families of ministry may be distinguished. First, there are ministries *within the church*. Here we expect to find men and women with abilities and insights which enable them to help others (1) to understand

and enter more deeply into the mystery of faith, (2) to create a sense of spontaneous and natural communal life, and (3) to enable the community to reflect on the meaning and demands of gospel teaching. Second, there are ministries *reaching beyond the church to a wider society.* Here we expect to find men and women who have been enabled to understand their lives in the light of the Christian symbols and who endeavor to bring this expanded consciousness to bear on facing up to the problems of the extra-ecclesial human context. Both families of ministry are essential.

There is danger today that our understanding of the moral problems of society, and of the need for commitment to solving them, may lead activists to underestimate the importance of internal ministries such as have been traditionally associated with clergy and other ecclesiastical figures. Though uneasiness with internal ministry, as a reaction against the clericalization of ordained ministry and the general "churchiness" of ecclesial life, is understandable, it would be shortsighted to allow abuses and deformations to crowd out an appreciation of the vital role of persons whose ministry is mainly internal. There is still need for men and women who would dedicate themselves primarily to creating the sort of worship experiences and teaching which cement and nurture the bonds of community which are essential for an effective outreach ministry.

The most important shift of consciousness is one which puts such internal ministries within a balanced, wholistic appreciation of the face-to-face outward looking basic community nature of the true local church. Christianity is finally not reducible to an ethical commitment to service, for such would only replace one form of reductionism with another, and would quite possibly end in a dehumanizing moral earnestness emptied of the depth which a rich spiritual life within a community can alone provide.

Lumen gentium, article 26, is a useful section to mull over in considering the nature of a basic community. There it is clear that the church is not to be considered first as a global institution with millions of Christians following out the programs prescribed by a pope. Rather, the church is the local community, and the local community is not merely the smallest unit of an international organization. The World Church exists only as a communion of local churches, each of which responds to the needs of its own particular peoples. Ministry is not a question of a college of office-bearers arranged with more or less authority depending on how close to or how distant they stand from the central authority. It is, rather, service done within and beyond a local community.

Within the Catholic tradition, of course, centuries of evolution have made ministry almost coextensive with hierarchy, and there have been documents enshrining the notion that lay apostolates are an extension of the hierarchy. Protestantism has little that approaches this exaggerated hierarchicalism, but that fact has not made the Protestant concept of ministry less "churchy" or inward looking. For a church to be caught up and entrapped by a churchy concept of ministry, an ideology of clerical authority is not necessary. But a thorough carrying out of the implications of *Lumen gentium* mortally undercuts the clerical mentality. As noted earlier, however, it is one thing to undercut such an ideology theoretically in a document, and quite another matter to draw the practical consequences.

What are the consequences of a basic community concept of ecclesial life? First, it is necessary that the community should be structured, as far as humanly possible, along the lines of local sociology. A church community structure among nomadic tribes on the plains of Africa might be quite different from the local community structure of a small, geographically stable Melanesian village. Secondly, it is necessary to include the input which will come from the traditional religious and mental outlooks of a people. Spiritual problems, religious expectations, and general mindsets differ widely from culture to culture. It is not so much a question of letting such things totally set the agenda for the Christian Church as it is a matter of structuring worship, teaching, and dialogue so that gospel teaching vitally and intrinsically interacts with cultural life and does not become a mere overlay. In Melanesia, for example, millenarism and the entire problem of coming to grips with the people's desire for change must be taken into dialogue about the meaning of life. It must not be allowed to be merely a "problem" that gets in the way of what expatriate churchmen consider the authentic concerns of the church. Thirdly, there is need to allow the practical consequences of the first two principles to actually affect the *official* constitution of the churches. I have here in mind the distinction between the happy initiatives of creative missionaries *as individuals* and the policies of missions *as institutions*. Fourthly, there is the issue of giving concrete examples to clarify what both the internal and outreach ministries might resemble. The following is not intended as a complete list, but may be useful to flesh out the principles already enunciated. There are two basic families of ministry.

1. INTERNAL MINISTRIES: Teaching, counseling, stewardship of material resources, overcoming of antipathies between members of the community, providing recreational services, aiding parents in educating children, providing help in times of sickness, loss of employment, or death, leading and preparing liturgical celebrations adapted to the culture, providing financial or personnel help for the local community, governing and arbitrating. The basic principle of internal ministries is the notion that the church is the local community. It should spring out of the cultural forms of communal life. It should not replace traditional fellowship patterns with something purporting to be universally required by the nature of the church. For the nature of the church is, in fact, nothing other than an enriching of what is already present. Ordained ministry is but one function within a basic community, and without insertion into an organic group ministering to the total needs of the people, ordained ministry runs the risk of elevation to a centrality quite foreign to the spirit of the gospel.

2. OUTREACH MINISTRIES: Promoting socio-economic development, working to overcome injustice, missionary preaching, catechesis of non-members, political action, elevating consciousness concerning the moral issues facing a society, social work among marginalized classes and oppressed minorities, involvement in unions, aiding the poor materially. A basic distinction must be made between outreach ministries of the community as church and the activities of individual members of the church who perform services on their own. There may arise a need for church organizations—either of single communities or on a broader, sometimes international, basis—to form explicitly church-related groups, (e.g., international relief services). However, it is no less an outreach ministry if a woman or man feels called to enter politics, even if she or he does not do so as a member of a church-related political party. Indeed, there is no requirement for institutional commitment in areas such as politics unless there are issues which clearly demand a public, ecclesial position taking as, for example, when a state's very legal structure is set against providing justice either for a class of people or for the populace as a whole.

The autonomy of secular society and the reality of pluralism forbid even an updated form of Caesaro-papalism. Christians should normally expect that they will be one spice in the recipe, rather like the mixing of salt in the concoction. History shows well that ecclesiastical involvment in public affairs is no guarantee of the righteousness of the church's cause. Private activities by persons of good will is ministry. For example, Christian physicians need not band together to provide a special Christian clinic if other organizations are present and want to do so. But it would be an outreach ministry for a Christian dentist to give up a day per week to serve a clinic on wheels that travelled to outlying villages not served by the regular medical establishment. If there are honest people in politics, it would be a mistake for a priest or minister to enter the arena merely because he or she would find it inviting.

The church's mission is service. But let us be wary of reducing that service to whatever project or preoccupation seems relevant at the moment. The church is a tree with many sorts of birds nesting in its branches, and it is not valid to construe it to be a monolithic power bloc pushing through its own particular programs at every instance of real or supposed need. The world is a complicated place, and it is the role of the laity to be present in its midst, but not as representatives of the official church thought of as having a "Christian" solution to every difficulty. A church program for literacy, for example, will be successful only if it is first a good program from an educational point of view. On the other hand, it may well be that an educator with professional competence might be inspired by a Christian formation to put that competence to work among illiterates. A bad program for hospital care or socio-economic development does not become good medicine or practical agriculture just because a concerned church wants to help. But a concerned union organizer may find some help from the community when running up against an unscrupulous employer, or a police officer working in a slum in Nairobi might have similar help when finding that there is nowhere for distressed prostitutes to turn. These examples point to the mutual interaction between internal and outreach ministries.

Those working primarily within the community solidify a communal basis for conscientizing the church's membership. Those with outreach ministries move beyond their spiritual homes into the wider community. One should not, however, absolutize the distinction between these families of ministry. Though the primary work of the priest or minister is within the membership, he or she will certainly also reach beyond it. And though a Christian judge's primary work is in the legal system, that does not mean that he or she might not also read a lesson at the liturgy or teach a class of youth in Bible studies.

The typology developed here is useful to restore a balanced appreciation of the community's services; it is not intended to erect rigid walls between ministries. And because we will later be concentrating on the function of ordained ministers, here we have merely made tangential reference to them. It is to be hoped that by heightening awareness that ministry is first and foremost a service in and by a communal body and its members, this scheme will serve to restore a sense of proportion regarding the ordained ministry's role.

Of Ministry and Ministries in Young Churches

How does this discussion come to bear on the Third Church? Is the clericalization of ministry a factor there also? The issue is complicated by the fact that in many nations missionary activity was perceived by the indigenous population as one part of a package deal. While in the Second Church historical forces led to a sacristy mentality which reduced the church's scope of activity to the private, inner, spiritual realm, in places such as Africa and Oceania the churches were considered part of modernization and social change. Thus, in Third Church regions one will find attitudes toward the church which are quite different from those common in the Second Church. This has both good and bad sides.

On the positive side, the church's commitment to education and health services has created a generally favorable attitude toward Christianity. In Oceania and large parts of Africa, for instance, the church's efforts have often been more extensive than those of the government. Given the inability of many Africans or Melanesians to drive a conceptual wedge between the secular and the sacred, the churches emerge in popular consciousness as deeply concerned with human and socio-economic development.

Another positive dimension that should not be ignored is the fact that certain lay ministries have been given greater prominence than they ever had in the parent churches of Europe and America. Missionaries were faced both with large numbers of people interested in Christianity and their own limited time and energies. In addition, they were often faced with a bewildering array of languages (in Papua New Guinea for example, there are 700 languages for a population of 2.9 million people). As a result, indigenous catechists were trained, and they bore the brunt of the direct apostolate in most mission situations. They may have had only a rudimentary knowledge of Christian doctrine, but missionaries worked with them and relied on them. An unpleasant aspect of this is that these ministers were often paid by the missionaries with funds gathered overseas, with the result that these catechists came to be considered extensions of the foreign priests and sisters rather than as persons carrying on an apostolate of the indigenous Christians themselves. Nevertheless, their ministry continues to be a vital one.

On the negative side, however, there is a subtle problem. Services have been provided in such a way that the indigenous population has been the recipient of benefits conferred by expatriates. As a result, local Christians, especially in remote areas, have come to think of the church as a service station dispensing goods (education, clinics, food, clothing, and so forth). The local Christians move with difficulty to a conception of themselves as church, and often interpret attempts by expatriate missionaries to make them active participants in service as niggardliness and a desire to cut them off. The enlightened modern missionaries who try to aid the people to see that "they are the church" often find themselves rather unfavorably compared with earlier generations of missionaries who liberally dispensed those same services.

The Columban sociologist and missiologist Fr. Cyril Halley has pointed out to me in numerous conversations that the role of the catechist has ensured that the church in Papua New Guinea—and the same can be said for much of the Third Church— *is* a lay church. Though the drawback of being considered a servant of the priest or minister rather than of the church as a whole remains, the catechists' ministry contains within it hints helpful for developing new kinds of pastoral ministries for the young churches.

Here, the key obstacle to be overcome is that centered around the passive role which Third Church members have adopted with regard to the proper role of the laity in ministry. Efforts to overcome this and help the people understand that *they* are, in fact, *the church* have been impressive. A national self-study in Papua New Guinea had as its major goal the theme "We are the church." While no one claims that there was a revolution in indigenous consciousness, important seeds were sown. Add this to the fact that the people do not generally split the world into sacred and secular, and the picture becomes encouraging. I believe that the Third Church may be psychologically much more ready for a wholistic approach to Christian service, not marred by a western sacristy mentality, if sensitive approaches can be developed which will instill a more active mindset in these Christians. We will speak more about this below.

What still remains a problem, especially for Catholic churches, is the entire issue of the clergyman-priest. As we have already noted, the clergyman remains the linchpin of both Protestant and Catholic churches. Unless there is developed a more balanced appreciation of the ministry of the church as a whole, there is every reason to believe that the growth of modern secular, scientific thinking will eventually lead Third Church Christians to develop a secular/sacred bifurcation of consciousness which will erode their present wholistic approach to religion as an integral part of life. The ordained ministry's dominant position in church life could easily lead people to believe that the church's sole business is the sacred.

The present institutional structure of the church is a copy of the parent churches. While there may still be time for changes, unless they are encouraged, the unspoken language of clericalism will certainly lead to undesirable consequences. The danger is that the Third Church may come to view ministry in the same way as western Christians in the Second Church. To different degrees and in novel ways, the possibility for this is present. To overcome present passivity, an appreciation of lay ministry as an active involvement in both church affairs and the issues facing the broader society must develop. Walbert Bühlmann's *The Coming of the Third Church* could well be read precisely as an expansion of this point.[5]

The Third Church has not been encouraged to take on novel shapes because its founders bear the genes of the Second Church. This is not to say that there are no missionaries working creatively to bring about just what is being advocated here. It is only that these creative initiatives have not yet become institutional policy. For the most part, Protestant mission boards, Catholic mission societies, and Roman congregations unselfconsciously pursue policies which insure that the Third Church will basically resemble its Second Church parents.

The shape of the ordained ministry in its clergyman model distorts an authentic concept of *diakonia* as a service in and of the total community in every realm of life. Though the following discussion treats ordained ministry in a way which might seem to be giving the leadership exactly the sort of prominence I am here trying to deny, it should be borne in mind that my aim is exactly the opposite. The preoccupation with the theology of ordained ministry arises precisely to redress the balance, not to create a new species of clericalism. What follows must always be placed in the context of Chapters 3 and 4 or run the risk of being misunderstood.

5

Church Office and the Sacrament of Order

In Chapters 5 and 6 we enter into complex doctrinal and historical questions in order to make positive suggestions for restoring the church to good health. Much will be said that will seem extremely technical to some readers. As well, much will be said that may be justly questioned by scholars as overly simplified. I have tried, on the one hand, to do justice to the nuances involved in the development of the sacrament of order and, on the other hand, to treat these complexities in a manner which will be understandable to the general reader. Dominant throughout is a desire to accent aspects of the theology of order relevant to the question of ministry in the Third Church.

The Place of the Sacrament of Order in Ecclesiology

One of the persistent defects of scholastic theology has been the seeming unrelatedness of sacramentology to a theology of the church as a whole. A large part of the modern renewal of sacramental theology has been directed at understanding the sacraments as celebrations of the church as a whole, as an integral part of ecclesial life. One of the most valid Protestant criticisms of Catholic theology has been the complaint that the sacraments seem to have a quasi-magical life of their own, cut off from the organic faithlife of the community. If this is true of the sacraments in general, it is nowhere more true than in the case of the "sacrament of holy orders." When linked to a theory of apostolic succession which saw the power over the sacraments transmitted from the "Twelve Apostles" and Peter to the bishops and the pope, the sacrament of holy orders became an essential part of Catholicism's confidence that the Church of Rome alone was the Church of Jesus Christ. The ideology growing up around this sacrament, in effect, became the supreme guarantor of the validity of Catholicism's claim to be *the* dispenser of God's saving grace.

Here our attempt is the modest one of showing that the sacrament of order must be placed within a theory of an apostolic church order if it is to escape disembodiment from the organic life of the community which quasi-magical understandings have brought about. The conventional Latin term for the sacrament is *sacramentum ordinis,* traditionally rendered in English as "sacrament of holy orders." It seems preferable to use the more literal "sacrament of order," since we thus avoid the pitfalls of recent historical connotations of sacral thinking which have tended to identify the sacrament with one of its elements: priesthood.

It is the conclusion of modern scholarship that the ancient church quite knowingly avoided the use of the priestly language of Greco-Roman or Israelite religion when it articulated its earliest understanding of its official ministry. The terminology utilized in the primitive church was basically secular and seems to have been chosen precisely to avoid the very sacral connotations which priestly terminology has subsequently added. The priesthood of the office-bearers of the church has often been treated as a power of the ordained themselves, causing the church to lose sight— at least at the popular level—of the uniqueness of the ministry of Jesus himself and the universal priesthood of all believers.

The priestly or "holy" aspect of the sacrament of order is best dealt with in the context of apostolic church order or constitution, not as a prerogative of the ordained. The ministerial priesthood of the ordained is but *one* aspect of their office, one means utilized by God to bring about the headship of Christ in the community as a whole. Centuries of overemphasizing the sacral has made it necessary to clearly subordinate the priest to a more organic, less sacral, ecclesiology of the whole community. Whatever is to be understood as specific and proper to the priesthood of the ordained is best grasped within the context of the ministry of the entire people.

It may seem too simple to maintain that the present shape of the church has crystallized around priestly concerns. In essence, though, this is my basic reading of the practical consequences of an unbalanced theology of the sacrament of order. I hope that the sharpness with which this view is presented will not alienate readers of a more conservative bent, but it is my experience that it is precisely on this point that debate must be joined if dialogue is to be directed to the crucial elements in my position. The statement intends no moral condemnation of the ordained hierarchy of the church. It does, however, underline my contention that a rethinking and restructuring of the ordained ministry is necessary if this important—but not dominating—function is to be put at the service of the total church's *diakonia* to God and world.

The sacrament of order is best understood when one stays close to the standard Latin terminology. Here we find the term *ordo,* a "rank," of office-bearers, which may be offensive to those who want to rule out hierarchicalism in the church, and may thus scandalize the theological left. But it emphasizes the collegial nature of office within the church, thus undercutting the position of those who would make office an individualized sacral conduit between the Godhead and the church. This, on the other hand, may scandalize the theological right. To discuss a sacrament of "order" avoids reducing the nature of office to merely holy matters, a tendency which has led the *ordo* of office-bearers to an excessive preoccupation with matters of cult and what might well be called the "other-worldly" dimension of Christian life.

To speak of a sacrament of order naturally leads to the question: "What sort of 'order' is meant by the word?" To which one should respond: "The proper apostolic order of the community." This insures in turn that attention will be turned to understanding office in the church in terms of the mission of the community as a whole, not as something at the summit of church life.

Insofar as the New Testament speaks of offices—and it does so only obliquely, leaving unsaid much more than it states—it speaks of them as being conferred on some members of the community in order that they may help to order the charisms which the church as a whole is given by the Holy Spirit. Hans von Campenhausen[1] and Hans Conzelmann[2] make it abundantly clear that to read New Testament terms such as *episkopos, presbyteros,* and *diakonos* as if they could be easily plugged into later sacral-juridical understandings of ecclesiastical office is to ignore a complex development of the meaning of these terms.

Though my own exposition of the matter intends to be Roman Catholic, the work of these two Protestant historians has been important in helping me better understand and come to terms with a dialectic in the early church's understanding of office. The difficulty is to do justice to what Catholics such as Eduard Schillebeeckx[3] and Carl Peter[4] term a *de jure divino* (which I will translate as "divinely willed") evolution in the understanding of the divine source of hierarchical office on the one hand, and what Protestantism, on the other hand, tends to see as a sacral-juristic deformation of a pristine purity. Schillebeeckx and Peter argue that what is conditioned by culture and history may also be divinely willed without thereby being considered forever normative. They articulate well the complexity of the dialectic whereby a state of affairs can be *de jure divino* binding at a given moment without precluding the possibility of future developments overturning the concrete forms those legitimate developments once took.

Classical Catholic positions, however, have tended to canonize the shape developments took by the end of the fourth century. Classical Protestant positions tend to recognize only the shape they had taken at the close of the formation of the New Testament. Both positions run the risk of being a-historical, that is to say, they easily ignore the vital question of the *theological* status of subsequent changes and fail to consider whether ongoing developments may be divinely willed for subsequent points in space and time. Here, however, we are merely trying to place the question of the sacrament of order in an integral, ecclesial context. The issue of the concrete form the sacrament will take in office-bearing is still being treated.

Our point is that the sacrament of order is the means whereby God signifies *(sacramentum)* and brings about *(res)* the proper apostolic order of the church. At a second level there is the negative element of criticizing the "sacralization" of the sacrament by reducing it to one of its constitutive elements: the priestly. For Catholicism, the Council of Trent (1545–1563) has been a major element in bringing about this reductionistic understanding of the sacrament of order.

Trent is important for a clear presentation of certain aspects of Catholic doctrine, but because it was a defensive council aimed at correcting what it believed to be the reformers' excesses, its canons are not a *full* treatment of the sacrament of order. The concern for two elements—the powers conferred and the permanent character impressed by the sacrament—make Trent's a one-sided theology. The sixteenth-century council's interest was in defending these aspects, not in articulating a complete sacramentology in a broader ecclesial context. We should not therefore use Trent for more than its Fathers intended.

Vatican Council I (1870) reflects a second characteristic attitude of the Catholic position by stressing the authority of the papacy and its powers. Vatican I's was not *new* doctrine. Rather, it upheld the authority of the office-bearers against liberalizing tendencies in the nineteenth-century European world.

Together, the two councils rest on the assumption that authority was given by Christ to the church's present rulers by a direct, lineal succession of office from the "Twelve Apostles" and Peter. Though historically minded Catholics have been generally persuaded that the question of apostolic succession is far more complex, until our own day the assumptions of these two councils have been central to the Catholic theory and practice of office and the ordination through which office is conferred. While ecumenical study groups have achieved promising solutions which make one hopeful that a mutual recognition of other churches' ordained ministries may be attained, the questions of the sacrament of order and apostolic succession remain primary theological obstacles to church unity.

What may be insufficiently recognized is the fact that the very rigidity with which Catholicism, at the official level, maintains the traditional doctrine is also the prime obstacle to allowing local autonomy in the Third Church. For it is clear that many of the solutions proposed for ending the dependence crisis in the Third Church (including those advanced in this book) seem "Protestant" to many Catholics, and are thus refused serious considerations.

How should the theology of the sacrament of order be approached if one is to remain faithful to the nature of the church as reflected in tradition, and yet open to new historical circumstances? First, one should recognize that the fences built around the sacrament of order have been erected to protect something extremely important. The sacrament of order has had a legitimate conserving function throughout history: insuring that the church's structure and order remain such that Christ may be encountered authentically by successive generations. Though our times are not the most auspicious for conservative agencies, it is only fair to say that in most societies and in most ages suspicion of tradition has not been as strong as it is today. In Oceania, for example, those persons who could faithfully transmit the rites and myths which gave the tribe contact with the very ground of its being and its sense of identity were the most revered. Such conservatism may, in fact, become more recognizably important even in the North Atlantic nations.

In dealing with church order, then, we should first be aware that the sacrament of order has a legitimate, conserving function. This is no argument for mindless conservatism, only a call to recognize that there is a cautionary side in office. But this aspect must be conditioned by an equally important dynamic side. Church order is not static but flexible. It is fluid internally because the community is alive; externally, because the community has a mission. And in times when one world order is passing and another being born, it is senseless to advocate that conservatism should be the dominant characteristic of God's people.

Most important of all, an approach to the sacrament of order must take account of the "apostolic" nature of the church. Not just any kind of order is the concern of the office-bearers, for long before anyone spoke of the *sacramentum ordinis,* there was concern for *apostolic order.* To discover the nature of the sacrament, then, one must first examine what is meant by an "apostolic" church.

Apostolic Church Order

One of the most basic failings of studies on priestly life and ministry has been the failure to treat them in the context of apostolicity. Reflection on the *powers* and *duties* of the ordained without getting at this basic element makes inevitable the slide into false presuppositions about priesthood and ministry that have dire consequences.

A second major failing springs out of an apologist mentality when examining ancient documents. Too often Catholic treatments on priesthood and episcopacy begin with a presupposition that both offices are to be found in the primitive church in much the same way as they are present to us today. The diaconate is also presumed to be there, though that question could easily be shelved, since, until recently, the diaconal order had practically disappeared from the Second Church.

When scholars discovered that our present arrangement of office into episcopal, presbyteral, and diaconal functions cannot be traced to Jesus or to Paul, a crisis was bound to develop. In the not very distant past scriptural and patristic texts, which superficially seemed to support the subsequent triadic division of office, were read as if that was what they *intended* to teach. The gross result was to gloss over the pluralism of the ancient church's division of office and treat it as a sort of confusion that was later corrected when the popes were able to bring aberrant church orders into line. There is scarcely a scholar, either Catholic or Protestant, who today believes that such an exegesis or history is valid. But the same practical versus theoretical dichotomy which bedevils the recognition of cultural pluralism still allows the church, at the level of policy, to proceed as if the present shape of ministry is the only one warranted.

Solid scholarship shows that there was a great variety of approaches to church order in the formative years of Christianity. In a remarkably readable summary of such studies, Walter Burghardt states that in the New Testament we find no finalized or absolutized pattern of ministry and office. Rather, there is a developmental process at work. "Development itself is canonical and therefore normative."[5] The ramifications are immense. In the New Testament we will find materials which will show that subsequent moves may have been justifiable or even happy expansions of the biblical witness, but there is no clear picture of episcopal, presbyteral, and diaconal office.

What we do find in scripture is a kaleidoscopic view of a variety of ministries in an *apostolic* church. In an apostolic church, variety and pluralism and even serendipity mark what we today popularly consider to have been a divinely established and eternally valid church order. That order was, however, not of a single sort, at least not *externally*. The concern of the earliest officers (to use a word they would not have used themselves) was the maintenance of an *internal* order which is best termed "apostolic." It is the mark of *apostolicity* which we must understand if we are to grasp the proper criteria for judging what constitutes a valid church order and the sacrament of order *(sacramentum ordinis)*.

What do we, then, mean by the term "apostolic"? There are two basic uses of the term which must be distinguished. First, there is the *theological usage* deriving from Lucan and Pauline scriptural language. Secondly, there is the traditional *ecclesiastical usage* which sees the Twelve governing the church and acting as the first missionaries. This ecclesiastical usage of the term, Conzelmann notes, has no historical value.[6] Because the theological usage and the traditional ecclesiastical (and largely legendary) usages are not distinguished, Christians usually think of the family of words springing from "apostle" as indicating the primitive church's foundation by and upon the "Twelve Apostles." In fact, that picture derives much more from the needs of later generations to validate their origins, their orthodoxy, and their orthopraxis than it does from the history of the Twelve.

In point of fact, we have almost no historical evidence that the Twelve functioned as the ruling body of the primitive community or as missionaries in the Mediterranean lands or inland Asia. The best way to summarize the function of the Twelve is to realize that they had a threefold *symbolic* role: (1) as an image of the New and True Israel; (2) as eschatological judges at the end of time when Jesus would return to earth; and (3) as the *shaliach* (representatives) of Jesus whose association with him during his earthly life and after his resurrection gave great weight to traditions regarding the Lord which were considered especially important in conflict with heretics in later ages.

Thus, the record of Luke-Acts and other primitive sources which speak of the Twelve as the supreme authority in the church and as missionary founders of various local churches should not be viewed as historical in the modern sense of the word. Contemporary usage of the term *apostle,* in other words, should be theological.

In calling the primitive church apostolic, one is making a *theological* statement (true in itself) that rests on a history far more complex than the ecclesiastical usage has understood. It was a third generation of Christians in the period around A.D. 100 which crystallized the notion of apostolic succession that today is enshrined in the classical doctrines of the historical church and the sacrament of order. It is the theological confession that the later church was integrally apostolic which is important for understanding the sacrament of order. We simply have no way of knowing in detail the historical reality of the body known as the Twelve.

The assertion that the church was apostolic meant that succeeding generations were confident that they had preserved the experience and doctrine of the apostles who had had intimate commerce with the Risen One. Other men besides the Twelve, especially Paul, were the *shaliach* of Christ. As the Gnostic crises began and appealed to special, *private* revelations of the true gospel, men such as Polycarp, Ignatius of Antioch, and Irenaeus articulated the notion that the teaching of Christ had been handed down as *public, apostolic tradition.* The guarantee of such men to be propounding the true gospel was that they stood solidly in the received apostolic tradition.

Paul, and presumably other apostles, were patriarchal figures in the first generation. When these leaders died, the authority of their ministry passed to those whom they had chosen to rule their churches. In that entire process, the nontransmittable, *personal* nature of the apostles' authority came to be understood as somehow enjoyed by their successors in the apostolic office. There was no universal practice or understanding of the meaning of this process of succession; documents coming from the second century show a variety of understandings and practices. But in all cases the new leaders were considered to be the guardians of apostolic tradition. There was a widespread tendency, though, toward considering the guardianship and leadership of the church as an "office" to which one must be legitimately appointed.

In time, the tradition which we will call the "Jewish Elder," or presbyteral, form of governance came to dominate. Von Campenhausen states that there were three principal strands feeding into the idea of office, each of which may be termed "embryonic forms" of the subsequent Roman Catholic, Greek Orthodox, and Lutheran thinking on office.[7] In Rome, for example, the bishop is the supreme cultic official of the congregation;

in Syria he is its spiritual example and sacral focus; and in Asia Minor he is the preacher of apostolic teaching. What seems common to all traditions, however, is the felt need to remain firmly founded on the apostolic experience of the Risen One, and to find ways in which to combat heretical distortions of that experience.

These "officers" had to preserve apostolic tradition if a given local church was to be recognized as authentic by other churches. There was a pluralism of concrete structures, but the early church was conscious of being a communion of local communities. Apostolicity was an essential mark, and involved an integral fidelity to the witness of the Twelve, who by this time had become a *theological symbol*. The theological teaching was that because the churches were faithful to the witness of the Twelve, they were the true community of faith.

The apostles' successors had the function of maintaining unity and apostolicity in a fast-spreading and far-flung church. Lists of leaders were drawn up to prove that the heads of the various churches could trace their tradition to that of the original apostles, and out of this has grown Roman Catholic and Greek Orthodox theories of lineal succession in the office of the church. But it is important to realize that the idea of lineal descent had a defensive purpose against the heretics. The laying on of hands, as a sign of installation in apostolic office, was a public display of the call by God of other men who were to carry out their guardianship function. In all cases, then, the central fact is the maintenance of tradition.

There are two theological issues which deserve at least a passing treatment: a question of method, and the ecumenical ramifications of apostolic succession. First, the question of theological method in developing our position. One will not find a theoretical understanding of apostolic succession if one reads the standard patristic or scriptural founts from which I have drawn my account of apostolicity. This is because of the nature of the early church and the intellectual methods then used. Early writers argue apologetically against what they consider abuses and mistakes, but their methods are not those of modern interpreters. Rather, the authors of the Pastoral Epistles, Clement, Polycarp, Ignatius of Antioch, and Irenaeus are involved in a world of practical common sense reasoning and fall back on arguments the forms of which are different from those of later generations.

In stating that defending a certain doctrine is a matter of preserving apostolic tradition, these authors are not giving a theoretical explanation of the sacrament of order or apostolic tradition. Rather, they defend the practices of their day by showing that what the Great Church is doing in their own time is consonant with the received apostolic tradition and that the heretics (for example, the Gnostics) have introduced new and spurious elements. Their arguments will only later be cast into more theoretical understandings of succession and ordination. What we are endeavoring to do is uncover the underlying thrust of their practice and concretize it around the notion that the office-bearers' primary function was that of guarding apostolicity. This is important for our second purpose.

The lineal descent arguments of the early Fathers have been used to deny validity to Protestant offices. It is extremely important to realize that the early Fathers were involved in apologetics, defending the Great Church from the heretics. Lineal descent arguments were used to bolster teaching on the preservation of public, apostolic tradition. They are not in themselves sufficient theoretical foundation for theories which say that non-Catholic churches are not apostolic because they lack lineal descent from bishops who enjoy valid ordination by the laying on of hands. This, of course, brings us to the center of the contemporary debate about the validity of Protestant orders. This issue requires a much more detailed analysis than we are giving to it here, but it may be useful to state that the teaching on apostolic succession should *not* be used for denying validity to churches whose ministry does not enjoy lineal, juridical succession.

To return to the main strand of our argument, it is clear that an authentic, apostolic church is one which preserves integrally the apostles' experience, teaching, and practice. The post-Easter encounters with the Lord form the basis of apostolicity. They are a never-to-be-repeated patrimony which is preserved and handed on in the apostolic succession of various communities, but not as something merely "past." Rather, succeeding generations' experiences of the Holy Spirit in the community authenticate the objective, historical tradition of the apostles and bolster a subjective, personal proof that their words are true "because the love of God has been poured into our hearts by the Holy Spirit which has been given us" (Rom. 5:5).

Apostolicity is a possession of the entire church, not just of its leadership. Its guardians are those who have been given the office of protecting the objective tradition of early apostles. Various shapes were given that office, yet that did not invalidate their authenticity. The Council of Jerusalem, for example, allowed pluriformity between Greek and explicitly Jewish forms of Christian fellowship, canonizing the principle that uniformity, either in forms of office or community life, is not required for being fully church.

Office and Offices in the Early Church

As already noted, it is dangerous to read contemporary understandings of episcopacy, priesthood, and diaconate into primitive Christian texts. A sounder methodology demands that one first examine the entire context in which reference to these offices or ministries appears. Eduard Schillebeeckx attempts to explain in contemporary theological language the thrust of the ancient understanding of office, as follows.[8]

1. The "offices of the church" (episcopate, presbyterate, and diaconate) emerged in the community as guided by the apostles (note, *not* by the

"Twelve"). The early church did not see these offices as merely human forms used to guide the church; they were for a purpose more theological than mere housekeeping or governance.

2. There is, however, "no direct link between the contemporary offices of the church and an act of institution on the part of Jesus while he was on earth." In other words, there is no way of proving that the actual shape which the offices took was laid down by Jesus himself, nor that the Twelve or Paul left any similar directions. The early church felt entitled to make decisions about the shape of the offices which were gradually established to guard apostolic tradition.

3. The emergence of these offices, however, should be interpreted, according to Schillebeeckx, as *de jure divino,* the fruit of the activity of the Spirit in the church. Though historical and doctrinal factors which led to these offices are intrinsic to the shape of their emergence and their *gestalt,* one would not be justified in attacking them as a multilating of the pristine spirit of the primitive church. Very early, certainly by the time of Ignatius of Antioch (c. 115), the existence of authority-endowed office-bearers, representatives of God, was considered essential to an apostolic church. What the historical factors indicate is not that office is incompatible with gospel, but that *de facto* the forms, divisions, and powers of the office of the church are to be regulated by the church.

The ramifications of these points must be clarified. First, the offices of the church were aimed at keeping the church integrally apostolic. They were considered to be of vital importance, and that function went deeper than the need to keep the church morally united or to settle practical disputes. The early church believed that the apostles had handed on a requirement that there should be men who would continue the apostles' own watchdog function of guiding the church. These officers would not have the personalized authority of the apostles (based on their first-hand acquaintance with the post-Easter events), but they would enjoy real, spiritual authority.

This is not an unimportant point. Since the Reformation, there has been a persistent attack on the Catholic notion of hierarchical authority. Even today, studies of the early church emanating from the reformed tradition tend to see the development of ecclesial offices as a deformation. One need not defend every aspect of the Catholic theory of office to see that such an attitude is a-historical. The German word *Frühkatholizismus* has often been used in a manner which calls into question the validity of the adoption of "early Catholic elements" in the postapostolic church. We cannot adequately answer the question here, but it is clear that to view the development of office as a major deformation of Christianity is to see the church as deviating from its pristine design at a very early stage. Rather than issue a blanket condemnation of the entire institution of offices, modern Catholic thought has taken what seems to be a safer road: identifying the belief of the church in order to make a selective criticism of elements which today may legitimately be altered.

Oceans of ink have been spilt to show that New Testament and patristic texts which witness to an institutionalizing of the church are a Catholic aberration from authentic apostolic ecclesiology. I believe that the position of Schillebeeckx is finally more satisfying. What is really at stake is the church's ability in *every* age to adapt itself to circumstances. If the Gnostics and the Marcionites created a situation where institutional cohesiveness and insistence upon authority derived "from the apostles" made it necessary to become more juridical in understanding the guardianship function of leadership, that was one historical circumstance. What emerges from it is best understood as a *de jure divino* impulse of God's guidance. Another age may require the dismantling of this structure without these subsequent demands being any the less divinely willed. The modern distrust of hierarchical institutions in the church derives from dissatisfaction with an outmoded authoritarianism. It is far less successful in disproving the still pressing need for an authoritative leadership which can help the community remain rooted in authentic apostolic tradition in new ages.

Secondly, Schillebeeckx's assertion that there is no direct link between the offices of the church and their institution by Christ requires explanation. *Episkopos, presbyteros,* and *diakonos* became the words used to depict three levels of office. The episcopate was considered the most basic, and there is no historical doubt about the fact that bishops were seen as successors of the apostles. By the third century, this belief had become general throughout the church, but the direct link of bishops with the Twelve as the apostolic founders of the key churches of ancient times is impossible to maintain except by realizing that the connection is primarily theological, not historical.

The function of bishops was to maintain apostolicity, but they can be termed successors of the apostles only in a secondary sense as they perform one function proper to the original witnesses of the Resurrection: maintaining their teaching. That function was the basic reality of apostolic office and later of episcopal office, but in the later church it could be exercised only indirectly, for the apostles' experiences (which constituted their role) were not repeated by subsequent miraculous appearances of Christ. There was no office of oracle to witness to the Resurrection anew and to guarantee its authenticity. Rather, the church was sent into the ambiguity of historical existence, armed with faith, hope, and love, there to puzzle its way through the murky waters of human existence. What we do have in the early church is the conviction that the guidance of the Spirit would be with its leaders to keep the community faithful to its head, Christ. The emergence of the elders (presbyters) helping the bishops in this activity in some churches springs from the Jewish patrimony. Indeed, the emergence of the first bishops is largely a matter of the presbyterate of elders requiring a head.

Thirdly, despite the fact that contingent historical and sociological factors determined the triadic shape of early office, this is not to be considered merely a human invention. In the first several centuries it simply became recognized that the Holy Spirit had led the church into a triadic form of office with Peter's headship of the apostles somehow carried on by the bishop of Rome. The process is one whereby later generations looked back at historical development and affirmed divine guidance of what had factually evolved. By the time of Cyprian of Carthage (c. 250), the episcopal form of government could be treated as something which had always been. Presbyters and deacons were the bishops' collaborators, but clearly subordinate to the men who exercised office directly in the name of Christ.

What one finds in the writings of bishops such as Cyprian, then, is an a-historical point of view. Cyprian, whose mode of filling the episcopal office influenced the entire Latin church, seems to know of no other ecclesiastical possibilities, and the conflicts of his age required practical solutions to pressing problems, not historical research. He acts as one with divine authority, without theorizing. Subsequent generations took over his self-confidence and the shape of the church—except for the development of papal office—became what it would remain down to the sixteenth century.

One might wish that Cyprian and those who have followed him would have had a more nuanced appreciation of the complexity of the earlier years of the church. For one thing it would have made the church far less rigid in its modern demand that the valid historical shape of office in Cyprian's age be retained in future ages. But even the a-historical view of Cyprian is a part of church history.

Fourthly, if we leapfrog back to the second century, it is clear that before the present theology of the bishops as successors of the apostles was clearly articulated and formalized, there was a *de facto* belief that the church had the power to regulate the form of offices. Ignatius of Antioch, early in the second century, clearly reflects a triadic form of office which became the rule for the Great Church. But even this picture was the result of historical events flowing into the important church of Antioch and later flowing on into other churches.

We can argue today about the ideal shape of office in the modern cultural and historical context precisely because there has been evolution in the past. Historical theology, then, gives us the dogmatic grounds for changing the structure of both church and office for new situations. To quote Schillebeeckx:

> What, then, emerges in the concrete from the foregoing is that there is a
> real need for the leadership of the church to consult the behavioral

sciences, and in particular religious sociology, in order to conduct a
suitable pastoral policy, especially in changed cultural circumstances.
What must emerge from pastoral experience, illuminated by sociological
investigation and research undertaken among groups, and seen against
the background of dogmatic possibilities, is what new divisions are necessary within the office of the church in order to ensure that it will function
meaningfully in the future, not only in the light of the situation in the
West, but also in the light of the situation in the East and the "third
world," with the meaningful models already there. Within the apostolic
criteria, meaningful development and pastoral suitability must be the
guiding principle in any such restructuration—that is to say, the guiding
principle for a *jus condendum* [a law for establishing something new], since
the apostolic criteria do not bind the church to a definitive structure of
her offices which might crystallize out into a rigidly fixed and unchange-
able *jus conditum* [an established law].[9]

For the Third Church no less than for the Second, the ramifications of
Schillebeeckx's principles are enormous. Today, too, there should be
office-bearers who will act with the authority of Christ in apostolic
churches, but the concrete shape that their office takes is determinable by
the church itself. While this strips us of the comfortable presuppositions
which Catholics have enjoyed, it also leaves friendly space for maneuver-
ability and creativity in the Third Church. The church is first and
foremost a communion of local churches, each with a right to its own
forms and life-styles. This principle, though, must be conditioned by
another important fact. Church history can be read as a search for means
to insure that local churches be in true communion with one another. In
the final analysis, papal authority, for example, grew out of the perception
that Peter's symbolic (and historical?) ministry was required to bring about
this communion. Dissatisfaction with the exaggerated uniformity which
today characterizes much of modern Catholicism should be fruitfully
tempered with the realization that in the modern world unity between
churches is more important than ever. This said, however, the fact remains that centralization is "in possession" in Catholicism, and ours is the
hour of winning back the rights of local churches for independence.

Ordination and the Authority of Office

The sacrament of order, we have said, is the symbol and the instrument
whose goal is maintaining and deepening the integral apostolicity of the
church. This brings us to the double question of the authority of the
office-bearer and the main elements of office. The two questions are
inextricably joined. As we have done throughout this chapter, we will
prescind here from the question of specific divisions within office, preferring to accentuate its unity. We are leaving until the next chapter an
examination of how office has been historically differentiated. This has

the unfortunate result of making the present argument abstract, but is necessary in order to clear the way for the later discussion. In it all, though, I have in mind the complexity of the historical development of the specific offices which we know as episcopacy, presbyterate, and diaconate. The central point which remains is the need to consider the office of the church within a community-centered ecclesiology. The nature and authority of office are determined by the mission of the church.

In early tradition, the office-bearer is anointed by the Spirit and approved by the community for the function of insuring that Christ remain the Lord of the church. In discharging that office the ordained minister helps the community attain its own full maturity as the body of Christ in a given place and time. There is a *dialectic* at play in exercising that role, one which is important to realize if we are not to succumb to the tendency to simplistic solutions of the problems of ordination. On the one hand, tradition has it that the ordinand represents Christ "over against" the community, in some way enjoying Christ's own authority to rule. On the other hand, an equally valid tradition holds that the ordinand represents the community and does not rule on his own. The first aspect of the dialectic tension has historically led to hierarchicalism, the second to congregationalism.

When dealing with dialectically related elements, the natural human tendency is toward reduction of tension. In the case of the authority of office, such a move is to be resisted. Those who would accentuate one above the other can do so, of course, with impeccable scriptural and theological warrants. Paul, for example, can be appealed to in order to recommend both a rigid authoritarianism and a docile humanity. The later Pastoral Epistles recommend attitudes of tact and yet confer an underlying authority to act decisively.

The modern dissatisfaction with Catholic leadership is found in those who want popes and bishops to insist on the rigor of traditional law just as much as it is found among those who believe authoritarian manners of acting are the real problem. The true solution, I believe, is to be found in neither attitude, but in authoritativeness. By definition, an authoritarian leader acts on the basis of his or her legal position and tends to be officious even when exercising authority with a gracious smile. Such an attitude derives power from position rather than from qualities which inspire confidence.

Contrariwise, who has not known ecclesiastical leaders who have abandoned the attempt to lead, unable to bear up under the pressure of congregations and dioceses which are hopelessly divided? Commissions and advisory boards are multiplied, but few are satisfied; movement stops; ennui sets in, and drift ensues, all in the name of a collegiality which ignores the elementary laws of social bodies. The key function of the leader is to persuade various factions to cooperate, enabling them to participate in obscure but still-shared goals. Because of his ability to articulate the latent ideals of the community, the authoritative leader can bring about exactly this sort of highmindedness.

It is difficult to phrase suitably or describe adequately the nature of the authority of the office-bearer. Tradition insists that it derives from God, not primarily from the community. Yet this cannot legitimately be made the excuse for binding the community to blind obedience to its leaders as if their authority were absolute. The matter is made doubly difficult in a church where the faithful have little say in choosing their leaders. However, in earlier periods of church history no conflict was seen between leaders exercising authority in the name of God while being democratically chosen.

The issue stems also from a general cultural crisis with regard to authority. In both traditional and modern societies this crisis cannot be gainsaid. It is simply present. And it requires that the church examine radically the specific nature of ecclesial authority. For Roman Catholic authorities have taken upon themselves trappings of feudal society which have little to do with the nature of Christian office, which is given to one who loves the Lord more deeply (John 21:15–17), rather than to one with secular and political talents.

Ordination is the conferral of power and grace *(dynamis kai charis)* to exercise office in the name of Christ, the Christ who, though he came not to be served but to serve, paradoxically showed no hesitation in giving commands to his followers. Such an understanding of the conferral of grace and power in ordination sounds painfully old-fashioned to those reared in the new theology; nevertheless, it is a good description of what occurs. The problem lies in how one is to understand the words "power" and "grace." If they retain a connotation of a magical conferral of supernatural power and grace, they will be unacceptable to most people today. It is to be hoped that our treatment of these words will avoid magical connotations while keeping away from the apologetic trap of trying to justify the oversimplifications of the Catholic practice of office.

The medieval concern with the powers conferred at ordination *(potestas ordinis)* centered on the ability of the ordinand to perform the priestly functions of consecrating the eucharistic elements and forgiving sins. There is no escaping the fact that the attempt to define the essence of ordination in these terms has influenced the Catholic understanding of the sacrament of order down to the present. The concentration on priestly power has been so great that Protestantism concluded that this was the whole Catholic doctrine of the sacrament of order.

As much as anything else this misunderstanding has clouded the horizon and made an ecumenical dialogue on the nature of ecclesial office impossible, since to the reformed tradition it seemed as if Catholics had removed power from God's sovereignty to give priests a power of their own unconnected with faith. Modern Catholic theology, however, has tended to return to the older, classical understanding of ordination as an admission to pastoral office and has made genuine dialogue with the reformed tradition possible once again.

In the modern Catholic understanding of ordination there is an emerging consensus that ordination ought ideally to take place after a period of observation has allowed the church to judge that the candidate possesses the Christian maturity and authoritativeness which come from a combination of character and spiritual gifts. Admission to pastoral office requires an ability to expound the word and inspire a community in a way that admission to a cultic priesthood, defined by the power of confecting sacraments, did not. Ordination, it is realized, can never make up for a lack of discernment and the ability to expound the word authoritatively. Considering ordination an admission to pastoral office instead of to priesthood may seem a subtle shift in semantics, but it is far more than that. Basic to the shift is the realization that a pastorate involves gifts of leadership, administration, and intangible spiritual discernment capacities, all to be exercised to help a community become more vitally the body of Christ.

In this entire context, then, the power conferred in ordination is not the magical power of the sorcerer. It is, rather, an authority to exercise public office in the name of Christ and of the community. The power of ordination, I believe, is coming to be understood in two ways: first, as a moral authoritativeness; and, secondly, as a conferral of the public right to act in the name of Christ and his church. The second will mean little if the first is not present.

Etymologically speaking, ordination is the act of being established (*ordinari*) among the members of the college of officers who oversee the church. That college functions to keep church order apostolic: faithful to the original experience of the risen Lord. To be ordained, then, is to be appointed to that college. It is a matter of entering into a life of nurturing and maintaining the order inspired by the Spirit as he leads human beings, as individuals and communities, to share in the mind of Christ, aiding the members of the community to exercise their specialized ministries both within the church itself and within the broader human community.

Before one goes into such questions as who has the power to "say Mass" or to "forgive sins," it is well to realize that the sacrament of order, *in the persons of the ordained,* functions collegially to build up the body of Christ. Too often the sacrament has been considered the *rite* by which men enter into the exercise of the office. I believe it is much more fruitful to realize that the sacrament is not a rite, but the activity of the college's members centering on this goal. The point may be subtle, but it is important.

The sacrament of order, in this perspective, is the historical sociological instrument whereby God works to maintain the community as the church of Christ. The rite of ordination is merely a mode of entrance into a specific and vital service, not the sacrament itself. The person of the office-bearer is sacramental as he or she becomes the concrete means through which the Spirit operates to bring about the community of faith which is the Lord's body and God's special people.

Office is a function in the church, present from the earliest times, aiming at bringing about an apostolic community. Before there were divisions of office into episcopal, presbyteral, or diaconal orders, there always were individuals exemplifying various models of exercising the office of the church. When one understands the principle clearly, it becomes evident that the shape office takes may legitimately vary from place to place and from age to age. Tradition will have a role in giving names and specific descriptions to the offices of the church but, at least in principle, the church is free to shape the offices in accord with the needs of different cultures and historical epochs.

The Roman tradition of Christianity allowed history and culture to shape the offices of the church which are now more or less universal in the Second Church, but later on the tradition seems to have forgotten its own history. What is *normative,* as opposed to merely contingent or sociological, is the tradition handed down from apostolic times: that the Spirit raises up men (and may raise up women?) who will exercise the function of discerning the signs of the times and of coordinating the charisms of the community as it lives the Christian life.

One can expect that the forms through which this authoritative function is exercised will be influenced by the culture and the sociology of a given people. Historically speaking, this is what has happened in the creation of the Second Church. What is important for us today, especially in the light of the emergence of the Third Church, is to avoid freezing the forms of church office in Second Church models. African, Asian, South American, or Oceanic modes of exercising office should be allowed to interact with the specifically Christian elements of ecclesial authority to create forms of official ministry which will serve to incarnate Christ vitally in their diverse patterns of life. In the following chapter we will examine some of the significant developments in the Second Church's forms of exercising the sacrament of order in an effort to focus our attention more concretely on changes which may be necessary for contextualizing the ordained ministry in the Third Church. For the moment, though, it will suffice to summarize our position.

The sacrament of order is the entire divine/human reality of symbolizing and bringing about the Lordship of Christ in the church through the activity of the office-bearing college. Ordination is the conferral of the grace and authority needed to help the community grow into the body of Christ. The rite is not to be considered the whole sacrament, but as an entrance into a college of persons chosen because of their ability to aid their fellow Christians to growth in faith. The activities (ministry of word and sacrament, governing, teaching, and so forth) of the ordained are means for the building of the community and depend upon both the power of the Spirit and the faith of the church for their efficacy. The exercise of office requires the authorization we call ordination; the powers of office are best understood as the authority to act in the name of Christ and the community. The essence of ordained ministry is that of aiding the community to meet the varied challenges of its existence. Hence there is nothing in the theology of the sacrament of order which allows or requires that the forms of its exercise be frozen in the manners in which it was exercised in the past. The Spirit blows where it wills, and the one enduring function of the ordained is to help the community discern the directions of its dynamic Lord.

6

The Historical Development of Ordained Ministry

The historical development of the modern form of Second Church ministry has been a gradual movement. From a widely varying but general ministry of supervision the ancient church's second and third generations evolved, within two centuries, the episcopal form of government which we now generally take to be normative. From the beginning there were deacons whose functions were as varied as the churches they served. Except for certain ceremonial and ancillary functions, by the beginning of the Middle Ages deacons had disappeared. From the beginning presbyters also were present in most churches. Their role was enhanced until theirs became the ordinary pastoral office in daily contact with the faithful when monarchical bishops had become more distant figures. In what follows, the rise of the presbyters and the reduction of their ministry until it was understood as "priesthood" is the element that will be stressed. A brief examination of that reduction and a reflection on its implications for a contemporary of the meaning of pastoral ministry, specialized ministries, and church life as a whole will be made.

Though our focus is on the presbyterate, that focus is to be understood in the light of the thrust of our entire study: the need to overcome clerical domination of the church while remaining faithful to both apostolic tradition and the task of reshaping that legacy for changed circumstances.

The Path of Reductionism from Pastoral Office to Priesthood

Christian church offices are not without a Jewish history. An important point to note, however, is that their roots do not lie in the postexilic Judaic priesthood. Attempts to make church officers primarily priests in the line of Aaron are misconceived from the start. The primitive church quite knowingly avoided the use of Old Testament terminology for describing its leadership just as studiously as it steered away from a rich Greco-Roman vocabulary. Nor did it attempt to build its office upon a Christology of Christ the priest. Of course, the New Testament book which we today know as Hebrews justifies ascribing that title to Christ, as do other important New Testament strata, though in a less emphatic manner. But priesthood is not the total office of Christ. His priesthood is always subordinate to other functions and priesthood is never the basic element in the office of those we today would call ordained ministers. Our question then is this: How did the church come to call its ministers *sacerdotes* (priests)?

JEWISH PRESBYTERS — CHRISTIAN PRESBYTERS

The first link in the chain is the Jewish system of governance by elders. The Jewish institution called the *sanhedrin* (council) is basic to understanding the development of office. Not everything in church office can be traced to this institution, but it is the foundation and model of the earliest form of leadership ministries. In his book *The Origin and Evolution of the Priesthood,* Father James A. Mohler has richly documented this and has succinctly summarized the state of research on the question.[1] After examining original sources and attempting my own synthesis of this exceedingly complex period in the development of Christian office, I concluded that Mohler's summary said all that needs to be said. For most of what follows I am indebted to him and to Father David Power's *Ministers of Christ and His Church.*[2] Readers who are interested in a more scholarly and detailed treatment of the subject matter of this chapter should turn to Mohler and Power and the sources they cite.

The Jewish sanhedrin was a council of elders (Greek, *presbyteroi;* Hebrew, *zeqenim*) who governed the total life of post-exilic communities of Jewry in both religious and secular matters (though the distinction is a contemporary one which would have been foreign to their wholistic approach to religious life). The center of their concern was *Torah,* the "Law," the fundamental charter of the Israelite community. *Torah* cannot be understood if one tries to grasp it with a modern, legal mindset. For *Torah* is not mere conventional law, or even divine positive law. Rather, it is both a revelation of God's benevolent choice of a people and the people's total response to the divine loving-kindness.

The institution of sanhedrin is not to be understood as merely that of the Great Sanhedrin of Jerusalem which is so often encountered in the Gospels. Besides this Sanhedrin of elders, who had an overseeing role for the entire Jewish people scattered throughout the diaspora, there were local sanhedrins in every Jewish community of requisite size. As *Torah* regulated every phase of interpersonal relationships and religious observance, so the sanhedrins served to arbitrate disputes and make decisions that affected the entire life of the local communities.

The sanhedrin was the earliest model for the authority structure of the Christian Church. Presbyters ruled, judged, formed links with the secular government, and insured that the community observed tradition. Like their Jewish forebears, Christian presbyters were not made remote from their people by office. They exerted their authority by influence and reason, seldom by coercion, for their communities were small, and formal or coercive legal procedures are seldom feasible in face-to-face communities. The Jewish style of leadership by elders became the model for

Christian sanhedrins and gradually became the rule even in the more charismatic, less structured style of the Pauline communities.

By the time of the writing of the epistle to Titus, church leaders could draw up quite un-Pauline-sounding requirements for leaders and yet claim Paul's authority for their action, as is shown by a comparison of the description of qualities needed for Jewish and Christian presbyters.

JEWISH PRESBYTERS	CHRISTIAN PRESBYTERS
None are to be appointed members of the sanhedrin but men of stature, wisdom, good appearance, mature age, with a knowledge of sorcery, and who are conversant with the 70 languages of mankind so that the court shall have not need of an interpreter (*Babylonian Talmud*, Sanhedrin, I, 17a).	This is why I left you in Crete, that you might . . . appoint elders (*presbyterous*) in every town as I directed you, if any man is blameless, the husband of one wife and not open to the charge of being profilgate or insubordinate. For a bishop (*episkopon*), as God's steward, must be blameless. . . . He must hold firm to the sure word as taught, so that he may be able to give instruction in sound doctrine and to confute those who contradict it (Titus 1:5–9).

The spirit of the two lists is similar. The letter to Titus is, of course, not of Pauline authorship, but was written in a later age when the more charismatic, less formal structure of Pauline Christianity was giving way to the need of the community to organize itself. It is interesting that the bishop is a member of a council of elders. He is not yet a monarchical figure who has a council, but who is independent of it.

Of more than passing interest today is the fact that both the Jewish and the Christian lists require that the elders be male. It has often been suggested that the Christian exclusion of women from the presbyterate—when there was ample example of female priests in Greco-Roman religion—is a reason for continuing to exclude them. Such reasoning ignores the fact that the roots of the Christian presbyterate's all-male character lie in the masculine nature of the Jewish community's sanhedrin, not in a conscious and reflective negative answer to the question of admitting women to priestly office!

Furthermore, contemporary research tends to strengthen our awareness of the influence of Judaism on the shape of the early church. The all-male nature of the leadership of Judaism explains the fact of the all-male Christian presbyterate much more satisfactorily than tortured, a-historical, theological explanations harking back to the maleness of Jesus. It is illogical to deny women ordination on *theological* grounds, ap-

pealing to early practices when those practices have *sociological,* not doctrinal foundations.

The majority of early Christian churches, especially in Palestine, would
have had Jewish elements in them. This would have been true throughout
the Mediterranean basin. The structure of the sanhedrin and its presbyterate, then, contributed heavily to the form of government adopted by
most churches as the first generation of apostle-missionary-founders
began to pass away in the last third of the first century. The Pastoral
Epistles, for example, are a reflection of this when they are written under
the aegis of a putative Pauline authority. Even the term *shaliach* (apostle)
itself springs from this environment and should make us very wary of
equating apostles with the Twelve. A Jewish *shaliach* was a representative
of the Great Sanhedrin of Jerusalem sent to diaspora communities to
announce decisions and to bring back news about their life. Paul claimed a
special apostleship, of course, founded on his experience of the risen
Lord, and most clearly adds the missionary note to the vocation of apostle,
but the ambassadorship which is the root of the Christian *shaliach* remains
rooted in its Jewish past.

Within the biblical picture of the Jerusalem community we have several
contradictory pictures of its governance. There is the symbolic one
wherein the Twelve, headed by Peter, rule after Pentecost (Acts 6:2–6).
Secondly, there is a picture where James seems to be the president of a
Christian sanhedrin which makes no mention of the Twelve (15:12–13).
Here the apostles seem to be present (vv. 22–23), but separate or distinct
from the elders who with James make the decision. Thirdly, we have
Paul's own account of the Jerusalem Council where neither the Twelve
nor a sanhedrin of elders is mentioned, but only the "pillars" of the
Jerusalem church—Peter, James, and John (Gal. 2:9–10).

From tradition, it seems most likely that James was the overseer of the
Jerusalem church until his death and that the presbyterate form of government was exercised there. James may have served as an *episkopos,* but it
is probable that he ruled more as a presbyteral president than as a
monarchical bishop even though his preeminence and power may well
make him deserve his designation as a prototype of the bishops who would
emerge by the end of the century. In any case, the term *sanhedrin* passed
away and its Greek equivalent, *presbyterate,* became the term by which the
governing body of many early churches was known.

Deserving of attention is the fact that the primitive church utilized
traditional Jewish organs of community authority while steering clear of
sacerdotal terminology. To be sure, this is partly explained by the fact that
the primitive community was still involved in Jerusalem temple worship
and had not yet completed the rupture that would carry it away from
Judaism (cf. Acts 3:1; 5:12; 6:7). But it can be explained also by the fact
that the church realized that something new was present in its fellowship
when it gathered to celebrate the Eucharist which would quickly become

its own distinctive worship (cf. 1 Cor. 11). Though the primitive church shunned Jewish sacerdotal terminology and advanced beyond its worship structures, it did not hesitate to utilize the ordinary authority structure of contemporary Judaism. As we shall see, by the middle of the third century, at the time of Cyprian of Carthage, the concept of a monarchical bishop would have made the Jewish roots of Christian office almost unrecognizable, but the fact still remains that the church chose a *semi-secular form of government* as its own in those first years.

As Christian self-understanding grew, and as the church expanded into the Roman world, it experienced a need for further adaptations, and this Jewish heritage begins to fade. But if one is looking for scriptural warrants for change and adaptation of the structure of ordained ministry and office, it is clear that the New Testament's picture is of a highly complex process of evolution begun already in the first century. In a Third Church context, then, a similar process would seem repeatable. If there are models of exercising office which may be more understandable to local Christians than those of the Second Church, these may well be suitable for use as the initial vehicles of indigenous office.

Another point deserves emphasis. Apparently Jesus did not leave clear instructions on the shape of office. The words we use today to designate bishops, priests, and deacons appear in the New Testament, but a close examination shows that at the time the meaning of these terms was in flux. If the organs of office had been the subject of an explicit mandate from Christ, this would hardly have been the case. One can only conclude that things were left flexible. In fact, it is much easier to trace the evolution of church ministries, as well as to show the pluriformity of ministries, than to find modern ecclesial offices in any recognizable form in the New Testament.

In the contemporary Third Church context, the preoccupation with finding men who will meet Second Church criteria in educational attainment, celibacy, and culture finds little to recommend itself. A group of Galilean fishermen are made the symbols of leadership in the scriptures. Whether they ever ruled as a group is less important than the fact that when the early church characterized its roots in scripture, it did so in a way which (1) was rather casual in its use of historical facts, (2) shows little concern with later hierarchical nit-picking theologies of leadership, and (3) continually has a semi-secular Jewish form of government lurking in its conceptual background.

Mohler summarizes the evolution of the Christian presbyterate from its Jewish forebear as follows:

> Modelled on their Jewish contemporaries, the Christian presbyters can be found in Jerusalem under the "Nasi" James, collecting and distributing alms to the needy, sharing with the Twelve decisions and judgments not only for the Jerusalem community, but for the diaspora as well, to which they dispatch apostles to promulgate their regulations. Paul and

Barnabas go around the diaspora appointing, ruling, and judging presbyters with whom Paul kept in touch by visits and letters of instructions.

In the Pastorals we begin to see a distinction between the college of
Christian presbyters and their guardian president, who is the father of
God's family and the steward of Jesus Christ. Although presbyters seem
to have been in the church from the beginning, the guardians do not
appear till Ephesus in 58. The distinction between presbyters and guardians is growing but not yet is there the monarchical trend of the second
century.

Presbyter-guardians must be morally upright and show the qualities of
prudent government illustrated by the loyal father of a Christian family.
They must be good and faithful stewards of the heavenly treasure left in
their trust by the Master. Presbyters should be chosen with care, corrected when erring, and recompensed especially when engaged in
preaching and teaching.

Christian elders, as their Jewish counterparts, were ordained by a
laying on of hands to judge and rule the community in synod. The
Christian elders appear to have been chosen by the Christian apostle, but
not without consultation. It would seem that they held the same place of
honor in the liturgy as their Jewish confreres.

As yet we have no Christian priesthood paralleling that of the Temple.
In the epistle to the Hebrews Christ is the sole high priest of his priestly
people. Not till the second and third centuries do we find priestly
analogies applied to the Christian officers, first to the bishops, then to the
presbyters and deacons.[3]

Clement of Rome, who died about the year 97, was probably the
overseer of the See of Rome in the last decade of the first century. Head of
the church of Rome, he nevertheless feels an obligation to admonish the
church of Corinth when certain factions begin deposing presbyters. Clement argues that their guardianship of the church (*episkope*) serves as a
center of unity in the place of Christ. Anyone who rejects them, rejects
him. People who are prone to sedition should leave the community so that
the community may live together in peace with its presbyters.[4]

To be noted here are two things. First, Clement's is not a fully self-
conscious papalism, but his letter does indicate that the Roman church —
both because of the importance of the Roman state and Peter's former
presence there—already very early in church history is not afraid to exert
influence and power outside of its own area. Lest one be tempted to make
Clement into a pope claiming universal jurisdiction, however, it is well to
note that similar letters from other bishops to other sees could be prof-
fered as well. The early church was a communion of local communities
with a lively interest in what was going on elsewhere. Secondly, Clement
understands the presbyters to have real authority, which they exercise in
Christ's name. It was not a monarchical authority, to be sure. Rather,
Clement's letter gives us a snapshot of an evolving ministry similar to that

shown in the Pastoral Epistles of the New Testament. It also shows us that authority is more and more becoming attached to office-bearers with definite powers.

Along with the presbyters who have a residential overview of the local church, there were also "apostles and teachers" in the church pictured by Clement. They had a role as charismatic teachers and preachers, but the direction of evolution was soon to subordinate them to the bishops. In the *Didache* we find a picture of Eastern Christianity where itinerant apostle-prophets make their periodic appearances and enjoy a position of respect in the local communities. It is possible that some of these apostle-prophets settled in towns and became heads of the councils of presbyters who had the task of overseeing these communities. It seems that at the time of the *Didache*'s writing such apostle-prophets outranked residential guardians and deacons, but already they were in the process of disappearing from the scene as formal, more juridical norms for governing local churches came into play.

Ignatius of Antioch (d. 117) gives a picture of a highly structured church where presbyters are the bishop's assistants and councilors. The guardian-bishop alone has the right of presiding at the Eucharist, but he may give another the right to do so in his name. The Antiochene model is not yet universal, but it will become the general pattern in the second and third centuries. For Ignatius the term *episkopos* clearly means a monarchical, residential bishop. In the Pastoral Epistles *episkopos* and *presbyteros* could be used interchangeably, along with *diakonos,* as general terms for official ministry. But in Ignatius the meaning that has come down to our own times is being crystallized. It should be observed, though, that other writings from the same time make it clear that itinerant ministries which followed the Pauline model still had an honored place. Even as late as the year 200 Irenaeus of Lyons used *episkopos* and *presbyteros* in a way which shows that the Antiochene vocabulary had not yet become mandatory in the West.

Still another factor must be considered. Mohler notes that there is a Johannine vision of the church, common especially in Asia, which tended to see each local church gathered around the mystically present Christ—its center of unity—as *the* church. The Pauline vision, however, came to dominate in the West. In it there is an emphasis on a global unity of everyone and everything in Christ, a unity represented by the ministers who exercise authority in his name. The Pauline view, united with the Jewish Elder tradition, dominates church development in the Latin West, perhaps because it was congenial to the Roman fondness for a large-scale design, and the fact that it was the church which stepped into the breach when Roman civil authority faltered at the close of the Empire.[5]

In the East, however, though monarchical bishops there certainly were, the western preoccupation with formal unity under the jurisdiction of the bishop of Rome never became a vital part of church development. In the present tendency to grant more autonomy to local churches, we can see an attempt to balance the Johannine and the Pauline visions of the church.

PRESBYTERS BECOME PRIESTS

Studies of the early church, notably those of Cardinal Daniélou, insist that a large part of the theological enterprise in the first centuries was a matter of the Christian church coming to terms with Judaism.[6] At first, the scriptures were those of the Old Testament, and it was important to give the correct interpretation of them. Only gradually, under the guidance of the church, did the New Testament canon form. Christian teachers and preachers, both during and after that formation, expounded their doctrine using allegorical and typological interpretations of the Hebrew scriptures in their Septuagint form. The church came to be understood as the New and True Israel; institutions such as the Israelite priesthood were understood as types and foreshadowings of the priesthood of the new law. As well, the need to assimilate popular attitudes toward the pagan priesthoods and religions formed a hard-to-evaluate cultural substratum in the rapidly expanding church. This pagan milieu undoubtedly had an influence on the unfolding of Christian office and must be remembered as one sees church office becoming more sacral.

These pagan and Jewish influences made it inevitable that bishops came to be thought of as priests. The word *sacerdos* makes its appearance and is applied to their ministry as Christian cult becomes more elaborate and strives to satisfy the pagan converts' need to participate in forms which will satisfy their spontaneous, cultural inclinations for religious experience and fellowship.

If one reads, for example, the letters of Cyprian of Carthage, *sacerdos* is used in a completely unself-conscious manner to speak of the *episkopus*. He often cites the Old Testament to bolster his teaching that the people must obey their priest (meaning bishop). Priests "celebrate the sacred mysteries daily." Presbyters are not yet generally called *sacerdotes* by Cyprian, but while he is in exile and unable to celebrate the Eucharist, they are authorized to do so. The picture that Cyprian draws of the Carthaginian clergy is one of presbyters and deacons as assistants of the bishop, but also one in which the bishop's office is clearly the key one:

> You ought to know that the bishop is in the church and the church in the bishop, and if there is anyone who is not with the bishop, he is not in the church. In vain they flatter themselves who creep up not having peace with the priests of God (i.e., the bishops) . . . when the church, which is one and Catholic, is not divided nor rent, but is certainly united and joined, in turn, by the solder of the bishops adhering to one another.[7]

Cyprian is an important figure, not because he advances a theoretical doctrine of episcopal power or sacerdotalism, but because he presumes that these teachings are accepted by all. In the wake of the Decian persecutions (c. 250–51), the church was troubled by all manner of divisive problems. One does not find Cyprian trying to prove a theological point of speculative merit; rather, he is trying to cajole the recalcitrant to return to the discipline which everyone had accepted before the controversies over the lapsed and heretical sacraments caused dissension.

Our point here is not to determine precisely where sacerdotal thinking attached itself to the episcopate, but simply to indicate that by the mid-third century it was well on the way to becoming an almost uncontested fact of life throughout the church. Neither Cyprian nor the many bishops he corresponds with (including Cornelius and Stephen, bishops of Rome) dispute the fact. The bishop is the priest of the church, and in his hands rests full juridical power to rule the local church. The Antiochene model found in Ignatius's letters has triumphed, and Roman legal thinking has begun to influence the West's understanding of the authority of those bishops.

At this time the bishop is still associated with the presbyterate and seeks the counsel and support of the deacons. The fact that the presbyters and deacons could oppose the bishops and create a major crisis indicates that the days of a strong presbyterate were not long gone. But we are clearly entering an era in which bishops are presidents with councils which they feel free to override and disregard. As the church gains adherents in the countryside, presbyters are increasingly made the ordinary pastors and are given habitual faculties to celebrate the Eucharist—the process whereby the presbyters will come to be considered *sacerdotes* with a lesser degree of authority than bishops has begun.

These presbyters are no longer residential members of a council of elders, together with deacons, but pastors in their own right. Nor were they celibates. The Jewish Elder tradition wherein mature, married men were the presbyters of the community was retained. As late as 722 we have a letter from Gregory II to the missionary bishop Boniface instructing him to ordain no one who has married "for the second time," a clear indication that the injunction of 1 Timothy 3 was still considered the normal rule for presbyters. There is no escaping the fact, however, that the teaching of St. Jerome on the superiority of virginity over married life exercised a major influence upon thinking about the single life as the ideal for the ordained minister.

Several religio-cultural threads are involved in the weaving together of celibacy and the ordained ministry. One of them is certainly the picture of Jesus as the celibate priest of the New Law. But, as Eduard Schillebeeckx points out, the gospel motivation ("for the Kingdom of God," Matt. 19:12) was not the initial one, nor necessarily the most important one. More important, though it is difficult to fully document them, were certain views as to the importance of sexual abstinence on the part of the person who was to offer the sacred mysteries. Much of this flows from both Jewish and pagan notions of ritual purity.[8]

Jewish and pagan rules for periodic abstinence from sexual relations on the part of priests were syncretistically mixed with Greco-Roman cultural fears of sexual pollution and gospel praise for celibacy in a way which, much later, would lead to a law binding all priests to remain single. In the question of the sacerdotalizing of evangelical ministry, as well as in the entire line of thought that leads to mandatory celibacy, one is, I believe, face to face with one of the early church's major attempts at contextualizing a Jewish apocalyptic message in a radically different historical and cultural situation. The problem (and the source of potential error) today lies in the tendency of many Catholics to see *that* contextual change as obligatory for all subsequent generations, and not merely the shape of one epoch's response to its context.

We have said little about the diaconate. This has been necessary, not because of a desire to downplay the diaconate, but because introducing an adequate discussion of deacons would have obscured our attempt to understand the main lines of the development of church office. In point of fact, the deacon became lost in the shuffle as ministry became increasingly sacerdotalized. Deacons were mentioned in any lineup of offices in the first several centuries. But as bishops became the high priests of the church and presbyters became their subordinate priests, the council-elder form of government—with its more communitarian emphasis—shrank to insignificance. At this point deacons may well be said to have entered an ecclesiastical limbo. Though they may have had a place in liturgy in the larger centers, their role was becoming more and more like that of an acolyte than of someone with an essential role to play. In places like Rome they retained the function of important advisors of the bishop, "his eyes and ears" as well, as one document put it. But when ministry was thought of as essentially sacerdotal, deacons lost any clear or important function in the order of office-bearers.

When one reads of the "golden age of the diaconate" from the time of Ignatius of Antioch till the Council of Nicea (325), it is clear that the deacons had important functions to play—administering finances, taking communion to the sick, caring for the poor in the name of the church, preaching, and teaching. The picture that emerges in that era is one wherein the diaconate was an important administrative, educational, and charitable ministry. It is probable that some deacons may also have celebrated the Eucharist, something which may be used, justifiably it is to be hoped, to prove our contention that the precise functions of office were once flexible. The diaconate disappeared as an important office permanently exercised when ordained ministry came to be identified as priestly service.

MEDIEVAL DEVELOPMENTS

From the time of the early Middle Ages down to the time of the Council of Trent (700–1545), we observe a gradual formalization and institutionalization of what had already emerged in many places by the middle of the third century. The process may be summarized as follows: (1) bishops became high priests in their dioceses; (2) Roman primacy came to be universally recognized; (3) priest-presbyters became pastors of the ordinary communities of faithful; (4) the diaconate disappeared as a general pastoral ministry in the "parishes"; and (5) monastic influence gradually began to affect the practice and understanding of clerical life-styles and piety, as monk-missionaries, such as Boniface and Columba, extended Christianity into northern Europe. During this time the sacrificial character of the Eucharist eclipsed other dimensions of the great sacrament and the priest was made its custodian.

The combination of suspicion of sexuality (crystallized by St. Jerome and St. Augustine) and the sense of a need for ritual purity in order to handle the Eucharist prepared the ground for the imposition of celibacy. It was a centuries-long movement made universally obligatory only in the twelfth century. In that entire process numerous factors intervened. Many of them were spiritual, but some of them had to do with things as mundane as priests leaving church goods to their children as inheritances and the desire of the church to keep a hold on its material wealth.

Medieval Christianity cannot be understood without reference to Benedictine monasticism and the later influence of the Franciscan and Dominican mendicant orders. Monasticism wore many faces; but it was Benedictinism (whether in a Cluniac or Cistercian form) which can be said to have had the most enduring impact. The missionaries who carried Christianity northwards from Italy and eastwards from Ireland and England were monks. Monks became bishops, and though (like Boniface) they endeavored to found a diocesan clergy, it is clear that monastic understandings of priestly life and ministry penetrated deep into the popular consciousness of what a priest ought to be, even when the monks themselves did not live up to their own high ascetical ideals.

The rejuvenating influence of the mendicant orders of Francis and Dominic was great, and again it is clear that the success of the monastic and mendicant orders greatly influenced the church's attitudes toward its ordained ministry. Nevertheless, as poorly educated as they may have been, secular priests bore the brunt of pastoral care in the years that carry us down to Luther and the Reformation. They may have had only the rudiments of doctrine and been scarcely able to read the Mass in Latin, but they were men of the people even as they shared their people's weaknesses for alcohol, wealth, sexual excesses, and superstition.

The key fact is that they were there to perform the rituals of birth, life, and death that gradually transformed pagan consciousness. The periodic attempts at reform indicate that the more sensitive bishops and popes wanted to upgrade these country priests, but that it was an almost impossible task. Both they and their people were descendants of the Germanic tribes which had overwhelmed the empire. Though the people of these tribes became Christians almost universally, the pagan substratum was never far removed from their understanding of the new faith. And when reforms were thought of, it was usually in the light of the ideals of monasticism and the later mendicant orders since these were the only models of a high level of spirituality available. This, then, is the root of the still present tendency to treat the secular priest as if he would be much more an ideal minister of Christ if he were more like a monk: celibate, living a life centered around the hours of the divine office, separated from the laity by special garb, and the like.

It is hard to define the moment when a proper understanding and practice of sacramental rites becomes empty ritualism or is colored by a magical mentality, but it is clear that medieval attitudes toward the sacraments and ministers who performed them did cross that borderline. When everyone was Christian and the faith had degenerated to the correct performance of certain rites, the need was felt for a major reform of ecclesial life, for sensitive men and women realized that gospel life was a much more radical response to God than a comfortable ritualism portrayed. And because priestly life-styles and ministry had to be changed if a renewed understanding of Christianity was to be practically implemented, it is not surprising that the clergy were vehemently attacked by the reformers of the sixteenth century.

Luther cut through the Gordian knot of medieval ritualism by skipping over the ten centuries of the Middle Ages to find his inspiration in the scriptural and patristic periods. In the Pauline emphasis on salvation through faith and the importance of preaching of the word, he found warrant for attacking the entire medieval doctrine and practice of office. The fluid structure of the New Testament period did not know the rigid hierarchicalism of the long ages which had seen the gradual juncture of Christian office with feudal society's institutions. For Luther it seemed possible to return to the pristine simplicity of the ancient church and to regain apostolicity without the elaborate structures of Catholicism. He did not, of course, intend from the start to do this; his program grew gradually. Nor did he totally escape history's burdens; for his own conservatism made him deeply fearful of the masses whose latent millenarism and desire for social reform he had touched. And when he was finished, he still had the clergyman at the center of his church, less monastic, to be sure, but still a person of considerable authority. Other branches of the Protestant Reform would try to be even more radically biblical, with the result that congregationalism without episcopal authority would bring with it the splintering of the church into thousands of independent bodies. At the time of Trent, though, all these consequences were still unforeseen, and Catholicism had on its hands the need to examine and reassert its belief in the nature of its ordained ministry.

The reformers exposed abuses in the life of the church, especially those which had obscured the centrality of personal faith as a response to the proclamation of the word. Priests, and often bishops, scarcely knew the scriptures. Worldly concerns and a belief in an almost magical efficacy of sacramental powers had divorced word, faith, and sacraments from one another. Salvation came to be considered a necessary result of receiving the sacraments almost as if they were tickets to eternal life or passports which could make up for an otherwise sinful life. Indulgences could be purchased and could supply for the punishments of purgatory. Priesthood had been split from pastoral life by the extension of monasticism. Private celebration of the Eucharist in the monasteries became one of the chief ways of earning a "cheap grace" which could excuse souls from the punishments of purgation, until gradually it began to seem that the primary purpose of the Mass and its priestly celebrants was that of rescuing sinners. Untold numbers of monastic priests had no direct ministry among the people, and scores of monasteries subsisted on the stipends given for saying Masses for the dead. Education for the pastoral, secular clergy was spotty at best and often completely missing. In this entire context, then, Luther insisted that ordination to a ministry which did not include a proclamation of the word was not valid ecclesial ministry at all. The Roman church, in the reformer's mind, had become totally corrupt and was unworthy of the name Christian.

FROM TRENT TO VATICAN II

Trent reacted by insisting that the sacrament of order was valid and permanent even when not connected with pastoral ministry among the people. The Council taught that a permanent character is conferred in the rite of ordination and that this character gives a spiritual power to confect the Eucharist and to forgive sins. According to the Council, Christ exemplified a priestly character in his act of sacrificial self-immolation. And since the Eucharist is communion in the cross of Christ, the priest must also be distinguished from the laity by a similar sacerdotal character which he receives at ordination. The bestowal of this power made the priest unique in the community.[9]

In the background lies the teaching of Thomas Aquinas, the doctrine that the laity's baptismal character was *passive*—giving them the power to *receive grace* from the church's public worship. The sacrament of order, on the other hand, gives the priest the *active power* to consecrate, forgive sins, and bless.[10] The church was, in effect, divided into those members who had active and passive powers.

The scholastic terminology that flowed into Trent's teaching did not mean to settle disputed philosophical and theological questions within Catholicism, but it did mean to undergird Catholicism's confidence in the sacrament of order as the means of salvation which benefited the Christian faithful independent of the merits or demerits of its ministers.[11] Unfortunately, the insistence on the *ex opere operato* character of sacerdotal efficacy in the sacraments is open to the crudest of magical interpretations. Literally, the term *ex opere operato* means "by the act being per-

formed" and intends to teach that God will grant the grace signified even
if the minister of the sacrament is unworthy. God is the giver of grace,
then, and the person who "does not interpose an obstacle" will receive that
grace if he or she receives the sacrament in good faith, intending to
receive it, not merely because the sacrament represents a "divine promise."[12]

The Catholic position meant to assure the faithful that God stood
behind the sacramental activities of the validly ordained minister. But this
position probably did not understand the radical, personalistic nature of
the challenge offered by the Lutheran appreciation of the act of faith,
which threw the entire question of salvation back upon a decision in the
heart of the believer. For the Reformation, faith was a total act of trust in
God. In the light of that sort of radical faith, the entire medieval system of
clerical mediation between God and humankind became somewhat
superfluous. Pastoral ministry for the Reformation was primarily the
ministry of the word which offered human beings a chance to respond
personally to the divine offer of salvation in Christ.

For the Tridentine Fathers this represented a denial of the efficacy of
the sacramental system. The entire evolution of Catholic thinking had
rested on an almost "physical coercion" view of clerical power in sacramental activity, and it was exactly this which was called into question by the
Lutheran view that the role of the official ministry of the church was
limited to proclaiming a word to which people responded in trust. The
medieval Catholic heritage had arrived at a point where popular faith was
primarily directed to the church's ability to deliver salvation through the
sacraments performed by validly ordained priests. God was viewed as
standing behind that system, but his was a presence mediated by the
sacramental powers of the church's hierarchy, not directly to the heart by
the proclamation of the word.

Reviewing the entire problem of Lutheran and Catholic visions of
ministry, George Lindbeck brings the proclamation/sacramental mediation issue to bear in the following question: "Is it not true that Roman
Catholics are irrevocably committed to the view that the legitimacy of
office ultimately guarantees the authenticity of proclamation?"[13] It would
seem that Trent's answer is yes. Office was viewed as undergirded by
divine power in such a manner that the sacramental celebration/
proclamation would *ex opere operato* confer grace. But that view never
successfully understood or met the Protestant concern for the *quality* of
faith and the unknowable mysteriousness of the divine activity in the heart
of the one addressed by the word.

The history of ministry in the Catholic Church from Trent to Vatican II
is chiefly one of the reform of the clergy and a paring away of the worst
abuses in matters such as traffic in indulgences. The basic Catholic confidence in the power of office was never seriously questioned. The Jesuit
movement gave a new model for clerical training and provided the church

with legions of better-trained priests. But the entire shape of priestly ministry remained that of a sacerdotal class, semi-monastic and celibate, performing an office of mediation. The underlying vision of the Catholic reform was to provide priests whose lives would exemplify the virtues of Christ by being lived solely for God in the service of their people. Celibacy, especially, was a means for emphasizing this vertical dimension. And it should not be forgotten that the Counter-Reformation did have tremendous successes in the area of clerical reform. The example of the Jesuits gave Rome confidence in the vigor of monasticism and semi-monastic service in the active life, thus making it possible for Catholicism to avoid a serious questioning of its structures of ministry.

The lamentable side of this four-century period is the lack of Catholic recognition that the reformers' insights were profoundly rooted in scripture and patristic practice. But while the reformers cut through the Gordian knot of feudal patterns of ecclesiastical power wielding, they never succeeded in overcoming tendencies which led to the splintering of churches into smaller and smaller units as theological and practical problems caused bitter divisions.

Trent and its doctrines can help us understand better the present resistance of Catholicism to changes in the structure of ordained ministry. Priesthood had become the dominant note in the sacrament of order. The priest was the guardian of the Eucharist understood as the sacrifice of the New Law. The Mass was the rite wherein Christ immolated himself to win the Father's favor for sinners. New seminaries insured that the priests were intellectually better prepared and became the only path to ordination. Discipline, especially celibacy, could thus be made more rigorous. Preaching was emphasized as a duty of pastors, but there was no pressure to consider ministry as intrinsically pastoral and connected to the proclamation of the word since the monastic priesthood was still considered to be valid. To consider the sacrament of order as essentially defined by *pastoral* responsibility would have been to undercut the very monasticism which was the spiritual heart of priestly life and would have derogated the priesthood as an order of men separated from the world to bear witness to the transcendent.

This separation of the priest from the laity by the sacrament of order has so penetrated Catholic thinking that even today the insistence that both clergy and laity form one church can scarcely supplant the popular view that the clergy *are* the church. Of course, one can point to the more precise understandings of theologians and the magisterium and prove that this has never been officially taught. But the emphasis on the dignity of priesthood and the powers conferred at ordination had this effect, even if it was never explicitly willed. Theology of priesthood was a theology of character and sacramental power. And clerical separation became a sociological manner of emphasizing the difference between the active and passive members of the church.

Trent's teaching was not meant to be a full theology of ordained ministry. Neither have we, in these few pages, given a balanced treatment of either the theological understanding or the praxis of that ministry. To some readers, this treatment will seem excessively narrow and critical. Has Catholicism, they will ask, done nothing right? First, it should be noted that I have concentrated on certain negative aspects of Catholic doctrine and practice because they undergird a structure of ministry which I have come to judge as holding back development of the Third Church. Second, there were many things which were very rightly done. History is a complicated affair. The operation of any organization is seldom perfect and the church is no exception to that truth.

The real strengths of the Catholic form of ministry lie in the entire area of liturgy and symbol, in a community-centered life wherein the symbols of the liturgy became a vital source of religious experience for the people. Hosts of dedicated religious and secular priests, anonymous for the most part, served their communities in a selfless manner, and their ministry, whether in Europe and America or in the missionary enterprise, was a profound service to the gospel.

It is perhaps a part of the unfortunate dialectic of history, though, that the very success of any model will demand a later criticism which will accentuate negative elements in order to make a point. The issue here is this: the post-Tridentine model of ministry is not the only valid form of office. Insofar as it is offered to the Third Church as *one* historical aspect of ministry, there is no quarrel with it. Insofar as it is proposed as the *only* one, I believe we must uncover its presuppositions in order to relativize it. Vatican Council II has given a much more balanced view of the nature of ordained ministry. It includes a good number of the reformers' teachings, and has created for us today the possibility of change, at least at the level of theory. Let us turn now to that council's doctrine on ministry.

Vatican II on Church Office

The first and most basic point to be grasped in regard to the teaching of Vatican Council II is that it has signalled a notable change in dealing with the church's constitution. The church is seen to be a community residing in local churches as well as being a World Church. This shift is not a new doctrine—only a move from a defensive preoccupation with the prerogatives and powers of the ordained ministry. It unites the medieval with the ancient by stressing the role and position of the laity in the Christian movement, and understands papacy, episcopacy, presbyterate, and diaconate as service functions within the church at large, not as the summit and most important aspect of ecclesial life.

Bishops are viewed as having the most basic office in the church, but their office is not seen as primarily priestly in nature. It is *pastoral*, and is meant to be exercised, not monarchically, but in collaboration with the laity and office-bearers of other ranks. The priest as well has pastoral office. Moreover, the stress on the *pastoral* office of the ordained makes it doubtful whether "priest" is the most apt word to use for the office of either bishops or their collaborators at the grassroots level.

The cultic role is only one aspect of pastoral ministry. Ceasing to call the ordained ministers "priests" might be a good way of shifting the emphasis back to the pastoral role which the council emphasizes. "Presbyter" might be a good word to use, though the simpler and more direct word "pastor" might do as well. Translated into everyday English, presbyters are "elders" or leaders in a community. Their function is that of shepherding, coordinating, teaching, and leading the liturgy. The authoritative discipleship of ministers ought to nurture the faith of the community and make it more conscious that Christ is in its midst. Moreover, the effectiveness of the presbyters' action springs not from their own power, but represents and symbolizes the community's faith that the Spirit is making the Lord present.

Differences in the various grades of church officers are not disjunctions such that the bishop exercises an office different in kind from the office of his presbyters. Both exercise a pastoral function, but at different levels. The bishop represents the unity of the church among *several* communities, the presbyter within a *single* community. While there will be need to spell out those differences in precise, legal terminology, still, to be faithful to the teaching of the council, it is important to emphasize the fundamental unity of office.

It would be dishonest to pretend that the documents of Vatican II are a revolutionary departure from past doctrine and practice. But it is equally true that *Christus Dominus* (Decrees on the Pastoral Office of Bishops) art. 1–7 defines bishops primarily as pastors of the faithful, and not as "holders of the fullness of priestly power" (the most usual pre-Vatican II definition). It is equally significant that *Lumen gentium* (Dogmatic Constitution on the Church), art. 10–11, begins with an examination of the priesthood of the faithful *before* treating the hierarchical constitution of the church and the ministerial priesthood (art. 18–29). Both the decrees on bishops and that on the nature of the church have much in them that extols the sacerdotal aspect of office. It would be the simplest matter in the world to cite numerous texts which will prove that the *emphasis* I have placed on desacerdotalizing ordained ministry is *not* in the documents. Nevertheless, I believe my points are fundamentally sound.

In the labored manner of ecclesiastical documents, the teaching of Vatican II has enunciated strands of thought which can be selected as more important precisely because of the fight that had to be made for their inclusion. To define office as pastoral rather than sacerdotal is a major innovation, the implications of which have not yet been allowed to work themselves out in practical ways around the world.

When one adds these points to the fact that no office, civil or ecclesial, can expect to gain popular approval if carried on in a feudal style whereby a position of authority in itself is supposed to guarantee authoritativeness, one is in a position to realize that something new has been made mandatory. Pastoral office in the twentieth century cannot be maintained coercively by curial regulations and decrees. Rather, it is part of an entire process of patient dialogue, combined with insightful leadership, which recognizes that the body of Christ is a people. And a people must function democratically if all segments of the community are to participate actively in its life. The division of the church into an *ecclesia docens et discens* (a "teaching and learning church") is too simple.

The Latin American experience of the past two decades is informative as an example where leaders have done a good deal of listening in order to become effective pastors who have not merely followed the guidance of their people, but have also corrected courses and made basic judgments about the signs and demands of the times. The Medellín conference and its documents were a first result. Seldom has an episcopal body issued authoritative and pertinent teachings so free from ecclesiastical beating around the bush. In a concrete manner the weight of the hierarchy was thrown behind a concern for social justice. But in the aftermath of Medellín, as many seemed to make the social justice agenda the sole apostolate, the bishops admonished Catholics to remember that there were other things to be considered. Among these were the positive side of folk religion and liturgical prayer.

The Latin American hierarchy seems to have gained an understanding of a practice of pastoral office within a community while maintaining their authority. It is today an open question whether or not they will be able to resist both local and outside forces who feel they have gone too far, but it is still clear that things will not soon return to a day when bishops would underpin an unjust social order.

The deemphasis of the sacerdotal has been said to have caused an identity crisis among priests. This is understandable and not altogether unhealthy. What has been undercut by the council's emphasis on pastoral office is the castelike nature of much of clerical life. Presbyters exercise the same ministry as bishops at a grassroots level. In fact, the bishop's ministry will usually be carried on through the work of the presbyters, mainly as a coordination of what emerges at the grassroots. The picture of ordained minstry, then, is one of a pastor among a people. The idea that one can be a pastor without a vital day-to-day contact with a community of the faithful is both a logical and theological contradiction. Herein, I believe, is the root of the so-called identity crisis of priests. Many thousands of them have almost no pastoral responsibility, and much of the work of diocesan priests in parishes has been administrative.

In the doctrine which considers priestliness as a "higher state" of life brought about by priestly character, it was enough to "say Mass" daily to enjoy the not inconsiderable prestige of "being a priest." But if the nature of office is not that of a state of life, the priest-teacher of mathematics, who at best says one or two parish Masses on Sunday, is rather a questionable reality. One can hardly be a *pastor* if contact with a community is restricted to a couple of hours once a week. It seems that many men have been attracted to the priesthood, not to become pastors but for other reasons: a feeling for spirituality, a sense that ordination would give them a recognizable and prestigious position, a desire to serve the church, and so forth.

While motives that bear on a desire for service or for deepening one's spiritual union with God are not to be impugned, these are not in themselves sufficient motivation for ordination. The sort of presbyter whose principal talents and joy in life lie in the area of enlivening a local community will feel no identity crisis in a shift from a priestly state-of-life spirituality to a pastoral-office concern. Such a man, I believe, will find in the teaching of Vatican II a liberation, since it will justify his desire to jettison some of the excess baggage of priestly caste separation and rectory culture in order to have more time to spend among his community members.

If the sacrament of order is the instrument through which Christ builds up his body, the church, several things follow. First, even the most venerable practices of piety borrowed by the diocesan or pastoral presbyterate from monastic, mendicant, or modern "religious life," are not essential to pastoral ministry. The pastor's spirituality revolves around a *sensus ecclesiae particularis* (a feeling for the church as a local community) and a felt call to serve local churches.

Secondly, if sociological, cultural, and historical changes have made traditional pastoral methods ill-adapted for community building, then research is needed to find suitable structures and life-styles for this task. Here one thinks immediately of the entire literature which has shown so persuasively that the traditional parish has been unable to reach out to groups such as urban workers in Europe or special groups of professionals in America. Other examples abound.

Thirdly, if one is concerned with the transition from mission to local church in the Third World, the first two points take on even greater importance in the face of rapid social changes of societal structures which do not even faintly resemble those of the European homelands of the missionaries. As we have stressed earlier, there is a great difference between evangelization structures in a contact situation and those models which promote local communities when faith has reached the stage which requires the missionaries to let go, precisely so that the young branches may find their own sources of nourishment and methods for contextualizing the gospel.

By way of summary, let us observe that the practice of ecclesial leadership has a history. Beginning from apostles who had intimate connections with the risen Christ, it took on the shapes required in the late Roman Empire and the medieval world. Theology explained the nature of the ordained ministry in manners understandable for the various eras of history through which the church was passing. Nevertheless, the essential point to recall is that ordained ministry is but one function within the church, a service of keeping the community faithful to the teaching and practice of apostolic Christianity. All subsequent developments are subordinate to that principle, and when one considers the shape of office for the future in diverse cultural situations, there should be a clear and enthusiastic granting of freedom to churches so that they may find forms of fellowship which will help them encounter the risen Lord who offers them his empowerment for the work of the kingdom. It would be odd indeed to be overly cautious when the central teaching which leadership is supposed to guarantee is one of confidence that the Lord will be with his people leading them in ever new situations.

PART THREE

Strategy for Third-Church Ministry

7

From Service Station to Basic Community

Orientations

From my own experience in Papua New Guinea and from conversations with confreres working in other young churches—particularly those of Oceania and various African nations—I have come to the conclusion that our problems and opportunities in most churches founded in the nineteenth-century missionary movement are very similar. Among the problems, the one that concerns me most is the lack of a long-term plan for making the transition from "mission" to "local church." It is around this issue that this chapter and the following one will revolve. Said succinctly, it is my contention that missions have fallen into the trap of carrying on in the traditions of their founders without being allowed to make the adaptations necessary to meet the dramatically changed social, historical, political, and theological climate of the late twentieth century.

The present function of the church does not differ much from the operation of a gasoline service station. You drive your car in to purchase gas, have the water and oil checked, have punctured tires fixed, and occasionally have major mechanical repairs done. The station, then, provides service for its customers. The attendants are active; the customers passive.

The mission station is similar to a service station; not that this is the theory behind it, but this is the way things have developed. Historically, this is most understandable. After initial contacts with the people and after surveying the territory, mission organizers selected key locations for "stations." The missionary, usually a priest, moved in and began to contact the people in a systematic way. Catechumens began their instructions, usually with the help of a native catechist brought from an older station. A house was built. The missionary would start a small clinic where he dispensed medical services and advice. Eventually the need for a school to provide systematic education for the children would be felt. At this point lay missionaries or sisters would arrive, and perhaps a brother as well. A church built of native materials would be built, and classrooms and a more adequate clinic for a full-time nurse to work in.

For the most part, these developments would be greeted with enthusiasm by the local populace as signs of modernization. After initial distrust had been overcome, little force would be needed to get parents to send their children to the schools, particularly when commercial developments made it apparent that education was a ticket to jobs, and jobs the ticket to the money which would purchase the clothing, kerosene lanterns, axes, fishing and hunting gear, and specialty foods which the people so much desired.

A generation or two would pass. Within fifty years virtually everyone in the locale would have become Christian. Outstations would have been established in the countryside around the main station, and more catechists would have been trained, either by the missionary or, increasingly, by the diocesan catechetical centers which would have gradually been established. Different priests, brothers, and sisters would come and go, all of them expatriates, but the station would go on. Gradually, the station would solidify as a fixed point in the life of the indigenous people, a place to go for certain services: sacraments, education, health care, economic advice and assistance.

In all of this process the service station character of the Missionary Standard Model is assumed. It is the counterpart of the *ecclesia discens et docens* of the Second Church (the learning and teaching church). The church means the clergyman and his ancillary staff, and to it come the faithful to be served. There certainly is service going on, and most of it is a service much desired by the people, but this sort of service establishes a service station mentality of activity on the one side and passivity on the other.

In this state of affairs how does one create a basic community wherein all will come to think of themselves as ministers? The Missionary Standard Model is basically paternalistic and subverts very important elements in an authentic conception of the Christian movement. Michael Hollis has put his finger on what I believe is the nerve center of the question when he says: "To develop the church without at the same time developing the ministry has deformed the conception of the church, of the sacraments and of the ministry itself."[1]

The presupposition on which the founders of the Melanesian missions worked was that the colonial era would go on indefinitely. The goal of education and development assistance was subordinate, in the case of the missions, to religious goals. There were serious quarrels between the mission and the government over policies which the missionaries perceived as exploitative, but the common ground between mission and government was always much more significant than their differences. Both believed that developments were headed toward a state of affairs where the indigenous population would be "westernized" to the point where a nation-state tightly wedded to the European colonial powers' world policies would be created. The colonies were to enhance the power and prestige of the homelands. The process would take generations.

The British colonial affairs offices, for example, recruited men and women who would spend a lifetime in the service of that grand design. The sons and daughters of overseas officers would replace their parents, marry, and raise families "in the colonies."

The paternalism of the missions was similar, and it has led to that deformation spoken of by Hollis. The post-World War II independence tide swept Europeans out of the colonies as political power was transferred to nationals. The present moment is one, as we have said, in which the new nations are endeavoring to change the colonial structures to make them more home-gown. The search is for new models, and the same should be the main concern of the church.

The Search for Models

The ordained ministry and the church, we have said, are related genetically in something like a chicken and egg evolutionary pattern. The church is the chicken that gives birth to its clergy, but the clergy in turn shape the church. Historically speaking, says Father Walter Burghardt, there can be identified five basic sorts of ordained ministry models.[2] Each has shaped and been shaped by the church's history.

First, the *pastoral model*. This is surely the central image of ministry in the New Testament and the early church. The New Testament presents a variegated picture of apostle-founders making provisions for their churches, but does not clearly define their power and authority. Various churches had their own particular emphases, but gradually bishops emerged as shepherds of the flock and guardians of the apostolic tradition. Vatican II has attempted to recover this vision of pastoral ministry. The council does not mean to jettison other images—particularly that of the sacerdotal ministry—but in its documents office is defined as pastoral in nature. That office is broader than mere cultic service, and its implications may deal a fatal blow to the priestly caste mindset prevalent in Roman Catholicism. This will probably happen not by frontally attacking the idea of the priestly state, but by a growing appreciation that one is ordained to be a pastor and nothing else.

Second, the *cultic model*. In this model the ordained minister is seen as the celebrant of the Christian mysteries. Historically, this model emerges as bishops become sacral figures in the midst of their communities and as liturgy becomes more elaborate. Presbyters gradually take on this same function and are known as priests. The sacraments are the instruments through which the grace of Christ is received, and to a large extent pastoral ministry is subsumed into cultic service.

Third, the *monastic model*. Originally, monasticism was separated from ordinary Christian communities, but Benedictine and Irish monks influenced church practice by their success as missionaries, educators, and pastors. They were celibate, wore special clothing, organized their lives around the divine office, and generally made ascetical practices the standard by which the seriousness of faith could be judged. Faced with a largely illiterate and often demoralized clergy, early medieval church reformers came to think of monastic ideals as appropriate for the secular clergy. At a later stage the mendicants provided refinements of this model, and when the church entered the modern era, the Jesuit movement gave this dynamic the shape it has taken down to contemporary times. We will later consider the confusion that exists in the Third Church because all of its priests have been formed in a semi-monastic or semi-Jesuit model; now it is enough to note that the life-style of priesthood is generally constructed around monastic ideals: celibacy, separation from the laity, special garb, and so forth.

Fourth, the *prophetic model.* The Protestant contribution to ministerial models has been to call attention to the minister as the preacher of the word in the community. The sermon becomes the central element of Christian worship services even when large parts of the Catholic sacramental heritage remain. The preacher serves the function of bringing the word to bear on the situation of the community, expounding it prophetically to touch the hearts of the faithful, and helping them to see concrete ways in which they are invited to respond to the Christ who offers them salvation. One of Vatican II's advances has been the attempt to utilize this Protestant model in its appreciation of the necessary link between word and sacrament. The rise of the social-critic priest is another example of how the prophetic model has an important role inside of Catholicism.

Fifth, the *jurisdictional model.* Important especially since Trent and reinforced by Vatican I and the 1917 updating of the Code of Canon Law, this model accentuates the notion that popes, bishops, and priests have authority over the various divisions of the church. Authority to rule in the name of Christ is spelled out in terms of jurisdiction over parishes, dioceses, and the universal church. Ministry is exercised by utilizing the powers and authority conferred on the ministers by sacramental ordination. Even teaching comes to be thought of as an authoritative propounding of official doctrine.

These divisions are not to be thought of as absolute. In practice, one or another has predominated in different historical situations, but in fact each of them is latent even when one or another of them becomes central. Each of them has a certain validity. We shall next consider how these models bear on our search for a viable model of ordained ministry for Third Church community building.

First, all the models spring from the history of the Second Church. Each of them is a response to concrete needs in its history, and, to be fair to them, one should realize that it is not a question of rejecting any of them so much as accepting them as relative, not absolute, in value. If Third Church needs can be met by one of them alone or by a creative blend of the five, that would be ideal. The problem is that present legislation is so constructed as to preclude the freedom to choose. This problem must be dealt with resolutely.

In this matter the basic truth is that the founders of the nineteenth-century missions were almost always trained by priests whose basic approach was based on Jesuit practice and theory. Thus we are dealing with the most recent updating of the monastic model of ministry, and this model was not understood as *one* shape ministry could take, but as *the* obligatory *gestalt*. Herein lies the problem. The orders and congregations who founded the missions saw no other possibility. Moreover, they were wedded to the colonial assumption that the rule of the missions would remain in European and American hands for many generations. That rule would change hands only when there were sufficient indigenous clergymen, trained according to Second Church specifications, to take over the direction of the church.

On the one hand this has sociological implications. Native patterns of authority might be deferred to as a means of making converts, but the vision of the finished church was something else again. It did not matter much how long it took, for the orders until recently had ample recruits to guarantee continuity. The diocesan seminaries which were established to bring about the gradual transition to local rule were, for the most part, run by religious priests and were carbon copies of European and American institutions. It was assumed that candidates for diocesan priesthood should be trained in a semi-monastic way of life, as if that were the only model for a true priestly life.

This sociological pattern has spiritual ramifications. The values stressed were obedience, discipline, and general docility to the Euro-American missionary clergy. The true priestly spirituality revolved around meditation, the divine office, regular daily life, and the developing of a celibate identification with Christ as the model for priestly existence. Within the community life of the seminary secular priests were being trained for pastoral ministry, without regard to the fact that for the secular priest the primary community ought to be that of the parish, not the comradeship of religious brotherhood between priests.

The nucleus of the entire system of seminary training was and is celibacy. As long as all candidates are bound to celibacy, they must develop strong bonds with their fellow celibates, especially in cultures where the single life for the sake of the gospel is simply not understood or accepted. In the Papua New Guinea seminary where I was stationed, our students were young men from twenty to thirty years of age. Most of them had entered the seminary system when they were fourteen. They thought little, initially, of being anything but likenesses of the expatriate missionaries. Gradually, however, they began to run into the reality of traditional Melanesian expectations and their own sexuality as they matured and their clans began to treat them as men and no longer as boys. The pressures grew for them to marry and to help their clans keep up their strength, wealth, and numbers. Then, too, they had their own desires for family life with wife and children to contend with. Most students found a real conflict between a desire to be priests on the one hand and the demands of the people on the other.

The seminary's response to this cultural challenge was to put more and more emphasis on spirituality. If a young man came close to Christ in prayer, it was thought he could overcome the "temptation" to leave. Staff members counselled seminarians in the light of their own experiences, trying to help them develop along celibate lines. Teachers tried to give a rationale for obligatory celibacy and defended the church's legislation. This may all seem well and good until one begins to realize that a seminary ought to be a place where men are trained for *pastoral* life where their service of a congregation would be paramount. But because of the need to give the students a protected environment, pains were taken to make the seminary itself such a happy home that there would be little need for the students to go outside into the world where they would have to stand alone against what the staff could only perceive as dangerous pressures from their own desires and those of their clans.

With the impetus for seminary renewal which resulted from Vatican II, more emphasis was placed on pastoral training. Everyone felt the need to give the students more practical experience in the field among the people. But this direction found a natural antagonist in the need to protect the seminarian. At most faculty meetings the question arose: "Are the students ready to work in the parishes?" And the "readiness" was not so much a question of whether they had something to offer or to learn from this sort of contact as it was a question of their capacity not to be swept away from the church's celibate ideal. Instead of being dominated by the need to educate for a pastoral ministry, our training was intrinsically conditioned by the need to unite celibacy with presbyteral life.

This problem was interestingly discussed on the occasion of the visit of Ronald Williams, head of the United Church Seminary. In the course of a discussion with me one night, Professor Williams said: "Our students settle down spiritually when they get married. I worry about them until they are into a good marriage. When they are, though, they begin to take prayer seriously and to accept the responsibilities of pastoral life."

At the time of Williams's visit, our biggest problem was conflict about how free our students ought to be to go to town. Like young bachelors everywhere, they had a marvelous ability to get invited to parties, meals, and socials. Their lives revolved around the seminary's sporting teams and the social life that postgame gatherings created. Even the more "liberal" members of the staff were concerned, not at the socializing in itself, but at its extent and the fact that so little serious pastoral concern was evidenced. Teaching and learning had become diversions in the midst of more important recreational pursuits. If one believed that a responsible student was one who tried to develop pastoral skills and attitudes, one would have to admit that in many ways the students' behavior was irresponsible.

In the years that followed, Williams's remarks began to percolate through my mind. What I came to believe was that we had created a situation where the main faculty effort in the seminary was centered on getting our students to adopt a semi-monastic life-style, and they were largely rejecting it. Our emphasis was on promoting a community life wherein the student would develop a celibate spirituality. That was the hidden agenda in our educational program.

No one should think that I am opposed to celibacy. History shows how celibacy and pastoral life can be fruitfully entwined. The critical question is directly related to how we have allowed the monastic model of priesthood to control Third Church ministry totally. *There can be no true attempt at developing indigenous forms of ministry until celibacy is made optional.* As long as it is required, seminaries worldwide will be engaged in the same frustrating enterprise as we were in Papua New Guinea.

Mandatory celibacy grew out of a complex history in the Second Church. While it may have been a fruitful development there, it is at least arguable that the Third Church should be allowed to find its own way. By insisting upon celibacy for all ministerial candidates, the church unintentionally has confounded pastoral life with one mode of exercising it.

The problem, though, is that while we are free to theorize about which sorts of ordained ministry are possible, practical action is precluded, and historical forces have come to make the entire Second Church institutional model dominant in the young churches. Two factors are most important here. First, there is the undeniable fact that modern popes, cardinals, and bishops have been influenced chiefly by the monastic and cultic understanding of ministry. Since the Middle Ages nothing else has been allowed to be tried as a viable alternative. Secondly, this problem is compounded by the influence of a jurisdictional model concept which emphasizes uniformity throughout the church.

In present legislation, the ordained ministry is sealed like a pressure hull on a submarine. No matter what forces assail it, the hermetically sealed environment within allows the clericalized institution to escape noticing changes outside. The council may articulate a pastoral theory of office, but practical judgements are not allowed free play, for such would be to jeopardize foreordained models. I believe that most readers will follow me in believing that what we are seeking for the Third Church is a viable pastoral model of ministry. Such a model may borrow from any of the other four, but a way must be found to cut ourselves loose from a long and ambiguous church tradition which has tended to solve ministry problems by falling back on the monastic tradition as the prime source of spiritual ideals.

Implementing a Pastoral Model of Office

Our argument has centered on the need to find a suitable pastoral model of office. Ordained ministry, we have said, is basically a responsibility for a community, not a priestly state of life, nor is it intrinsically wedded to elements of spirituality and training proper to religious orders. My first caution, then, is directed to the members of missionary congregations in churches where they form the core group of ordained ministers.

Missionaries must be aware of several things. First, there is a profound difference between being an expatriate missionary in the contact-evangelization moment, and being an expatriate pastor in a third- or fourth-generation church. In many places missionaries have become foreign pastors without ever really reflecting on that transition. Secondly, great care must be taken lest the practices and spirituality of religious orders and missionary congregations not be unfairly accentuated in the younger churches. This is done not merely by emphasizing, for example, the Holy Spirit devotions of the Divine Word Missionaries or the Sacred Heart devotions of the Jesuits. Much more dangerous is the unspoken assumption that to be really serious as a Christian is to take on the ascetical practices of religious. A Second Church example may be useful in illustrating this danger. Is it not true that many European and American Christians have imbibed the attitude that *the* way of perfection is through the religious vows, and that lay spirituality is at best a matter of taking on such practices as daily Mass and meditation? The church can easily lose sight of *general* gospel teachings (everyone is to be leaven in the dough of society) by emphasizing *special* counsels (some may be invited to leave house and home to dedicate themselves to special works).

Thirdly, there is the issue of promoting one's own congregation at the expense of the ordinary pastoral ministry. Theoretically, religious congregations are supposed to foster the diocesan or secular priesthood. Practically, it has been a common experience that the solitary life of the diocesan priest has proven difficult. Resignations from the ministry among the diocesan priests have been high, with the result that many have thought that a religious community life would be a good help in maintaining perseverance.

No one, of course, should condemn a young man who feels a desire to become a Franciscan or a Marist. That is not the issue. It is rather that instead of offering a suitable manner of exercising the normal pastoral ministry in the diocesan presbyterate, the church has, in recent years, permitted a steady slide in the direction of promoting vocations to the religious or regular priesthood. Even some mission bishops, have thought this a good practical response to the question of perseverance. Because of such thinking in the early 1970's, the Vatican reversed its long-standing policies, removed its earlier reservations, and adopted a more positive attitude toward religious orders who were recruiting members in the Third Church before the diocesan presbyterate had been securely established. My feeling on the matter is that the earlier legislation discouraging this recruitment was sounder ecclesiologically and missiologically. However, I believe also that freedom must be given to experiment with new forms of the diocesan ministry if there is to be success in obtaining the sort of persons necessary.

What might such a diocesan, pastoral ministry resemble? The controlling principle must be local needs and indigenous social life patterns. In Papua New Guinea, for instance, there are two basic indigenous patterns of life: the coastal and the highlands societies—small hamlets and scattered clan-based family units respectively. In addition, there is the factor of rapid urbanization and new forms of social life emerging in the cities: first among the unemployed and the laborers; secondly, among, the educated "elites" with jobs in government and the private sector. Thus, what might at first seem like a simple question of identifying natural communities and attempting to serve them becomes complex, for there are at least four very different sorts of communities. This does not invalidate the basic principle, however. It means only that simple solutions, such as the often mentioned plan to ordain rural catechists, need critical and skeptical consideration.

In a rural coastal village or the scattered hamlets of the mountains, the main station/outstation arrangement of the mission offers us a system already in existence and perhaps capable of utilization. But the situation in the sprawling confusion of the cities in many lands presents immense difficulties. Small groups of people from various districts (for example, from Tari or the Sepik River) tend to congregate and maintain a way of life quite similar to what they knew at home. But often clashes occur, and the groups are divided even more deeply by differences in educational and economic levels. Such complicating factors are less an argument for a traditional "parish" than a challenge to ecclesial ingenuity to create a broader sort of community built on common faith.

Besides the need to identify or to create basic communities, there is a second major challenge which is not so often recognized: the basic conservatism of the masses, both urban and rural. One of the great mistakes of the past two decades of discussion on the shape of local churches has been the tendency of many liberals to ignore the fact that many, if not most, of the people are relatively happy with the present station arrangement of the mission and are reluctant to change. Many seasoned expatriate missionaries, men and women, know well that their younger colleagues often misjudge the readiness and desire of national Christians to make changes, and they are thus confirmed in their judgment that there is little of positive value to be found in the new theology.

Such a position, though, is *descriptive* of the situation, not *critical*. An analysis of the conservatism of the masses would also show that to retain the present structure of the church is to confirm Third Church members in their passivity in the rural homelands and to condemn urban Christians to death by spiritual strangulation. For the passive Christian sees the church as a place to receive services, rather like the way one drives into a service station to be served with gasoline. This state of affairs has the advantage of making the missionaries feel wanted for day and night they are sought after for their help. But it puts off the day when Christianity is part of the basic community, a power springing from their hearts, a force for the creative transformation of society because people realize that they are the church and have a mission.

It will not do merely to call people together to ask them what sort of ordained ministry they want. They simply will not understand the question. Prior to that must come some sort of a program of "conscientization." As used by Paulo Freire, that term means an elevation of popular consciousness through literacy programs. Though the attainment of conscientization (critical self-awareness of oneself as an active agent) is promoted by Freirian-type programs, and though it may be useful in many Third Church situations, we would be unfaithful to Freire himself to imagine that it must be tied to literacy promotion.

What I am personally proposing is that a method must be developed to bring Third Church members to an awareness that *they* are the church and that *they* are persons capable of carrying on the Christian mission. Then the question asked above (What might normal pastoral ministry resemble?) can be posed in the proper ecclesial context. Consciousness needs to be raised and self-confidence developed in order to move people from being adherents of a foreign mission to being active members of a local church with a sense of its own mission. The importance of asking a question which will be understood cannot be stressed enough. It is not just intellectual clarification which is required. This is one of the strengths of Freire's methodology.

Freire envisions pilot programs wherein dialogue takes place to identify felt needs of a people and the development of consciousness-raising methods in experimental groups which will not merely elicit answers, but will become part of a process in which people experience their own capacities to determine the future of their community. Theory alone is not enough. It must be joined to praxis. And if there is no willingness to follow through practically then it is better never to begin the process of consciousness-raising.

An example of what happened during the National Self-Study of the Catholic Church in Papua New Guinea is instructive, for it was the beginning of a conscientization process which was not allowed to come to term precisely because ecclesiastical authorities were not ready to follow the lead of grassroots groups. For several years most parishes and dioceses participated in the Self-Study by following a program of questions aimed in a twofold direction: (1) gathering the laity's opinions about future directions; and (2) helping them come to realize in the process that "they are the church."

The Self-Study had successes and failures, but it gradually trailed off into insignificance. One reason for this was that the national Christians began to make suggestions which were unacceptable to expatriate authorities, especially bishops and priests. Some of the suggestions were somewhat shallow and shortsighted, but even in such ideas one could learn what the people were really thinking. In many cases that thinking was quite different from the missionaries' views of what they *ought* to be thinking. Nevertheless, even the view that the people ought to be able to use the missionary's truck whenever they wanted it constituted a point of dialogue on the nature of the church and the wealth of the mission from the *people's* point of view. Where else can one begin?

Initially the Bishops' Conference in Papua New Guinea had accepted the idea of the Self-Study because it was perceived as a means of catechizing the populace and bringing home to them some of the teachings of Vatican II. Those teachings took on surprising shades of meaning when they were filtered through national thinking processes and back to the floor of various meetings. Few will say it as flatly as this, but it is my belief that the Self-Study was allowed to die because to go further with it inexorably led to a situation where the mission would have had to change radically many of its cherished forms in order to follow through on what the people were saying.

Of course, most organizations have smooth, diplomatic ways of allowing such things to cease without creating a public scene. This is what happened to the Self-Study in Papua New Guinea. Were someone to suggest today that the Self-Study be reopened, and were the idea acted upon favorably by the Bishops' Conference, it is likely that the ordinary faithful would respond only halfheartedly. Why? Because they have learned that many missionaries enter into dialogue as a one-way process of instructing a passive laity, not in order to draw practical consequences from the dialogue. Nevertheless, people do forgive and can be persuaded by sincerity. This being so, dialogue may again be possible.

Restructuring Ministry around the Basic Community

A foreign missionary places himself or herself in a methodologically suspicious position by attempting to sketch out a hypothetical model of a future church and a possible model for implementing a pastoral model of office for the basic community in that church, yet even when one enters into an open-ended, free dialogue, there must be at least some agenda in mind. It may be totally changed by the time one is in the position to move into practical action, but the acuteness with which one proposes the issues for discussion almost always determines the sharpness of the debate itself. Insofar as I have a theological position before starting, it is the one I have put forward throughout our study: the shape of the church should determine the shape of the ordained ministry whose role is one of helping a community become more self-consciously the body of Christ.

In restructuring ministry around the notion of the basic community, we are involved in the double wrestle of contextualization, on the one hand, and a vision of the church which starts from the grassroots, on the other hand. Certain elements are normative when one thinks about ministry: the witness of scripture and tradition leads to an expectation that certain men (and women) will be singled out by God and granted charisms which will fit them for the ministry of creating an apostolic community. They are people with a profound *sensus ecclesiae,* a feeling for the meaning of the church and the Christian message.

This is what the church has meant to protect by its insistence that the church is hierarchical and that the authority of office is not merely an authority granted by the community. It is conferred on the office-bearer by God. More accurately, it may be described as a capacity for authoritative ecclesial leadership. It is difficult to phrase theologically the nature of that authority, especially since the feudal forms through which it has been exercised in Catholicism since the Middle Ages have been largely discredited in the eyes of many, while popes and bishops especially are still operating in this mode. The way authority will come to be exercised, then, ought to depend on the second member of the double wrestle: *the culturally acceptable norms of a given people.*

When the double wrestle is taken seriously and there is a readiness to think freely and allow experimentation at the grassroots level, what is then to be said? I believe Father Schillebeeckx has given us at least a hint of a proper approach when he says, "There is a real need for the leadership of the church to consult the behavioral sciences, and in particular religious sociology, in order to conduct a suitable pastoral policy, particularly in changed cultural circumstances."[3] Sociology should be of service in identifying meaningful units which may fruitfully be considered as the basic communities which constitute the local church. As we have said, this is not simple, for there is much flux in the Third Church, more perhaps than in western nations. So it is a matter of realizing that patterns of life, even in such remote places of the world as the islands of Oceania and the rain forests of Zaire, may be changing, but they also constitute the primary datum for church building.

How does this differ from the research that went into decisions on how and where to build mission stations in the first place? In several ways. First, the mission station was erected in a first-contact or primary evangelization moment as a structure for creating a mission presence in a given locality. Second, the station was built up around expatriate clerical, religious, and lay personnel as the logistics base for their evangelization work. We should be open to the possibility at least that the structures suitable for a mission may not be the best ones for a local church. It may be that in some parts of the world the old main station may well fill both purposes, but one should not *presume* that it will until both sociological investigations and popular consciousness-raising have been carried out.

Third, the sort of thinking that went into the building of the mission station was rooted in the notion that the local church would eventually resemble a large European or American parish. At a time when the notion of parish is being questioned in the Second Church, it is highly debatable whether the Third Church should hitch its future totally to this model.

Fourth, the sort of thinking that led to the building of the mission station presumes that the full-time, fully trained, fully paid clergyman will be the mainstay of the church. This too is something which should be left open for discussion. All I am saying is that the sort of research envisioned here is much more open-ended than the investigations made when the stations were first established.

Here I would caution that I am thinking mainly of the Melanesian world. There people live together in small village communities. It is true that because of both government and mission influence larger units have been formed, but on the whole the village or village cluster is the next largest unit above the clan and family. I would envision a series of questions addressed to the issue of whether or not such villages and village clusters should be the fundamental unit of the basic Christian community. The answer may be either negative or affirmative. If the answer is negative, then the questioning process simply moves on to weighing other alternatives. Let us, though, for the sake of illustration, imagine that the village or village cluster does seem appropriate as our basic Christian community unit in the rural area. What follows from this and the theological principles we have been enunciating throughout this study of the ordained ministry?

As faith matures and people come to grips with the meaning of the gospel, various gifts can be expected to emerge. Some may have an ability to be peacemakers; others may have insights into scripture; others, the capacity to organize; others, the skill to counsel; others, the aptitude to teach; others, the talent to create liturgical songs. Ordained ministry would be nothing else than the ability to coordinate these and other gifts and authoritatively blend them in a meaningful community life. In worship, especially, this leader would have the task of calling the community's attention to the deeper faith dimension of their daily lives by leading them in the celebration of reconciliation when they have been untrue to their calling and by periodically joining in eucharistic worship.

The key theological principle ought to be the *right* of each basic community to enjoy a complete ecclesial life. Ministry is a pastoral office and includes the elements of teaching, worshiping, and coordinating. But if Catholicism is to take seriously its own doctrines on the importance of liturgy for the formation of a church, it has to find structures of ministry which will allow basic communities to worship in a complete round of sacramental celebrations creatively adapted to local lifeways and culture. To insist on the clergyman model of priestly ministry is to betray obligatory *theological* principles merely because *historical and cultural* factors have made it illicit to implement other models.

My first concrete proposal is that a ministry of village pastors be instituted wherever investigations lead us to believe they could aid in the creation of basic Christian communities. They need not be men or women who have received a long and costly training, but they would require ongoing formation and supervision. Sermon aids and workshops, for example, would have to be prepared to keep them moving ahead, learning to see more deeply into the meaning of the gospel and developing the necessary pastoral skills. But it is undoubtedly true that there are suitable candidates for such a ministry once personal, spiritual characteristics become the norms for selection, instead of educational attainment and the willingness to embrace celibacy. Pastors such as these should be fully ordained presbyters with the authority to preside at the Eucharist.

My second proposal involves the men we today call priests, who in the Third Church are the pastors of large mission stations. When village presbyters become the normal, everyday pastors, these priests could well become the coordinators of a number of village presbyters, functioning somewhat as deans do in the present structure. They would not be the immediate pastors of any basic community, but would serve as "mini-bishops" to several such churches. They would presumably be better educated, and thus able to help out the village pastors on regular visits to them. Perhaps they would chair meetings of the presbyters and deacons of the basic communities and help them to devise common plans. This could be an interim function for expatriate missionaries who could then be gradually replaced by local presbyters who had proven themselves capable of exercising this supervisory function.

Basic communities and larger clusters of such churches are not enough for a full ecclesial life. Thus we come to the diocesan level of church organization. In a very real sense it is not the basic community, but the diocese, whose unity is symbolized in the person and ministry of the bishop, which is the local church of Vatican II's teaching (cf. *Lumen gentium*, art. 20–21). We have emphasized the basic community and the presbyterate in the present study precisely because of the incompleteness of the teaching and the deficiency of the practice at the grassroots level.

Our stress, though, should not obscure the fact that it is the bishop who finally is the pastor of the faithful. His is the fullness of office, and the presbyters and deacons are his associates, not free-lancers operating with their own agenda. Bishops are first and foremost the pastors and teachers of their flocks, not as feudal lords, but as men of the people, not as businessmen who supervise the finances of the church (though over this they must have final control), but as reflective, spiritual energizers with insight into broader questions. To carry on that immense task they require uncommon spiritual and administrative talents if they are not to be submerged by the tumult of the times, for theirs really is the task of creating the atmosphere in which everything else we have spoken of will take place.

The core of our concrete proposals is the need to identify the basic communities and make them truly the foundation of ecclesial life. Institutional impressiveness is vain and empty pomp if it is not founded on local churches where faith lives and life is full. Pastors need not be clerics separated from their people by semi-monastic life-styles. Indeed, religious usages may easily become a barrier to a more wholistic approach to the gospel. Life lived according to the "canonical" evangelical counsels is an important witness to some elements of the gospel, but Jesus' teaching is directed to ordinary people and their concerns: family life, schools, businesses, farms, food for the table, and roofs over their heads. Since the religious tend to have these things provided for them, they lose sight of some of these realities. Their perspective gives them a point of view which it is important to hear in the church, but it is not necessarily the best mindset for the ordinary pastor.

And so I believe the basic pastoral ministry of the church is best kept in the hands of ministers who live a common life with their people. Married persons may be swamped by the problems of keeping their conjugal relationship alive, clothes on their children's backs, and the need to provide security for themselves and their families. But the gospel message that life is not to be entirely taken up with such concerns may be more convincingly and pertinently exemplified by the sort of pastor who combines all these concerns with Jesus' message than by religious or semi-monastic presbyters whose lives revolve around other matters.

There is scant possibility that such village pastors can undergo "full" seminary training, or that sufficient celibates can be found to undertake this ministry. I am, therefore, advocating the ordination of proven married persons to the presbyterate. Most traditional Melanesian and African village communities range from one hundred to a thousand persons. Today those communities are served by regular services at the main stations and by periodic visits to outlying communities by the missionary pastor. Between visits, if they are fortunate, there may be a catechist or a prayer leader to bring people together for community prayer, but in no way is the village or the village cluster the basic unit of ecclesial life. This state of affairs must be addressed and questioned.

How can pastors such as we are advocating be identified, trained, and put into service? Numerous possibilities exist. In many places catechists are already virtual pastors and could form a cadre from which pastors might be chosen. This manner of selection runs the risk of obscuring the proper ministry of catechists—teaching—but it well might be that catechists de facto could provide an initial source of village presbyters.

Second, mature married laypersons ought to be the ordinary personnel pool of potential candidates for the pastorate. The ministry of village presbyters will not usually be a full-time office. It is more likely to be a part-time office exercised by a committed Christian with a profound *sensus ecclesiae*.

Another possibility will be discussed in the following section: instituting the order of deacon as a special ministry in the church. Persons who have proven themselves in such services as caring for the sick or administering the financial and physical assets of the community could be called to the presbyterate.

What is the likely result of not taking seriously the challenge of identifying basic communities, making them the normal and basic unit of ecclesial life, and providing them with pastors? Latin America and the Philippines furnish examples of what happens when full liturgical life becomes impossible because of the lack of presbyters. Folk religion easily takes over, bringing numerous elements of dubious value into church life.[4] Instruction in sound doctrine is not given. Sacraments are only occasionally celebrated. Scripture is seldom read and expounded. At one level people feel the need to be religious, and at another they are barred from being so in a fully Catholic manner. Nonsacramental devotions which do not require presbyters are devised. These borrow from pre-Christian religion in manners which are syncretistic in the bad sense of the word. Nearly everyone in Latin America and the Philippines is nominally Christian and Catholic. But it is no secret that the church in these countries stands at a crucial juncture in its history and requires massive reform so that the gospel's central message may be heard.

Much of the modern literature and thinking on basic communities emerges from Latin America and the Philippines and is aimed precisely at correcting the present situation. What seems especially poignant is the similarity that exists today between the churches of Oceania and Africa, and the Latin American situation of two hundred years ago (in the seventeenth and eighteenth centuries, when the first-contact evangelization period reached the point it has reached elsewhere in the late twentieth century). The church did not change its structures in Latin America and the Philippines, and the negative results are clear. But the situation today is immensely more dangerous than it was in 1650, 1750, or even 1850.

Today the assault from scientific and technological thinking and political and economic changes, which has made the future of Christianity so problematic in the Second Church, is present also in the Third Church. If steps are not taken to contextualize the Third Church in an adequate way, no one can do more than guess at the consequences. The future of the Christian movement is being written in the villages and cities of the Third World. It would be tragic not to act because the Second Church is caught up in historical obstacles with little theological content. The conservative may argue that the guidance of the Spirit will always be present in the church, but it may well be that the Spirit's voice is calling for institutional reform.

The Order of Deacons

The Second Vatican Council has called for the institution of the order of deacons as a normal and permanent ordained ministry in the church. [5] Central to both the Second and Third Church debate about the diaconate has been a fear that ordaining deacons to a vague "ministry of service" runs the risk of depreciating the ministry of the laity. The argument contends that we have only just recovered an understanding of lay service in the church. If we begin to ordain the most promising laymen and/or laywomen, will we not once again be clericalizing ministry? It is not easy to refute this argument.

A second family of difficulties arises when one tries to define precisely the powers and authority of the office of deacons. The question runs somewhat as follows. What can a deacon do that a lay person can't do or that a catechist in the Third Church doesn't do? Lay readers, ministers of communion, prayer leaders in isolated communities, and social workers today perform most of the duties performed by deacons in the ancient church. Do we really need a special order of ordained men and women called deacons?

Thirdly, to speak plainly, there is little clarity on the office and role of deacons in the ancient church. For example, Acts 6:1ff states that the first deacons were chosen to perform administrative chores in order to free the apostles for prayer and preaching. They were apparently chosen for a ministry of charitable service. Yet immediately afterwards Acts 6:8ff depicts Stephen as performing a ministry of miracle working and preaching. In the Pastoral Epistles it is most difficult to pin down the difference between the deacons and the presbyters. In the patristic writings, too, a variety of pictures is present. In Justin's *Apology* deacons distribute the Eucharist. In Cyprian of Carthage's epistles they help the presbyters administer the church while he is in exile, but are otherwise shadowy figures with a charitable ministry. In the *Didaschalia* of Syria women as well as men are deacons. Elsewhere deacons appear as counselors of the bishops, preachers, and ministers of baptism, and are generally prominent persons in the community.

As ministry became sacerdotalized in the third and fourth centuries, the diaconate began its downward path until, by the Middle Ages, it was little more than a ceremonial step on the road to priesthood. That has been its position until modern times when Vatican II presented us with two images of the ministry of deacons. Some Council Fathers were enthusiastic about the diaconate and wanted deacons restored to a position of prominence. Others saw the married diaconate as a dangerous first step on the way to optional celibacy for priests. Men of good will championed and opposed the reinstitution of the ministry, and article 29 of *Lumen gentium* was the compromised result.

There the deacon's role is primarily liturgical: distributing communion, celebrating marriages, teaching, and preaching. Also indicated is a role in unspecified "works of charity." Commentaries on *Lumen gentium* bear out my point on the compromise nature of the decree's teaching.

Ad gentes (the Decree on the Missions) has a much more important role for deacons:

> Where episcopal conferences consider it opportune, the order of deacon may be restored as a permanent state. . . . It is advisable that men who exercise the ministry of deacons, in fact either as catechists preaching the word of God, or who, in the name of the bishop or parish priest, are heads of distant communities . . . be confirmed and situated in that order by the imposition of hands (a matter of apostolic tradition), and thus be more fruitfully joined to the altar in order to better and more fruitfully clarify the meaning of their ministry by means of the sacramental grace of the diaconate (art. 16).

In *Ad gentes* one notes that diaconate is considered a subordinate *pastoral* office, not merely as a higher grade of the order of acolyte.

Subsequent legislation has, however, tended to follow the list of duties to be found in *Lumen gentium* and thus reflects the desire of more conservative factions, which feared that the diaconate might compete with the presbyterate (as happened in the second, third, and fourth centuries) or eventually lead to optional celibacy for presbyters if deacons with the ability to be pastors were to emerge and be proposed for presbyteral ordination. *Ad gentes* would seem to have a sounder theology of the diaconate because it appears to recognize deacons as holders of pastoral office, even if only for "distant communities" deprived of presbyteral ministers.

To develop this notion further we might consider that ordination is admission to the office of the church and that office is centered on helping communities to become more self-consciously the body of Christ in a given place. Before there is a division of powers and authorities among bishops, presbyters and deacons, there is the notion of a college of persons with special sensitivity to the nature and mission of the church. Ordination is admission to that office, the prototype of which is episcopacy. Presbyters and deacons are associates of the bishop, helpers, and advisors, but they are also persons with authority in their own right as representatives of God.

How might this be translated into the terms of our argument for an ordained ministry at the service of basic communities? It is clear that the idea of a pastor having authority as the head of a local community steadily and inexorably devolved in the direction of presbyters, so that presbyter and pastor are *de facto* reciprocal terms. Presbyters have thus been given the authority to be the ordinary ministers of the sacraments, the normal presidents of the eucharistic assembly. I believe that this is something which need not be touched or changed, but this should not hinder us from ordaining certain individuals as co-workers of the pastors and giving them a recognized place in the administration of the community for performing certain functions (for example, in dispensing charitable services in the name of the church, or in works such as preaching and presiding at marriages and funerals).

The key point to be observed, though, has a twofold dimension: first, the diaconate is not something which should obscure or supplant lay ministry; secondly, it is not an office which is a substitute for the presbyter's when there are insufficient pastors. The deacons of a community should help both pastor and community, not take over anyone else's role. The sort of person given the diaconate should have two basic qualities: a feeling for church and gospel, and an ability to deepen ecclesial life as an officer of the congregation.

Because the office of deacon has liturgical, teaching, administrative, and service dimensions, it might be well to envisage *several* deacons within a *single* community according to the community's needs and the deacons' special talents. Their office is not a matter of special powers to do what the laity cannot do, so much as it is a sharing of the office of pastoral responsibility among several individuals. When one thinks of the communitarian life of many Third Church peoples, the advisability of having a group of several deacons assisting the pastor becomes persuasive.

Deacons need not receive a long, specialized training in seminaries. Short courses and seminars would suffice. But it is easy to imagine that in the course of their activities many of them will grow both in stature and in their understanding of pastoral office. Thus they might easily become the cadre of persons from whom future presbyters could be chosen.

Modern educational theory moves increasingly in the direction of realizing that men and women cannot be trained as children for jobs which they will perform all their lives. For either presbyterate or diaconate, ongoing training in informal settings, along with updating and sharing of experiences are viable alternatives to long periods spent in formal seminary training. Putting more faith in this form of training would give the church a chance to utilize the services of persons who at various stages in their lives have something special to offer. It would also be a fine manner of restoring to local congregations the right of participating in the choice of their pastors.

In the question of the diaconate it is most important to realize that the diaconate is a part of the office of the church, not a catchall ministry. Time will be required to create structures for a fruitful diaconate, but the task will not be difficult as long as it is recalled that all office is a pastoral function, and that one creates institutional offices where there are needs, not on an *a priori* basis.

The Ordination of Women?

Since we are mainly concerned with the Third Church, the question of the ordination of women must necessarily be colored by the infinite variety of concrete sociologies of male/female relationships in various cultures. Besides the fact that there is neither "male nor female" as long as we are Christ's (Gal. 3:28), there are also suitable times and seasons for eveything under the sun (Eccles. 3:1–10). People close to the issue in the various churches are the only ones who can make judgments on the signs of the times and the opportuneness of the move. It has been observed, for example, that Catholicism in the Philippines and Latin America is already largely viewed as "something for women" and consequently condemned by males. One need not be a male chauvinist to realize that circumspection is necessary, here and elsewhere, to implement a policy which will really advance gospel interests.

The key question is theological. Are women fit candidates for being taken into the office of the church? If that question is answered in the affirmative, the issue of the opportuneness of the move can be fruitfully debated.

If one accepts the *possibility* that women are capable of being ordained, the issue revolves around two questions: (1) the aspect of opportuneness in a given cultural setting (which *may* make deferring the ordination of women advisable); and (2) the issue which Anne Carr has called "engendering the future"[6] (which may make it *obligatory* to go against cultural values that would indicate the need for caution, because insight into the gospel and the signs of the times might make one understand that courageous action is required to overcome an insidious form of sexual oppression).

A recent Roman curial statement gave a negative answer to the question of ordaining women to the presbyterate.[7] This statement represents itself as theological and develops along the following lines in barring the ordination of women. (1) The presbyter represents Christ, and Christ is male. (2) Church tradition has never allowed the ordination of women. (3) The denial of female ordination is not the result of a desire to suppress women, but because New Testament and apostolic witness forbid it. (4) A basic symbolism in the economy of salvation is preserved by keeping priesthood masculine. These require comment.

Throughout this study I have tried to show that to reduce ordained ministry to sacerdotal dimensions is to reduce that service in an unacceptable manner. The basic task of the ordained ministry lies in helping a community to root itself in apostolicity by becoming a people founded on Christ and serving the world in his name. The ordained minister is not the center of the community; rather, he or she is the person whose authoritative personal leadership helps members of the church discover their personal vocation to serve both within the basic community and in the world outside of the church.

It is clear that Jesus was a male person and that he viewed the world from the perspective of Israelite, patriarchal images of God as Father. Furthermore, it is a simple fact that the presbyter has long been seen as someone representing Christ in the midst of the community as an *alter Christus* (another Christ). It is easy to see, then, how the Congregation for the Doctrine of the Faith could conclude from the masculinity of Christ, the paternity of the Father, and apostolic practices rooted in the all-male Jewish sanhedrin that women could not represent Christ as presbyters. Moreover, given the entire history of the issue, it is not too much to say that the burden of proof lies on the side of those who would change the present legislation which allows ordination only of males.[8]

However, it is unfortunate that the Congregation's statement would claim to be theological in rejecting female ordination not just for the present moment (which may be prudent), but for all time. The arguments are, I believe, inconclusive and do not warrant an absolute negative.

First, there is the basic principle. The declaration is finally based on the notion that the priest is, in a most special way, an *alter Christus*. On the face of it, that notion seems unassailable, but it must be put over against the basic nature of office. It is much more true to say that it is the community which is the *alter Christus* than it is to say that the ordained minister is. The church is Christ and each member of the church is a member of his body. The minister's basic function in the community is as a representative of the community's faith that Christ lives in its midst as its head. That faith is the prime matter of ecclesial life. It is the subjective attitude of open trust and confidence which allows the Spirit to work in the church. The minister is primarily an exemplar of this open, trusting, and fiducial discipleship which allows the Lord himself to be the church's head. *Discipleship* is a mark of the entire community, and the leadership of the church should be entrusted to the sort of person who exemplifies this discipleship.

Second, the leadership function is a matter of *apostolic concern*, that is to say, of the sensitivity and capacity necessary to keep the church rooted in orthodoxy and orthopraxis.

Third, the leadership has a function of *overseeing* ecclesial life, not as a master but as one who serves. Authority there is, but it can be entrusted only to a person who can combine guardianship with a servant mentality.

These three marks are symbolized when the ordained minister functions as the *president of the eucharistic meal*. The presbyter does this not as an *alter Christus* but as the representative of the church's faith as it incarnates Christ in the multitude of its daily activities. There is nothing intrinsically masculine about any of these activities. An excellent article by Edward Kilmartin addresses this issue clearly and seems to me most instructive in insisting that the ordained minister is not a direct representative *of Christ* but the representative *of the church* united in faith.[9] If a woman has the capacity to do this, there would seem to be no reason to bar her from admission to office.

Besides the theological reasoning for the possibility of women's ordination, there are numerous historical and sociological arguments to be considered. Together, I believe, they constitute a datum which may make women's ordination even obligatory. For the elevation of women's consciousness is one of the most profound movements of our times. Though stronger in Europe and America than in other places, it is likely to grow as others become more aware that women have been denied human rights to develop themselves and participate actively in the shaping of society at large in more than a merely domestic manner.

It is, however, not clear what the enduring significance of the women's consciousness movement will be. A valid conservatism may enter here and urge caution. But caution should be exercised to help us understand better the implications of embracing the women's movement rather than to block its unfolding. This is an argument for establishing avenues of dialogue, on an international and intercultural basis, to weigh what might be the church's contribution to helping women achieve fuller personhood and a share in decision making. It is not an argument for giving a negative response to the movement pressing for women's ordination.

Second, women themselves are not agreed upon the sort of ecclesial, ordained ministry they would like to carry out. Many feel that to step into the present role of the clergyman, so that we would then have "clergy-women" as well, is not worth the effort. Women's ordination should be part of a restructuring of the ordained college as a whole, not merely the giving to them a position in a model which is destined for destruction.

Steps should be taken to determine two issues: (1) Are there communities which could be better served by women presbyters, either as pastors or co-pastors, than by male presbyters alone? (2) Are there experimental or pilot ministries which should be embarked upon and which should be opened up to women?

Finally, I have a suggestion which may seem more radical than any thus far considered, but which, in fact, may be the easiest and most practical way to begin the entire process of change. Women have come to exercise offices such as cabinet ministry and premiership in numerous nations around the world, even very conservative ones. Might they not be appointed cardinals and placed in a position where they would have visible and real authority in the shaping of international church policies? The cardinalate has never been reserved to the ordained. The nature of the office has generally been considered as special assistance to the pope.

Thus, even if some would view ordination as questionable for women, the possibility of placing them in high offices where they would serve as executives of the papacy and electors of future popes seems feasible. The Vatican's diplomatic service could be enlivened, too, by the presence of women as the envoys of the pope both to governments and national churches. If the church expects to have a role in the shaping of the international women's movement, it must show that it is really serious about enfranchising them in its own life. It is not enough merely to put them in advisory positions at a third and fourth level in the bureaucracy; they have a right to actually exercise power as executives and decision makers.

Ironically, it is probably easier to overcome prejudices by beginning at this higher level than it would be to try to place women in pastorates at the grassroots. One of the really great strengths of Catholicism is its worldwide unity and visibility. It has negative effects in its ability to hinder local initiatives. But it could also have great positive effects by showing leadership in the women's questions.

Some might feel that to introduce the question of women's ordination into the debate about the pastoral ministry of the church is to open a pandora's box better left shut. Whether to do this or not will depend greatly on the position one takes with regard to "engendering the future." The church need not wait to be shaped by cultural movements. It is surely more faithful to the spirit of Jesus' wineskin-breaking ministry to shape the future by recognizing the equality of women than to be shaped by a cultural past of nontheological and relative value. And even in places where many have not come to accept the women's movement, might not one part of the gospel's leaven be to disseminate the truth that in Christ there is neither Jew nor Greek, slave nor free person, male nor female? This seems at least worth considering.

The practical decision about the role of women ministers in the Third Church is, of course, even more fraught with complexity than in the Second Church. In the final analysis, though, the question comes down to this: granting that the step is theologically permissible, how great a priority does the issue enjoy in the discussion of creating a healthy ordained ministry for basic communities? That question will be answered differently in different cultural settings.

Like other issues confronting the Third Church, the answers are best left in the hands of local Christians. The Second Church has a responsibility for letting go the reins of power, and not once again setting the Third Church's agenda. But insofar as the issue of women's rights to participate fully in a life broader than traditional domestic roles is part of the gospel's agenda, to that extent the World Church does have an obligation to clearly reform its policies. This will not be easy. There is a sexual bias that runs through ecclesiastical thinking as surely as it runs through almost every society. Unmasking it for what it is can only be painful, for women no less than for men.

8

The Basic Community in a World Church

An Initial Perspective

The World Church is a communion of local churches and is healthy to the extent that its basic communities are sound. These communities are the foundation stones of the dioceses which Vatican II generally considers to be "particular" or "local" churches in the fullest sense of these words.[1] Numerous crucial decisions face Christianity in the volatile conditions of modern complexity, some of them far more challenging and exciting than the prosaic business of pondering church structures. I hope it has been evident that I see issues such as peace and justice, world poverty, population planning, the creation of national and international political frameworks for furthering human development, and other such challenges as being more vital to the future than debating models of ordained ministry. Nevertheless, the model of ordained ministry chosen determines, in large measure, the way in which the gospel will be brought to bear on the more crucial issues.

Ultimately, the enormous number of questions that cloud the horizons of humankind are matters of the human heart and its need to come to terms with the possibility of *agape* and *dike* (love and justice) as God's healing presence within individuals and between groups. The Christian message is concern for the reconciliation of competing and hostile forces within individuals, groups, nations, societies, social classes, races, and the human race as a whole. There is but one world, a troubled world in the grip of what the Judeo-Christian-Muslim traditions call sin. It would seem that liberal faith in the perfectability of the human has been proven ineffective for it does not supply the inner resources that are necessary to overcome the irrationality of sin and to bring about the global reconciliation between all creatures and God that is captured in Jesus' symbol of the Kingdom of God. For we continually find ourselves caught by the inability to be truly human.

Langdon Gilkey, in reflecting on his experiences in a prison compound in China during World War II, came to believe that the central religious problem of his fellow internees and himself was the call to sacrifice what individuals and groups seemed to need for the sake of the common good.[2] Each original group of inhabitants of the Shantung Compound carved out a comfortable life for itself. But the war had a habit of moving on, and part of its progress was the dumping of new internees on the compound. Resources were stretched—food, clothing, space—and the holders of these power-conferring commodities were faced with the need to share. Few acquitted themselves with dignity. Fewer still could manage magnanimity. Gilkey was especially struck by the fact that few of the missionaries interned with him did better than the "godless." Often they did much worse. To be human in the Shantung Compound meant sacrifice: giving up what you thought you needed, often what you really *did* need, in order to create the possibility of a minimally humane life for all.

Gilkey sees the Shantung experience as a miniature of the problems facing humankind in its global existence, and his record of life in the prison compound is both moving and profound. In story form he lays out the basic human problems which the gospel must speak to if it is to have relevance to life. In the final analysis, Jesus' teachings are about what makes life human. What one wears, eats, or possesses is less important than extending compassionate care for others because they are children of a common Father.

Church life is the attempt to make present the life of the man who uttered the parables of sin and its forgiveness, of greed and sharing, of life in abundance that illustrate the human dilemma. It is the trust that his Spirit can bring about inner wholeness which is the very condition of entering the dynamic of *displacing self-concern* in its narrow sense and *replacing it with effective compassion.* In that dynamic of religious conversion scriptures are read and expounded in the attempt to open hearts to the fact of sin and the possibility of repentance leading to wholeness. Sacraments are celebrated as the signs of our recognition of our condition and as the instruments of our regeneration. But because, paradoxically, sacraments and prayer have also become identified with a narrow, ethnocentric, un-Christian self-concern, many who have a concern for the global issues of peace and justice have grown impatient with the church. Understandable as that attitude is, it is unfortunate, for the basic human problem still remains the narrowness of the human heart. The teachings of the Judeo-Christian-Muslim traditions unmask that narrowness. They give, moreover, a message of hope that evil can be overcome and that God's kingdom will come, indeed, *is* present as the leaven in dough which is already rising.

What is required, then, is a renewal of ecclesial life on both world and local levels which will help persons displace self-preoccupied sin and replace it with loving, self-forgetting compassion. We have pointed to the basic community as the place where this sort of life begins and have argued that freedom must be given to structure the church around this insight. A reform of the grassroots pastoral ministry is one of the foundation stones of that process. At the next level, there are required bishops who are able to elevate local concerns and help basic communities focus themselves on broader, but equally pressing issues.

There still remains the question of the structure of the World Church and its unity. In a shrinking world of increasing interdependence, communion between churches will be necessary if what is begun with such hope in the villages and cities of the world is to be carried through to completion on a broader scale. The following sections, then, are a schematic attempt to deal with the structures of the World Church from the bottom up. For it is no less a ministry of service to humankind to help to unify all Christians at a world level than to assist the village, the urban neighborhood, or the suburb to coalesce around the struggle for human development.

It is at the world level that the scandal of Christian divisions becomes most catastrophic. Christians preach a doctrine of unity under a common God only to find themselves shamefully divided. The parent of many Christian churches remains Roman Catholicism, but there are millions to whom its claims to be the *mater et caput omnium ecclesiarum* (the mother and head of all churches) are nothing less than arrogance.

In what follows I write about the World Church as a Catholic. Nevertheless, I am painfully aware of the incompleteness of ecclesial unity. I utilize Roman Catholic terminology in speaking of the World Church, not because I believe all other churches must come to our table under our conditions, but because it is futile to try to do more than deal with one problem at a time. I speak of Roman Catholicism and its world structures with a hope that a reform of its structures may make available a vehicle useful for bringing about the world unity of all churches and ecclesial communities that the ministry of Peter has symbolized for centuries, but which it has been unable to bring about in recent generations.

The Ministry of Episcopal Conferences

Between the first and fourth centuries the role of bishops was being clarified. This was the era par excellence of bishops. The local church became the community centered around a bishop-pastor. However, there were numerous questions—especially regarding heresy—which necessitated a larger unity among churches, a unity which could aid local communities in settling disputed matters. The great councils were one response, but along with them came the increase in the prominence of the Roman bishop as the pope of all the churches. Authority devolved more and more into the Roman bishop's hands, and by the early Middle Ages most of the significant features of the Roman primacy and its claims had come to be accepted.

The East, the First Church, was never completely happy with some of the more imperial aspects of those claims, and a complex history might be well summarized by saying that a schism was simply waiting for an excuse to happen—and this, not merely for theological reasons. What is of significance here is the fact that the papacy gradually came to be the central organ of ecclesiastical authority, and a gradual shift of emphasis saw more and more power flowing into papal hands.

In too few histories of this evolution is the *theological* dimension of this transition highlighted. It is common enough for those who see the papacy as the Whore of Babylon to judge the whole movement as a deformation, pure and simple, of the church. But it is much more accurate to realize that the claims of Rome were based on a deep, existential need of the church for a focal point of unity. One may decry the centralization of Catholicism and believe passionately that the imperial court style that has characterized it is wrongheaded and un-Christian; but the fact still remains that the papacy filled a felt need.

Today Catholicism is struggling to return initiative and power to the local church even if at times many are tempted to question whether that is really the name of the game which is being played out. In discussing episcopal conferences and international synods of bishops I mean to address the issue of local initiative and autonomy, for I believe that the long-term significance of the present moment is that it allows us to go back once again to the sort of issues which led to the formation of the papacy and to renew the papacy in a way which will balance out both the need for local autonomy and for international unity.

Bishops, according to the documents of Vatican II, are members of an episcopal college and pastors of the World Church.[3] The key issue is to adjust the teaching on the corporate responsibility of the bishops for the whole church so as to harmonize it with the role of the papacy and the Roman Curia. I view the issue more as one of *praxis* than *theoria*. Transferring to others the authority which one is accustomed to exercise oneself is a task sure to test one's maturity and good sense. One can scarcely expect to accomplish this overnight. The dramas of the years since the close of Vatican Council II have been periodic episodes of high intrigue punctuated by returns to the Curia's "business as usual routines"; but the need for change is still there. It is a matter of seizing the initiative by utilizing the insights of the council and putting them into practice.

In what follows, "episcopal conferences" are to be understood as national or regional groupings of local churches (in the persons of their bishops).[4] On a theoretical level, bishops' conferences have been recognized and given great scope for initiative. On a practical level, however, the traditional lines of papal and curial authority remain intact, and *real* authority remains in Rome. In recent centuries the lines of authority ran directly from pope to individual bishops. Each diocese was considered to be directly under the pope in all matters. The principle was concretized in the 1917 revision of the Code of Canon Law, where it is made clear that each bishop exercises jurisdiction in his diocese at the pleasure of the pope:

> Bishops are the successors of the apostles and are, by divine institution, appointed to the particular churches which, with ordinary jurisdiction, they rule under the authority of the Roman Pontiff (Canon 329).

Moreover, in the Code, the pope's authority extends directly

> into each and every church, to each and every pastor and to all the faithful, and is independent of all human authority (Canon 218).

This need not be taken as a purely negative formulation of imperial papalism, for it is meant to insure that in urgent cases every Christian has the privilege of appealing to the pope. But one might well ask whether the *right* of such an appeal to the pope has been allowed to degenerate into too much intervention into the daily lives of local churches by the pope. Side by side with the recognition of the principle that local churches have a right to relative autonomy, there continues to exist a curial functioning that deals directly with individual bishops and dioceses. On the one hand there is a recognition of episcopal conferences as having certain authority over national and regional church life; on the other hand there is what often seems to be an intentional obscuring of exactly what powers to shape church life these bodies have. And in the ambiguity of this situation the curia is asked for permissions as in days of yore.

Bishops' conferences seem nervous and afraid that they may overstep their ambiguous powers. And so the curial mode of action in the church seems to keep the World Church an international institution which operates under a common law in all places and cultures. This is done in spite of the theoretical recognition of the principle of cultural relativity and the principle of subsidiarity. Until this ambiguity is cleared by a Roman policy that *encourages* major regional initiatives, there is little chance that the principle of relative autonomy within a communion of interdependent local churches will ever be able to operate effectively.

Bishops' conferences would have an important ministry if it were clear that they had the ordinary authority to direct affairs for a group of dioceses. Their first service would be at the local level itself. Though there are vast differences within single nations, the fact still remains that the policies of one diocese cannot be formed in isolation from those of another. Cyprian of Carthage faced a situation similar to ours. A strong believer in the rights of the individual bishop, he was faced with problems confronting the whole of North Africa in the aftermath of the Decian persecutions. His summoning of regional synods, not unlike modern episcopal conferences, was his response.

Because of his strong belief that no bishop could be ordered around by another bishop, Cyprian also held that the decisions of a regional synod could not be made absolutely binding. He relied on the sensitivity of individual bishops to the need for a greater unity to lead them to forego their own private opinions. He was thoroughly impartial in his disdain for intervention from the outside, an attitude Cyprian showed in his rather cordial dislike of the policies of at least one of his fellow bishops in Rome. (That conflict was solved in Cyprian's own case by martyrdom, and for the church as a whole by the subsequent extension of papal authority in ways he would not have liked.)

The entire issue of an *intermediate* authority between individual bishops and Rome is as lively today as it was in the third century. But with a difference. Today some fifteen centuries of practice have brought about a state of affairs where the central authority has a clear domination over both individual dioceses and national churches. This the papacy did not enjoy in the third century.

Rome could, however, *encourage* the creation of strong episcopal conferences today and make it clear that they should be creative, without the fear of reversal. In such a state of affairs the presupposition would be in favor of subsidiarity if Rome would presume that local bishops know the situation, are seriously weighing alternatives, are faithful to apostolic teaching, and have an eye turned to the international ramifications of their decisions. For bishops do have a worldwide responsibility, not just a ministry within their own dioceses.[5] Conferences of bishops would have to be aware of modern communications; no decision can ever again be purely local. But that should not change the fact that the basic presumption in church life should favor local autonomy.

My experience in Papua New Guinea and numerous conversations with men and women working in other nations convince me that the ambiguity referred to above has led to a situation where bishops' conferences are afraid to organize themselves into strong bodies with binding powers for the shaping of national policies, for fear that their decisions might be reversed by Rome. In addition, one finds anxiety in the individual bishop at the prospect of losing autonomy with regard to the practical affairs in his own diocese. He fears this would be the result of giving authority to a national conference of bishops. In other words, individual bishops do not want to lose personal power to a collective body. In the second place, there is an exaggerated respect for the papacy which has been engendered by long years of study of church history and canon law. This has made bishops unable to consider Vatican II's teachings on the local church to be as important as papal centralism.

To overcome both obstacles, strong encouragement will be necessary; and such encouragement can come only from Rome. Only then will bishops feel impelled to set up strong conferences with the power to enact policy decisions at national and regional levels. At the moment, lacking this encouragement, few conferences create strong secretariats for seriously studying issues; fewer still are willing to take the steps toward local initiative which these secretariats might advise. And lacking these structures, local churches are perpetually in the position of not developing well-thought-out policies for liturgical life, for human development, for clarifying the moral values at stake in political choices, or for any of the myriad of other such matters confronting the church. These issues are too large for individual dioceses and too local for the papacy or the World Church to grapple with effectively.

For this reason it is clearly necessary for the ministry of national and regional episcopal conferences to be recognized and made operative. It is to be expected, as well, that there will be issues too big for these conferences to handle. Thus we come to the subject of international synods.

The Ministry of International Synods

The next step up the ladder in the World Church is the international synod of bishops. The Council describes the synod as follows:

> Bishops from various parts of the world, chosen by ways and procedures established or to be established by the Roman Pontiff, will render especially helpful assistance to the supreme pastor of the church in a council to be known by the proper name of Synod of Bishops. Since it will be acting in the name of the entire Catholic episcopate, it will at the same time demonstrate that all the bishops in hierarchical communion share in the responsibility for the universal church.[6]

The Council wished to establish the synod to assist the pope. Herein lies the seed of controversies that have attended its every meeting. Some have wanted the synod to have legislative power relatively untrammeled by curial or papal intervention, and not just to be a body giving advice to the pope. Other issues have also called forth dissatisfaction from many quarters. For example, would giving the synod broad powers undercut the papacy and lead to a form of conciliarism? The dilemma is not an easy one.

To what extent ought the bishops to have the initiative in establishing an agenda? It has been painfully evident that Pope Paul VI saw the synod as *his* meeting. Should it be otherwise? Though the pope must not be denied the right to propose agenda items, I believe that the normal order should be to allow proposals for discussion to emanate from the grassroots. The pope has a unique perspective and must be able to make himself heard. But first the synod must deal with matters flowing from this question: What are the matters which episcopal conferences feel are too large for their churches to decide upon alone? The synod ought to be a forum where such questions can be debated and policies decided.

In the past the agenda has been limited by the pope and *decision-making power* barred from the start. The questions of clerical celibacy or birth control are but two issues which bishops have wanted to debate, and about which discussion was cut short or forbidden. It should never become evident that synods are bound by foreordained agenda that block discussion of matters which would "give pain to the pope." As long as this remains the case, we are dealing with an imperial court where the pleasure of the monarch determines both the direction and content of discussion. In no way is it an expression of confidence in the guidance of a Spirit who may initiate movement from the grassroots level as well as from the top.

To most moderns, it appears that in the adoption of agenda the curial point of view prevails (even though questionnaires are sent out to episcopal conferences). Unfortunately, the Curia does not have a reputation for encouraging dissent from its own positions. This statement may seem unfair to the multitude of men and women who work for serious reforms within the Curia, but at the very least these men and women have a serious public relations problem. I believe that there is a problem of substance as well. Institutions obey laws that respect no persons. Fine individuals can work in archaic institutions.

In the case in point, to all appearances we have a problem with two visions of the church operating simultaneously, each competing for acceptance. Vision one follows the Code of Canon Law and sees the pope exercising jurisdiction directly over individual dioceses with the right of intervening in local churches whenever he sees fit. Vision two sees things from the bottom up. Local bishops, in consultation with the laity and with their ordained collaborators, shape the life of the diocese. Because dioceses exist in nations and regions with common problems, conferences of bishops shape policies among the various dioceses. Because national questions have international ramifications, the synod exists to promote debate and decision at the international level. Direct papal interventions would come only as a last resort in serious issues.

The concept of the synod springs from the second vision. But that concept is in competition with the first vision. No one can predict the outcome of the conflict between the two visions. What is, however, clear is that the future of the synod as a free body will be a clear indicator of which vision is in the ascendancy. In the end, one's concept of the papal ministry will decide whether one wants to allow the first or the second to prevail.

The Papal Ministry

No consideration of the ministry of the church can be complete without treating the papacy, nor is there any question so likely to excite strong feelings as a consideration of that office. It is a simple fact that from the sixth to the sixteenth centuries, Second Church history has largely been shaped by or in reaction to a succession of heroic, saintly, cowardly, or worldly popes. Prescinding from the *historical* facts of Peter's position in the ancient church (a hotly contested issue), and of how far back we can date the emergence of strong Roman claims for a primacy of honor and jurisdiction over the World Church, there arose both a *theological* outlook and a *psychological* climate which explain how those claims were once generally accepted.

The Letter to the Ephesians represents the theological dimension. The first chapter is a magnificent recital of the significance of Jesus Christ for the whole human race, and ends in a paean-like account of the church: ". . . he has put all things under his feet and made him the head over all things for the church, which is his body, the fullness of him who fills all in all" (Eph. 1:22–23). Ephesians was widely considered a Pauline epistle. Though this is now doubted, it still remains fact that its putative Pauline derivation gave it great prestige. Moreover, its ecclesiology is a universalist ecclesiology wherein the World Church has priority. The papacy came to answer to a felt need for symbolizing and realizing that worldwide unity. The psychological side of the process rises out of the migration of the Germanic peoples and the loss of a preponderant imperial Roman military power after A.D. 410. The papacy answered the need of the Roman world for another visible center of unity.

The intrinsic faith issue surrounding the papacy regards the following question: Are the primacy claims of the papacy theologically defensible? Most Catholics accept them even though they may have problems with the exercise of papal ministry. The difficulty lies in the answer to other questions: What sort of papacy will best minister to the World Church's needs? Can the papacy be structured in a modern manner which will (1) make it an effective instrument of unity, (2) exemplify meaningfully that unity, and (3) help the World Church achieve vigor and decisiveness in facing the dilemmas of Christianity in the modern world?

In a Third Church perspective the issue becomes the following: How can the papal ministry help the young churches achieve their autonomous, local cultural dimension while simultaneously guarding against the temptation to cut themselves off from the World Church? For the dark side of the insistence upon local churches and contextualized theology is the danger of splintering the church into national and regional bodies. No one who has worked with Third World intellectuals will underestimate their anger at the international status quo. Many see everything that emanates from the northern hemisphere as an unjust oppression of their peoples. The tight organization of Catholicism is just one example of a structure which will have to prove itself their friend if it is to receive allegiance and affection.

Vatican II has attempted to articulate a balanced understanding of both papal and episcopal ministries. *Lumen gentium,* art. 18, for example, sees Peter as "the visible and perpetual foundation of the unity and communion of faith." According to conciliar doctrine his ministry continues in the papacy. Given the decentralization thrust of contemporary missiology and ecclesiology, the papal ministry becomes *more* important, not less. It is not a simple matter to create a World Church with great local diversity and

still be faithful to the Pauline vision of the church representing the fullness
of Christ. We are a World Church with a dazzling assortment of histories
and cultures, but we also have a vocation to be one church. The pope's
ministry of encouraging both unity and diversity is a dizzyingly difficult
dimension of ecclesial life which cannot validly be swept under the carpet
if tensions are to be met and solutions to world problems are to be
addressed.

All Catholic Christians may agree that they are trying to live a life
faithful to the gospel. But in Tanzania, for example, they may come to
believe that only a high degree of socialism will bring about the social
justice spoken of by the prophets and accepted as a part of his message by
Jesus. Men and women in Tanzania may find themselves judging negatively the very capitalism which United States Catholics may believe is the
best possible way of guaranteeing individual freedoms and the production
of goods and services to benefit the masses. The Tanzanians may point to
inequalities within the United States, and to the fact that untrammeled
American-inspired transnational corporations are instruments of
economic exploitation. The Americans may counter with the fact that
socialism inevitably puts curbs on individual rights, restricts the flow of
news, and tends to make anyone who opposes the state into an enemy.

Both groups read the same Bible and come to quite different conclusions about its meaning. Each suspects the other of a breach of faith in
coming to exactly those judgments which seem most precious to their
respective points of view. One group may believe that the moral fiber of a
people is eroded when the self-assertive attitudes favoring competitive
capitalism are promoted. Another sees issues as being so complex that the
attempt to implement international social justice schemes will lead to
curtailing individual rights in areas where truth is so confusing as to
preclude practical, universal norms for solving problems. In the more
narrowly ecclesial realm the same is true. What seems to one group a
legitimate pluralism in theology is heresy for another. But one thing is
common to the Catholics in every group: a desire that the pope speak out
clearly in defense of *their* position. Here the pope finds himself in a
precarious predicament.

Perhaps too much is expected of the papacy, but that expectation points
to a live faith that wants Peter to lead. If he remains content with a merely
symbolic ministry, his role may be trivialized. Issues are embarrassingly
concrete and do not yield to homiletic exhortations to end the arms race or
to overcome racism when issues like economic exploitation are solidly
rooted in military power balances.

In the New Testament (Acts 15), we see Peter prevailing in the controversy over the observance of the Jewish law, but it is James who presides
over the meeting and issues the edict. It seems to have been Paul (Gal. 2)
who pressured Peter to take the stand he did. This is certainly a confusing picture which belies Luke's attempt (Acts 2:44–47) to make the

primitive church an idyllic community of peace and concord. Very evidently, Peter's historical ministry did not unfold itself in a court walled off from dissenting opinions. Equally evident is the fact that it was exercised through structures over which he had little direct control. The monarchical papacy of the Middle Ages and modern times is not the only model that has functioned, nor must it always operate as it does today.

The present functioning of the papacy seems to please few, either those on the left or those on the right. But the *theory* behind the papacy, once one leaves aside its court style of operation, has probably never been as necessary or acceptable as it is today. I was once asked to give a radio talk entitled "Peter and the Papacy" for the Papua New Guinea National Broadcasting Commission. I drew up my talk on fairly conservative dogmatic lines, not softening even the teaching on infallibility (but putting it in a context of consultation with local churches). The surprising thing was the response which that talk drew from Protestant missionaries. Many felt acutely the need for an international spokesman. The contrast of this reaction with the feeling common among our Catholic seminarians at Bomana was striking. For them the papacy is something heard from only when decrees are issued on moral, liturgical, and ecclesiastical questions, many of which seem tragically beside the point and out of touch with their Melanesian concerns.

Among the bishops of Papua New Guinea there is an openness and sensitivity to the needs of the local church. That sensitivity expresses itself in a desire to find forms of ministry, worship, and general ecclesial life more adapted to the local scene. It shows itself further in an opinion that more autonomy must be granted to the local level. But when it comes to the point where the individual bishop or the episcopal conference should devise a policy which would depart from universal law, the fear of being rapped on the knuckles by a Roman congregation causes paralysis.

One incident illustrates this well. In many sections of Melanesia there exists a form of "trial marriage." Marriage in Melanesia is not a matter of a commitment between two persons witnessed on a single occasion by a representative of the community. Rather, a couple is given permission to live together to see how things will work out. There will have been long, preliminary discussions between key relatives of the two clans involved, and initial exchanges of gifts called the bride-price. When an agreement is struck, there are degrees of living together, ultimately culminating in full cohabitation with conjugal rights. But it is not a matter of two young people "playing house." It is serious business in which both clans have a vital stake. If the marriage progresses as the community hopes it will, it is eventually sealed with a final exchange of gifts (and by that time there may be a child or two as well) to recognize the passing of the woman from one clan to another. In no way is the trial marriage a permissive relationship.

From a Christian moral point of view there is a problem. Can the couple receive the Eucharist during the trial stages of the marriage? Or are they "living in a state of public sin"? According to western norms they are in public sin. But is this an issue for adaptation since Melanesian marriage is something quite different from western marriage? It would seem that decisions in the matter should rest with the local church and its bishops.

What actually happened? The matter was raised, perhaps prematurely, by priests who were confronted with trial marriages on a daily basis and who wanted an official sanction for what many of them were already allowing. Several moral theologians expressed the opinion that the bishops ought to function as the ordinary magisterium and affirmatively decide the matter at the local level. When the issue was brought to the attention of Rome, however, it was regarded as an immoral solution and the rest of the bishops sided with Rome against their fellow bishop who had believed the custom compatible with gospel teaching. They demanded that he clearly cease to sanction such trial marriages and that he expressly forbid the giving of rights to eucharistic communion to those in them.

It is not intended here to accuse the pope of intervening in the case. But his ministry is exercised through the Roman congregations, and their activities tend to make national priests and seminarians suspect the papacy's grasp of the local scene's cultural values and practices. It would be a tremendous loss to the local church if such attitudes of suspicion were to become engrained. At a time in the formation of local churches in which there is a strong tendency to consider local values as absolutely normative, there is an equally great need for a ministry that will help local Christians to realize that they are a part of a worldwide *catholica,* a people offering a worship of service and prayer across the globe. The Third Church, too, can be ethnocentrically narrow.

Papal ministry is a positive and creative office. Its basic function is to symbolize the worldwide, global unity of Christians and to help men and women of many nations expand their horizons to the cosmic dimensions of the Christian movement. It is a helping ministry, directing efforts to aid local churches grow in the Spirit of Christ.

Unfortunately, the present picture is far different. Because of a complex set of circumstances, basically historical, the papal ministry has been exercised through the Roman Curia and seems to function in a negative manner, hindering local developments, keeping ambiguous the juridical powers and rights of local churches to chart their own course through a maze of particular problems and opportunities. The papal office's dilemma is a serious one. What may seem to some a legitimate contextualization of the church in indigenous culture appears to others as giving in to a materialistic spirit of the times, flattening out essential contours of practice and doctrine, contours which define the gospel message as contrasted with worldly attitudes.

This is merely another way of saying that the contemporary historical scene is complex and presents the church with confusing issues. The only way out of the difficulty, though, is through it. There is no single solution unless it be that of giving freedom to local churches to muddle their way through the hundreds of questions which rise out of the encounter of Christ and culture. In that process the initiative ought clearly to be placed at the grassroots level.

In Roman Catholicism, this will happen only if positive encouragement is given by the pope. Central to that task is the opening up of the structures of ordained ministry so that basic communities are construed as the foundation stones of the World Church. This, of course, is the central argument of our study—the need to encourage the development of a form of ordained ministry at the basic community level so that renewal and reform may take place from the bottom up. Centuries of centralism have created the paradoxical situation where grassroots renewal must be first encouraged from the top.

CONCLUSION

Pipe Dream or Realism?

When all is said and done, perhaps a word about the realism of the basic community as the foundation for a concept of ordained ministry is called for. Is what we have been discussing and arguing toward a mere pipe dream, or is it realistic?

Good theory is supposed to lead to good practice. But, as everyone knows, there is a great chasm between the dreams of writers and the realities of life. Given limited resources and the difficulties of making concrete changes in human societies, what is actually possible? This leads to a discussion which, though brief, intends to focus on what I believe is the chief roadblock on the way toward restructuring the church's ordained leadership. We have seen indications of what I view as the central problem, but have until now steered clear of the critical issue.

Roman Catholicism's shape today is centered on the clergyman priest and the religious orders. Growth in this direction has had a long and complex history, full of saints and sinners, insights and blunders of immense proportions. But at bottom is the fact that the clerical state is rather like the Roman Empire's *cursus honorum.* Responsibility, in the final analysis, is vested in those who have come up the ladder through the seminary system. Immense strengths have been given to Catholicism by following this arrangement. The question is whether this model of leadership is adequate for shifting to the set of priorities implied in a basic community model of church.

It is arguable that the church has gradually moved into a situation in which there are only "regular" or "religious" priests. "Diocesan" or "secular" priests have been formed in a semi-religious model both in the seminary and by their life-style's requirements. The technical and canonical fact that they own property, do not live in community, and do not follow an approved "rule" is relatively unimportant when set alongside the similarities between the lives of religious and diocesan ministers. What the church really has is a situation where perhaps 40 percent of its presbyters are formally religious and 60 percent are informally so, the latter living with their bishop as a quasi-religious superior.

What does this mean? At the very least it means that real authority is exercised only by men who have a certain "class attitude" toward ecclesial issues. Even more, it comes to mean that what will be allowed to change

151

depends upon the permission of that clerical class within the church. None of this is new to those reading the liberal Catholic press during the years of Vatican II and immediately following. Nor will this point of view seem particularly radical to people such as the U.S. Catholics who have participated in movements such as the "Call to Action," or to equivalent liberal groups in other nations.

Still, in spite of widespread dissatisfaction with the present state of affairs, little really changes. The clergy are still firmly in control, and "underground churches" have lost their appeal.

The so-called vocations crisis (the shortage of new recruits for the clergyman model of ministry) is an indication that clerical life has lost its appeal. One can point here and there to orders or dioceses or nations in which this is not the case. But by and large it seems that young people are voting with their feet by not presenting themselves in large numbers to seminaries and novitiates in a trend which shows little sign of reversing itself. In this context it is interesting to note that most Protestant churches are not afflicted by a similar vocations dropoff. In the light of the Protestant experience one is wise to be reluctant to judge that modern youth has no spirit of sacrifice or desire to serve God, gospel, and humankind in pastoral ministry. My own interpretation of the entire phenomenon is that there has been a fundamental shift in lay attitudes as to what constitutes Christian ecclesial life, and the clergy have not been able yet to read the signs of the times.

What, though, does this have to do with the Third Church? First, it ought to lead us to a willingness seriously to consult its membership about the relevance the present shape of the church has to their concerns. What I would like to do here is point out what seems to me to be the roadblock to doing this.

The main focus of my study has been the missions (now on the point of becoming churches) founded in the nineteenth-century missionary movement, particularly in Oceania and Africa. There one finds the direction of the church still largely in the hands of either foreign religious priests and bishops, or led by indigenous clergy with a large emotional stake in the present ecclesial models. Both groups will need positive encouragement to suggest the sort of dialogue which might lead to another model. This can come only from Rome.

But Rome is caught in a very serious bind. The centuries-long process that has led to the centralizing of ecclesial decision making in Rome has been one in which prescriptions for clerical life have made the papacy the clergy's spiritual and emotional homeland. The religious orders, especially, report directly to the papacy through their superiors general who are among the papacy's chief collaborators. Thus the missions, even more directly than parts of the world where diocesan bishops are relatively more important, depend upon the papacy both for direction and financial support. To be sure, I am not advocating revolt. I mean only to indicate that the religious orders which staff and are so important in the direction of the younger churches must become deeply conscious of these "political" realities. The anomaly is that religious orders, although their vows ought to free them of worldly concerns, have come to a juncture where they are supporting an ecclesiastical structure which is very much this-worldly. While the religious orders ought to be a radical way of life in the church, but also somewhat in tension with it (exemplifying the world-negating or world-indifferent aspect of part of the gospel teaching[1]), their actual function is somewhat different. They have, in effect, been co-opted by the ecclesiastical institution, indeed they are almost indistinguishable from it, thus becoming conservative rather than innovative forces in church life.[2] Early in the twentieth century Troeltsch and Harnack gave a criticism of Catholicism which seems to have lost little validity with the passage of time. Troeltsch saw Catholicism essentially wedded to its medieval form.[3] Harnack believed that the religious orders were the "monasticism of the modern period," and part of the institutional church's opposition not to secularism and the erosion of spiritual values, but of its bolstering of its own power.[4] My own point is that the continuation of the sort of thinking which sees religious life as the *ideal for all the church* leads to fundamental dislocations in the theology of the ordinary pastoral ministry of the local church. It also has negative effects upon religious life, for it must compromise itself and its true nature in order to attract large numbers of candidates so that the orders can serve their civil service function. Moreover, because they are both within and outside of the main decision-making bodies of the church, they find it hard to realize their actual impact on the church as a whole. The nut of the problem is that religious life was never meant to give the dominant shape to the ordinary pastoral ministry, but that is what it does today.

At another level, in the context of the process of moving from the status of missions to that of becoming local churches, the problems of religious life in the Second Church tend to spill over into the Third. Second, each religious order is preoccupied with the problems of its own particular missions: providing the personnel and finances necessary to keep the present state of affairs running. Even the drastic reduction of recruits for the orders has not yet led them to critical reflection on the question of whether or not one era has ended and another begun.

At this point, though, my own thinking encounters genuine puzzlement. What should the orders do? From one point of view it is not the work of North Americans or Germans to plan for Nigerians or Fijians. Direction of the local church ought to be in the hands of local bishops. On the other hand, as long as the orders provide the bishops with priests to replace dying and retiring missionaries, nothing will ever change. The crunch will not come for perhaps another twenty-five years. The generation of missionaries sent out in the heyday of post-World War II expansion in the fifties and sixties will be serving into the nineties.

It is possible, of course, that vocations will increase. But even if they do, is it right to continue to send men to be foreign pastors in the young churches? Or is it time seriously and critically to evaluate the *theological* issues posed by cultural relativity and ecclesial growth with a view to encouraging national Christians in the young churches to assume full responsibility for their future? Needless to say, expatriates with expertise in certain areas may be invited for either short-term or long-term service. But is it not a form of cultural and religious imperialism to continue to insist on the following of Second Church models when these entail dependence upon the parent churches?

Again I find myself returning to the papal ministry. It would seem that a thorough and free airing of these and similar questions is called for. Given the present arrangement of Roman Catholicism, the initiative for such debate can come only from the papacy itself. In the end, of course, the debate will have ramifications for the Second Church, the full impact of which can hardly be imagined.

If the Third Church were to opt for a basic community model and restructure its ordination policies accordingly, choosing men and women for pastorates and stepping outside the seminary system to train them, the basic shape of the church would be mightily changed. At the very least the semi-monastic or quasi-religious shape of the clergy could expect to give way to something more adapted to indigenous sociological patterns. Certainly celibacy and religious life would survive, but never again would their structures determine the shape of the church as a whole. They would assume the voluntary character which they ought ideally to have had in the first place.

In it all, though, it is the papacy which must lead. This will not be easy. For centuries its leadership has created a cadre of ordained leaders intensely loyal to its directions. To take the initiative in encouraging local churches to solve their problems in the way *they* see fit can, to cautious papalists at least, seem only a weakening of Roman authority and church unity. I see that very issue, though, more as a challenge to creative leadership than a weakening of the papacy's true role of providing an inspirational leadership, and of helping local communities overcome the temptation to become insular and parochial.

In any case, gazing into crystal balls is rather unprofitable. What will prove more fruitful is a courageous attempt to confront the present with confidence that the Spirit breathes at all levels of the church. Jesus' teaching on the nearness of the kingdom and its demands and possibilities, not a concern for the preservation of the past, constitutes the mission and service of the church. In fact, the manner in which he broke through the wineskins of postexilic Judaism ought to validate the principle that authentic Christian spirituality is gained by courageously letting go of security rather than by holding on to the past.

This very act, done in an apostolic manner, will give the church greater credibility when it speaks for justice for the oppressed and asks the powerful of the world to make room for the powerless. We cannot have it both ways. Either we are on the side of authentic human freedom and development or we are not. Being on the side of true liberation cannot leave the church itself untouched. If it does, one can only suspect that the church's central leadership is firmly fastened to the status quo. In such a case it can be seriously questioned whether the church has a rightful claim to speak for its wineskin-bursting Lord.

Notes

Preface

1. See James Bergquist and P. Kambar Manickam, *A Crisis of Dependency in Third World Ministries: A Critique of Inherited Missionary Forms in India* (Madras, India: The Christian Literature Society, 1974). The authors note that "just as dependency upon western models and goals makes economic development with justice impossible today, so dependency upon western missionary-inherited models of ministry may threaten the emergence of vigorous and involved Christian service in local situations.

"Our concern is not for the wider theology of ministry (in an abstract sense) but of its function. The reason for this more restricted view is not that theological foundations are unimportant. To the contrary, theology and function are inseparably inter-related. Ministerial functions ought to reflect a kind of theology which affirms the biblical interaction between being and doing, for the biblical witness refuses to divide the announcement of God's gifts from contextual human response, or to separate thought and action. But there lies the problem. Most, if not all, of the churches under review in this study can demonstrate impeccable credentials in their purely 'theological' statements about what ministry ought to be and do. Yet the actual types of ministry appear to fall short of what the theological visions embedded in church constitutions, confessional statements and the minds of church leaders intend them to be—thus calling into question both theology and functional form. In ministry, as in other endeavors, practice has lagged behind theory" (pp. 2–3).

2. Ibid., pp. 22–32.

3. The term "Basic Christian Community" has become common to denote the perception and judgment that the church stands in need of a reform at the grassroots level. Presently the parish is conceived to be the basic unit in the life of the church. Often, however, because of local conditions the parish is ineffectual in creating the type of face-to-face community which many religious psychologists and sociologists judge necessary for enabling integral Christian life to thrive. The parish structure is commonly established for the convenience of the ordained priests as a *locus* of their sacramental ministry, not as a face-to-face community where people can meet together to bring their faith to bear on their total life.

The thrust of the basic community movement is towards the development of intimate communities of Christians at a grassroots level. In the context of the present study, we are interested in formulating a concept of ordained ministry which springs from an idea of the church as just this sort of basic community. The argument is that the needs of the basic community—in various cultural contexts—should determine the shape of the ministry, not vice versa.

Chapter 1

1. Shoki Coe, "In Search of Renewal in Theological Education," *Theological Education* 9 (Summer 1973): 238.

2. See *Gaudium et spes* (Pastoral Constitution on the Church in the Modern World), article 4: "To carry out such a task [serving the world], the Church has always had the duty of scrutinizing the signs of the times and of interpreting them in the light of the gospel. Thus, in language intelligible to each generation, she can respond to the perennial questions which men ask about this present life and the life to come, and about the relationship of the one to the other. We must therefore recognize and understand the world in which we live, its expectations, its longings, and its often dramatic characteristics."

3. In a book valuable for its attempt to improve upon fashionable or ideological approaches to the question of underdevelopment, Mende exposes the inadequacy of post-World War II development doctrines and asks, "Can we fully identify the reasons which have led this first experiment in aid to its failure? Do we know enough about the particular mixture of motives, circumstances, and aims which induce apparently inert societies to embark on their own transformation? Can we define the real impact of external factors on their endeavors? Or can we ever command the objectivity to assess to what extent our own experiences are or are not relevant to their reality and to their aspirations?" Tibor Mende, *From Aid to Recolonization: Lessons of a Failure* (New York: Pantheon, 1973), p. xxviii.

4. Freire says, "The liberation of the oppressed is a liberation of men, not things. Accordingly, while no one liberates himself by his own efforts alone, neither is he liberated by others. . . . The correct method lies in dialogue. The conviction of the oppressed that they must fight for their liberation is not a gift bestowed by the revolutionary leadership, but the result of their own *conscientização*." See Paulo Freire, *Pedagogy of the Oppressed* (New York: Seabury, 1973), pp. 53–54.

5. See Paul Tillich, *The Socialist Decision* (New York: Harper & Row, 1977), p. 145.

6. Peter Berger, *Facing Up to Modernity: Excursions in Society, Politics and Religion* (New York: Basic Books, 1977), pp. 162–81.

7. According to David Martin, the concept of secularization as a worldwide, "unitary process" is too simple and, in effect, invalid if understood in that way. The popular notion of secularization is one of a unitary process which is supposed to be working across the globe to weaken and enfeeble a dimension of life called "religion." Thus modernity, the bearer of secularization, is supposed to spell the end of religion. Martin, however, notes that, "All institutions expand and decline for a wide variety of reasons, and religious institutions are no exception. For example, the contemporary decline in religious institutions may be part of the general malaise which is offsetting every kind of social institution in a time of rapid social change" (*The Religious and the Secular*, New York: Schocken Books, 1969, p. 16). See also Martin's *The Dilemmas of Contemporary Religion* (New York: St. Martin's Press, 1978) and *A General Theory of Secularization* (Oxford: Basil Blackwell, 1978), especially Chapter Two, "A Theory of Secularization: Basic Patterns" (pp. 12–99).

8. Peter Glasner, *The Sociology of Secularization: Critique of a Concept* (London: Routledge & Kegan Paul, 1977), pp. 100–18.

9. See Lesslie Newbigin, *Honest Religion for Secular Man* (London: SCM, 1966), pp. 11–43. I have found it interesting to note the reaction of indigenous Melanesians to Newbigin's account of secularization in India and elsewhere. My students often said something like, "He describes it like it feels for our people." Events in contemporary Islam show, though, that some religious formations do not intend

to sit passively as modernization erodes their customary spiritual values and way of life.

10. Simon Barrington-Ward sees spirit possession movements as offering "a new centre and new boundaries potentially coterminous with a renewed society," and characterizes the movements as a "glimpse of reintegration," a new access to divine power (made necessary because of the dislocations and sense of impotence caused among tribal people by the incursion of modernity into "traditional" societies), a "new way of living and relating to others and a new future surpassing all that local cults could offer" (see " 'The Centre Cannot Hold . . . ' Spirit Possession as Redefinition," in *Christianity in Independent Africa*, edited by Edward Fashole-Luke and others [Bloomington: Indiana University Press, 1978], pp. 468–71).

Kenelm Burridge sees the Melanesian "Cargo Cult" in similar terms as a millenarian movement aimed at bringing about a "new situation and a status which, providing the basis of a new integrity, will enable life to be lived more abundantly" (*New Heaven, New Earth: A Study of Millenarian Activities* [New York: Schocken Books, 1969], p. 171). At the risk of oversimplification in comparing complex religious and social adjustment movements, I would observe that such "cults" express the spontaneous needs and religious feelings of their adherents — strong desires for a reintegration of a shattered cosmos and a method of securing a meaningful participation in that cosmos. One of the effects of colonial changes in traditional societies was the marginalization of the bulk of the populace. Traditional Christianity seems to have been unable to minister to this problem and the cults become paths on which the marginalized can tread back to self-respect and meaningfulness.

11. Newbigin, *Honest Religion*, pp. 27–29.

Chapter 2

1. See Walbert Bühlmann, *The Coming of the Third Church* (Maryknoll, N.Y.: Orbis, 1977), pp. 19–24, where Bühlmann gives both the statistics which prove the inevitability of the shift of the Christian population's majority to the southern hemisphere and the likely consequences of that shift.

2. Paul Tillich, *Theology of Culture* (New York: Oxford University Press, 1959), p. 42.

3. John L. McKenzie, *A Theology of the Old Testament* (Garden City, N.Y.: Doubleday, Image Books, 1976), pp. 279–80.

4. Ibid., p. 332.

Chapter 3

1. Dulles (*Models of the Church*, Garden City, N.Y.: Doubleday, 1974) requires a method of analysis that is able ". . . to harmonize the models in such a way that their differences become complementary rather than mutually repugnant. We must refrain from so affirming any one of the models as to deny, even implicitly, what the others affirm. In this way it may become possible to gain an understanding of the Church that transcends the limitations of any given model" (p. 185). He cautions that the church should not operate as if it had a pre-ordained blueprint valid in all details. Rather, "within the myriad possibilities left open by Scripture

and tradition, the Church in every generation has to exercise options. It becomes what its leaders and its people choose to make of it" (p. 188).

2. One of Lonergan's lifelong preoccupations has been the attempt to bridge the gap between Catholicism's traditional dogmatic method and modernity's realization of the historical relativity of truth and its expression. The confusion experienced in modern Catholicism, in Lonergan's view, is not a matter of a collapse of faith but of a modern approach to theology as part of a cultural attack on what he calls a "classicist" ideal of culture. "Classicist culture, by conceiving itself normatively and universally, also had to think of itself as the one and only culture for all time. But modern culture is culture on the move. It is historicist. Because human cultures are man-made, they can be changed by man. They not only can but also should be changed. Modern man is not concerned simply to perpetuate the wisdom of his ancestors. For him the past is just the springboard to the future and the future, if it is to be good, will improve all that is good in the past and it will liquidate all that is evil. . . . Ours is a time that criticizes and debunks the past, that preaches an ideology, that looks forward to a utopia.

"It is also a time of confusion for there are many voices, many of them shrill, and most of them contradictory.

"Such a time of confusion . . . calls beliefs into question. . . . So to confusion there are easily added disorientation, disillusionment, crisis, surrender, unbelief. But . . . from the present situation Catholics are suffering more keenly than others, not indeed because their plight is worse but because up to Vatican II they were sheltered against the modern world and since Vatican II they have been exposed more and more to the chill winds of modernity" ("Belief: Today's Issue," in *A Second Collection,* Philadelphia: Westminster, 1974, p. 93).

3. Juan Luis Segundo, *A Theology for Artisans of a New Humanity,* 5 vols. (Maryknoll, N.Y.: Orbis, 1973–74).

4. Gustavo Gutiérrez, *A Theology of Liberation: History, Politics, and Salvation* (Maryknoll, N.Y.: Orbis, 1973).

5. See John Howard Yoder, *The Politics of Jesus* (Grand Rapids, Mich.: Eerdmans, 1973), pp. 64 ff.

6. For example, Yoder criticizes the standard interpretations of the gospel as giving a "personal" and not a "social" ethic. His position notes the standard interpretation: "The 'ethics of the Sermon on the Mount' is for face-to-face personal encounters; for social structures an ethic of the 'secular vocation' is needed." According to Yoder, however, "Jesus doesn't know anything about radical personalism. The personhood which he proclaims as a healing, forgiving call to all is integrated into the social novelty of the healing community" (ibid., p. 113). The entire sixth chapter ("A Trial Balance") is valuable for making the argument that a "spiritual" or "personalist" interpretation of Jesus' teaching deprives Jesus of the "Jewishness of his context" and the presence of Amos which should be "ringing in our ears."

7. In Freire, problem-solving education (in contradistinction to banking-deposit education) is a process of dialogue wherein "men develop their power to perceive critically *the way they exist* in the world *with which* and *in which* they find themselves; they come to see the world not as a static reality, but as a reality in process, in transformation" (*Pedagogy,* p. 71). If the liberator is trying to liberate human beings without authentic dialogue which leads the oppressed to awareness

that they are movers of the world and its structures, according to Freire, places the "liberator" in a dangerous position. If the liberator is not involved in authentic dialogue, he or she is dehumanized.

8. John Dominic Crossan, *In Parables: The Challenge of the Historical Jesus* (New York: Harper & Row, 1973), pp. 55 ff.

9. Ibid., p. 120.

10. Freire, *Pedagogy*, pp. 164–66.

11. John B. Cobb, Jr., *Christ in a Pluralistic Age* (Philadelphia: Westminster, 1975), p. 21.

12. In *Lumen gentium* (Dogmatic Constitution on the Church), article 5, the church's mission is a participation in the mission of Christ himself, who has given the Spirit to the church to empower it to carry on that work. "The church, consequently, equipped with the gifts of her Founder and faithfully guarding His precepts of charity, humility, and self-sacrifice, receives the mission to proclaim and to establish among all peoples the kingdom of Christ and of God. She becomes on earth the initial budding forth of that kingdom. While she slowly grows, the Church strains toward the consummation of the kingdom and, with all her strength, hopes and desires to be united in glory with her King."

13. Ancient Israel used its religious faith in the divine call improperly in failing to realize that God was calling it to a higher righteousness. According to Gerhard von Rad, the divine call in the past was illegitimately used to give confidence that Israel would be blessed in the present. The prophets, however, introduce "a fundamentally new element, which is that only acts which lie in the future are to be important for Israel's salvation. The old traditions said that Jahweh led Israel into her land, founded Zion, and established the throne of David, and this was sufficient. No prophet could any longer believe this; for between him and those founding acts hung a fiery curtain of dire judgments upon Israel, judgments which, in the prophets' opinion, had already begun; and this message of judgment had no basis in the old Jahwistic tradition" (II:185). Roman Catholic self-confidence in its institutions reminds one of nothing so much as the earlier Israelite confidence in the validity of its institutions. One might fairly wonder if what von Rad finds as the theological innovation of the prophets —a pronouncement that the old covenant was broken (II:186–87; 212–17)—might not be true *mutatis mutandis* of modern confidence in the institutional church. See von Rad's magisterial *Old Testament Theology*, Volume II: *The Theology of Israel's Prophetic Traditions* (New York: Harper & Row, 1965). Von Rad does not ask the question in the manner in which I have posed my questions about the validity of present confidence in institutions, but I think it is fair to draw the comparison between the pre-exilic Israelite faith and Catholicism's confidence in itself.

14. In Chapter Sixteen, "The Unity of Hope," Cobb notes that living "from our past" is not a real option, for, "If we seek life by clinging to past realizations, we do not live at all. It is only a question of the pace of death. The one who holds to the past and repeats it does not enliven the past but only joins it in death. However, the one who turns from the past in openness to the new finds the past restored and revitalized. The new possibility allows for the appropriation of the past in its continuing immediacy whereas the attempt to hold on to it or to repeat it does not" (p. 243). Cobb wants a reinterpretation of Christianity in this future oriented key, seeing in Christ the source of the images of hope which arise only through

"creative transformation," the code word which, according to Cobb, unlocks the meaning of Christ.

15. We have used the term "wineskin-breaking mission" to stand as a shorthand expression for two elements: (1) Christ's rupture of the standards and expectations of Judaism in his own day; and (2) the "reversal logic" of the gospels as it upsets normal human standards of judgment. Langdon Gilkey, in a most significant introduction to Christian theology available only after my own work was completed, makes substantially the same point, but from another (and perhaps clearer) point of view. Gilkey notes that humans "affirm" a certain goodness to life, but that "taken undialectically" that affirmation is false because it does not account sufficiently for the negative elements in life (estrangement, alienation, social and personal evil, etc.). Gilkey's point is that a certain pattern of affirmation, negation, and affirmation at a deeper level defines "the unique form of Christian symbolism." In the life of Jesus himself we have the life, the death, and the resurrection. This same pattern recurs in all of life, the key to Christianity being that its most basic symbol structure bears witness to faith in God's creative and re-creative power in individual, corporate, and cosmic life. The "world" tends either to affirm life as unambiguously good or evil. Christianity, on the other hand, does affirm life, but does so in the light of the experience that negative forces make an unambiguous affirmation naive; and, therefore, faith entails an act of affirmation of life's goodness, but at a deeper, chastened level. This dialectical dimension is what we are referring to in the present study when we maintain that the wineskin-breaking side of Christ's mission is a present reality and must be continually taken into account lest political or liberation theologies become naively utopian. See Gilkey, *Message and Existence: An Introduction to Christian Theology* (New York: Seabury, 1979), pp. 181–94. Gilkey is uniquely sensitive to the problem of the idolatry involved in making an undialectic act of faith in Christ (making him into a "Superman," pp. 186–87), as well as to the problem of understanding the church undialectically (pp. 233–40).

Chapter 4

1. In language which may strike moderns as quaint, one of Freytag's informants describes the liberation felt by Melanesians when they embraced the gospel: "In earlier ages we were not as we are today. A great wickedness utterly enveloped us. We lived together in great enmity. . . . When the Lord sent us His servants, hunger, fear and war were our rulers. . . . And since then [i.e., the arrival of the gospel] we have here in the brightness of the light of God a great work, a good road and secure sleep" (*Spiritual Revolution in the East*, London: Lutterworth, 1940, pp. 23–24). The Melanesians experienced the liberation as freedom from fear of sorcery, enmity with neighbors, and as a road to a better total way of life. Freytag's book may over-glamorize the successes of the missions, but it is a healthy corrective to the more common contemporary report that the missionaries were destroyers of a previously happy and peaceful way of life.

2. Paul Tillich was convinced of the importance of sacraments in the Christian life (see his *Systematic Theology*, Vol. 3, Chicago: University of Chicago Press, 1963, pp. 120–28). His explanation of how God utilizes the sacraments as vehicles of his personal communication is tied to his idea of symbol: "To put it in terms of the

theory of symbolism, the sacramental material is not a sign but a symbol. As symbols the sacramental materials are intrinsically related to what they express; they have inherent qualities (water, fire, oil, bread, wine) which makes them adequate to their symbolic function and irreplaceable. The Spirit 'uses' the powers of being in nature in order to 'enter' man's spirit. Again, it is not the quality of the materials as such which makes them media of the Spiritual presence; rather, it is their quality as brought into sacramental union. This consideration excludes both the Catholic doctrine of transubstantiation which transforms a symbol into a thing to be handled, and the reformed doctrine of the sign character of the sacramental symbol. A sacramental symbol is neither a thing nor a sign. It participates in the power of what it symbolizes, and therefore, it can be a medium of the Spirit" (p. 123).

3. See Lonergan's *Method in Theology* (New York: Herder & Herder, 1972), pp. 130–32, 267–69.

4. In the introduction to his autobiography, Gandhi says, "I simply want to tell the story of my numerous experiments with truth" (*An Autobiography: The Story of My Experiments with Truth,* Boston: Beacon, 1957, p. xii).

5. For example, see Bühlmann's Chapter Twelve, "Untapped Potential: the Laity," pp. 261–69.

Chapter 5

1. Hans von Campenhausen, *Ecclesiastical Authority and Spiritual Power in the Church of the First Three Centuries* (Stanford: Stanford University Press, 1969), pp. 293–301.

2. Hans Conzelmann, *History of Primitive Christianity* (New York: Abingdon, 1973), pp. 112–19.

3. Eduard Schillebeeckx, "The Catholic Understanding of Office in the Church," *Theological Studies* 30 (1969): 569–71.

4. Carl J. Peter, "Dimensions of *Jus Divinum* in Catholic Theology," *Theological Studies* 34 (1973): 244–45.

5. Walter J. Burghardt, "What Is a Priest?" *Way Supplements* 23 (Autumn 1974): 57.

6. Conzelmann, *History,* p. 41.

7. Von Campenhausen, *Ecclesiastical Authority,* pp. 120–21.

8. Schillebeeckx, "Catholic Understanding," pp. 568–69.

9. Ibid., pp. 570–71.

Chapter 6

1. James A. Mohler, *The Origin and the Evolution of the Priesthood* (Staten Island, N.Y.: Alba House, 1969).

2. David N. Power, *Ministers of Christ and His Church: The Theology of the Priesthood* (London: Chapman, 1969).

3. Mohler, op. cit., pp. 30–31.

4. Clement of Rome, *Epistle to the Corinthians,* chapters 36–38, and 54.

5. Father Mohler utilizes the book of J. Colson, *L'évêque dans les communautés primitives* (Paris: Cerf, 1951), asserting that in Irenaeus of Lyons we begin to have a

convergence of the Pauline and the Johannine traditions of church order. Mohler sees them as complementary. "The Pauline tradition emphasizes world unity in Christ who is the unique chief of the redeemed world without distinction of sex, status, or nationality. Thus the local churches are members of his body under the one head, Jesus Christ or his representative. . . .

"The Johannine tradition . . . emphasizes the incarnation, the Word made flesh and united to man. Thus in each community Christians gather around the living incarnate representative of Jesus Christ, the center of unity. The local presidents . . . are the chief witnesses to the apostolic tradition guarding against false teachers and presiding over their communities in cult, court and service, surrounded by their college of presbyters.

"So Paul's emphasis on the one body of the Church to the neglect of local autonomy is balanced by the local supremacy of the Johannine tradition. These are still the normal patterns in the West and the East today, although there has been a move towards decentralization in the West since Vatican II" (Mohler, *Origin*, p. 48).

6. In *The Theology of Jewish Christianity* (London: Darton, Longman and Todd, 1964), Cardinal Daniélou shows that earliest Christianity expressed itself in the context of the Jewish apocalyptic thought world. In *The Origins of Latin Christianity* (Philadelphia: Westminster, 1977) the cardinal shows how western, Latin Christianity is explicable only when the persistence of Jewish influences is taken into account. For example, this is seen in Tertullian's anxiety to overcome the Jewish element in order to create a form of Christianity adapted to the Latin mind (see Mohler, *Origins*, pp. 140–61). Analogously, Third Church Christians have their identity shaped by the reaction against Second Church understandings and models. For a contemporary example of the same dynamic found in the Latin reaction to Jewish Christianity see Choan-Seng Song's *Christian Mission in Reconstruction: An Asian Attempt* (Maryknoll, N.Y.: Orbis, 1977).

7. Cyprian of Carthage, *Epistles*, 66,8.

8. See Eduard Schillebeeckx, "The Explicit Motivation for Clerical Celibacy in the History of the Church," Chapter Two of *Celibacy* (New York: Sheed and Ward, 1968), pp. 51–72. The most detailed and important study of the question is edited by Joseph Coppens and published by the Louvain University Press (*Sacerdoce et Célibat: Études historiques et théologiques*, 1971), especially the articles by L. Legrand (*Le célibat et la continence dans l'Église primitive: leurs motivations*, pp. 333–71), and by A. M. Stickler (*L'évolution de la discipline du célibat dans l'Église en Occident de la fin de l'âge patristique au Concile de Trente*, pp. 373–42).

9. Council of Trent, "Decree on the Sacrament of Order," Canons 1–8. See Denzinger-Schönmetzer, *Enchiridion Symbolorum*, 34th ed. (Freiburg im Breisgau: Herder, 1967), Nos. 1771–78.

10. In the *Summa Theologica*, III, q. 63, a.2, it is clear that the baptismal character is passive and that of the sacrament of order is active. The former empowers one to receive and the latter to pass on grace (*nam ad tradendum aliquid aliis, requiritur potentia activa . . . ad recipiendum autem requiritur potentia passiva*). See also his *Commentary on the Book of Sentences, IV, distinctio iv, q.1, a.1*.

11. Council of Trent, "Decree on the Sacraments," Canon 8 (Denzinger-Schönmetzer, No. 160).

12. Ibid., Canon 6 (Denzinger-Schönmetzer, No. 1606).

13. George Lindbeck, "The Lutheran Doctrine of the Ministry: Catholic and Reformed," *Theological Studies* 30 (1969): 611.

Chapter 7

1. Michael Hollis, *Paternalism in the Church* (London: Oxford University Press, 1962), p. 51.

2. Burghardt, "What Is a Priest?" pp. 61–62.

3. Schillebeeckx, "Catholic Understanding," pp. 570–71.

4. "Folk Religion," like everything else in human life, is ambiguous, that is to say, partially good and noble (insofar as it expresses human transcendence and participation in the divine), partially bad and apt to lead humans to inordiante fear of or fascination with the "holy." One of the most important and delicate aspects of contextualization is the dynamic of helping the people discern the difference between these two dimensions of the religious. "Folk Religion" is enjoying new favor in liberal circles, and our own study's emphasis on contextualization is consonant with that new appraisal. Latin American and Filipino Catholicism's problems, however, ought to be a signal of what happens when aspects of Christianity are overlayed with folk religion and when a full ministry of word and sacrament is made impossible because of short-sighted ordination policies.

5. The key texts of Vatican II for the restoration of the diaconate as a permanent state are *Lumen gentium* (Dogmatic Constitution on the Church), article 29, and *Ad gentes* (Decree on the Church's Missionary Activity), article 16.

6. Carr notes that there is a clear tradition barring the ordination of women, analyzes the factors that go into the shaping of that tradition, and suggests that to be authentic to the deeper thrust of Christian faith the church must take account of the modern experience of women, one of "a new emergence into fuller personhood, central to which is an awareness of mutuality and equality with men that seeks to overcome sexual stereotyping and generally passive role models for women" (p. 73). Carr is sensitive to the question of merely ordaining women to a discredited "clerical state" and makes it clear that the sort of church and ministry women aspire to engender is not that model. She believes that the ordination of women "would further the transformation of the priesthood: by admission of those who have traditionally only served, the sign will be clear. It will transform the ministry from a predominantly cultic role to a ministerial one, from a symbol of prestige to a symbol of service, releasing the imagination of half the Church's population into fuller operation as the Church moves into the future" (pp. 72–73). See Carr's "The Church in Process: Engendering the Future," in *Women and Catholic Priesthood: An Expanded Vision,* edited by Anne Marie Gardiner (New York: Paulist Press, 1976).

7. Congregation for the Doctrine of the Faith, "Declaratio circa Quaestionem Admissionis Mulierum ad Sacerdotium Ministeriale," signed by Franjo Cardinal Seper, October 15, 1976, *Acta Apostolicae Sedis* 69 [1977]: 98–116.

8. The relevant portion of the Code reads, "Only a baptized male validly receives sacred ordination" (*Solus vir baptizatus valide recipit sacram ordinationem*). *Codex Iuris Canonici,* No. 968.

9. In an important and tightly reasoned article ("Apostolic Office: Sacrament of Christ," *Theological Studies* 36 [June 1975]: 243–64), Kilmartin says, "The

presence of Christ is given as personal presence through the faith of the Church. Therefore it obtains a certain objectivity. It is neither dependent upon the faith of the minister nor on the faith of any particular community. . . . The apostolic officer is a sacrament of the efficacious presence of Christ and the Spirit. But taking this statement a step further, and employing the Scholastic distinction between a *sacramentum, res et sacramentum, et res tantum* to express levels of significa-tion, we should more accurately say: The apostolic officer is *sacramentum* of the Church united in faith and love, which in turn as *res* is also *sacramentum* of Christ and the Spirit, the *res tantum*. In this way apostolic office is correctly ordered to the Church, sacrament of Christ, and to Christ, Sacrament of God. . . .

"A direct representation of Christ through the ministry of the Church would be possible only if there existed a ministry which could operate independently of the faith of the Church" (pp. 259–60).

Chapter 8

1. Throughout the book we have used the expression "local church" and have meant "basic community," in the sense of a small, face-to-face community. Our terminology differs somewhat from the usage of Vatican II. There the usual term for a local church is *ecclesia particularis* (i.e., "particular church") and the referent is the diocese—for example, see *Christus Dominus* (Decree on the Pastoral Office of Bishops), article 11: "The diocese is a portion of the People of God entrusted to the pastoral care of the bishop aided by his presbyterate . . . in such a way that . . . it constitutes a particular church, in which is truly present the one, holy, catholic and apostolic church of Christ" (*"ita ut . . . Ecclesiam particularem constituat"*). See also *Lumen gentium,* articles 23–26, for similar terminology.

It is my own judgment that the theology of episcopacy is better developed than that of the presbyterate. This is so, not just in the case of Vatican II teaching such as *Presbyterorum ordinis* ("Decree on the Ministry and Life of Priests"), but charac-terizes the whole of the Catholic dogmatic treatment of ministry. The episcopate received close attention at the Council. The presbyterate received only passing attention and most of what one finds in the decree is fairly conventional.

Our conversation in the book has centered on the theology of the presbyterate and the role of the presbyter in the formation of the basic communities which we have called also "local churches." It is, however, good to recall that our terminol-ogy does differ from that of the Council.

2. "The only hope in the human situation is that the 'religiousness' of men finds its true center in God, not in the many idols that appear in the course of our experience. If men are able to forget themselves enough to share with each other, to be honest under pressure and to be rational and moral enough to establish community, they must have some center of loyalty and devotion, some source of security and meaning beyond their own welfare" (*Shantung Compound: The Story of Men and Women Under Pressure*, New York: Harper & Row, 1966, p. 234).

3. See *Christus Dominus*, article 47; *Lumen gentium*, articles 18–19.

4. *Christus Dominus*, article 38.

5. Ibid., article 3.

6. Ibid., article 5.

Conclusion

1. See Ernst Troeltsch, *The Social Teaching of the Christian Churches* (Chicago: University of Chicago Press, Midway Reprints, 1976; original edition, published in 1912), pp. 87–89. One of Troeltsch's central points is that the gospel was essentially indifferent or hostile towards "the world", and thus Christian ethics is a compromise made necessary by the historical process as Christianity became the dominant religion of Europe. Monasticism in Catholicism is seen by Troeltsch to be an authentic development which helps the worldly church keep the world-denying aspects of the gospel before its eyes. Rather than live with the tension, however, the church eventually absorbed monasticism and domesticated it (see pp. 241–45).

2. Those close to Catholic mission thinking realize well that there has been great controversy about their identity among the religious orders which staff most Catholic missions. Are they, when working to establish young churches, primarily *religious* (i.e., members of a community with a set of constitutions, goals, life-style, and spirit) or are they primarily *missionaries* (i.e., members of the church's out-reach team, helping to found new communities)? The issue is not an easy one to resolve. In point of fact, most religious communities in the missions live a schizophrenic existence.

In this connection, it is interesting to read Johannes B. Metz's *Followers of Christ: Perspectives on the Religious Life* (New York: Paulist Press, 1978). Metz makes it clear that religious life should be thought of as a radical way of life: in practice, it has been co-opted by the institutional church and its members become the civil servants of the hierarchy, often themselves called to become hierarchs. "Have not the religious orders moved too far into that middle ground where everything is nicely balanced and moderate: so to speak adapted to and tamed by the institutional Church?" (p. 15). It is my contention that the confusion present today with regard to the position of religious orders will work itself out only when something like Metz's thesis—religious life is a radical way of life—is recognized. This will allow us to concentrate on the normal form of pastoral ministry by presbyters. Today the theology of the presbyterate is too clouded by issues which are important in themselves, but which throw us off the track of identifying a working model of pastoral ministry for basic communities.

See Ralph D. Winter's interesting "Protestant Mission Societies: The American Experience" in *Missiology* 8 (April 1979): 139–78, for a perceptive interpretation of the relationship of a religious order (as a *para-church structure*) to the church as a whole.

3. Troeltsch, *The Social Teaching*, pp. 1007–13.

4. Harnack's lecture on monasticism sees monasticism at a dead end in the years before the Reformation. Then the Jesuit movement arrived and aided in the process of the church achieving domination over the state where Protestantism did not overcome Catholicism. One need not subscribe to Harnack's anti-Jesuit and anti-Catholic attitudes to realize a truth in what he says; the modern "congregations" or "orders", which dominate the work of the "missions", tend to guard the present ecclesiastical order. Harnack sees these modern orders ("those elastic and pliant creations in which the spirit of the Jesuit Order has found a point of contact

with the institutions and needs of modern society" [pp. 113–14]) as part of the church's opposition to the culture of the Renaissance and the Reformation, in other words to modernity (see Adolf Harnack, *Monasticism: Its Ideals and History* [London: Williams and Norgate, 1913], pp. 109–14).

Bibliography

Ahrens, Theodor. "Christian Syncretism: A Study of the Southern Madang District." *Catalyst* 4 (1974): 3–40.

Berger, Peter L. *Facing Up to Modernity: Excursions in Society, Politics and Religion.* New York: Basic Books, 1971.

Bergquist, James, and Manickam, P. Kambar. *The Crisis of Dependency in Third World Ministries: A Critique of Inherited Missionary Forms in India.* Madras, India: The Christian Literature Society, 1974.

Bernard, John Henry. "The Cyprianic Doctrine of the Ministry." In *Essays on the Early History of the Church and Its Ministry*, edited by H. B. Swete, pp. 215–62. London: Macmillan, 1918.

Bläser, Peter. "Valid Eucharist Without Valid Ordination?" *Theology Digest* 21 (1973): 39–45.

Bovenmars, Jan. *Ordained Ministry from Trent to Vatican II.* Bomana, Holy Spirit Seminary, Papua New Guinea. Privately printed, 1974.

Bowman, S. Loren. "Some Contributions to Planning the Future of Theological Education." *Theological Education* 11 (1974): 23–49.

Brown, Raymond E. *Priest and Bishop: Biblical Reflections.* London: Chapman, 1970.

———. "Priestly Character and Sacramental Ordination." *The Priest* (February 1975).

Bühlmann, Walbert. *The Coming of the Third Church: An Analysis of the Present and the Future of the Church.* Maryknoll, N.Y.: Orbis, 1977.

Bunnik, R. J. "The Question of Married Priests." *Cross Currents* (1965): 409–31; (1966): 81–112.

Burghardt, Walter. "What is a Priest?" *Way Supplements* 23 (1974): 55–67.

———, and Thompson, William G., eds. *Why the Church?* New York: Paulist Press, 1977.

———, ed. *Woman: New Dimensions.* New York: Paulist Press, 1977.

Burridge, Kenelm. *New Heaven, New Earth: A Study of Millenarian Activities.* New York: Schocken, 1969.

Burrows, William R. "Theologizing in the Melanesian Context Today." *Verbum SVD* 18 (1977): 89–109.

Campenhausen, Hans von. *Ecclesiastical Authority in the Church of the First Three Centuries.* Stanford: Stanford University Press, 1969.

"Christ in Melanesia: Exploring Theological Issues." Special issue of *Point.* Goroka, Papua New Guinea: Melanesian Institute, 1977.

Cobb, John B., Jr. *Christ in a Pluralistic Age.* Philadelphia: Westminster, 1975.

Coe, Shoki. "In Search of Renewal in Theological Education." *Theological Education* 9 (1973): 233–43.

Colson, Jean. *La function diaconale aux origines de l'Église.* Brussels: Desclée de Brouwer, 1960.

169

Congar, Yves J. M. "My Path-Findings in the Theology of Laity and Ministries."
    The Jurist 32 (1972): 169–88.
———. *Lay People in the Church*. Westminster, Maryland: Newman, 1965.
Congregation for the Doctrine of the Faith. "Declaratio circa Quaestionem Ad-
    missionis Mulierum ad Sacerdotium Ministeriale." *Acta Apostolicae Sedis* 69
    (1977): 98–116.
Conzelmann, Hans. *History of Primitive Christianity*. New York: Abingdon, 1973.
Coppens, Joseph, ed. *Sacerdoce et Célibat: Études Historiques et Théologiques*. Louvain:
    Editions Peeters, 1971.
Crossan, John Dominic. *In Parables: The Challenge of the Historical Jesus*. New York:
    Harper & Row, 1973.
Crouzel, Henri. "The Sacerdotal Character and Tradition." *Theology Digest* 23
    (1975): 157–63.
Crowley, Patrick. "The Diaconate for the Present Age." *The Clergy Review* 58
    (1974): 787–803.
Crowley, Paul. "Celibacy and Ministry." *African Ecclesiastical Review* 17 (1975):
    85–92.
———. "Christian Community and Ministry: Reflections on the AMECEA Ple-
    nary 1976." *African Ecclesiastical Review* 17 (1977): 201–8.
———. "The Ministry in Africa." *The Clergy Review* 60 (1977): 26–32.
Daly, John. "Caught Between Cultures." *African Ecclesiastical Review* 17 (1975):
    93–100.
Daniélou, Jean. *The Origins of Latin Christianity*. Philadelphia: Westminster, 1977.
———. *The Theology of Jewish Christianity*. London: Darton, Longman & Todd,
    1964.
Denzinger, Henricus, and Schönmetzer, Adolfus, eds. *Enchiridion Symbolorum*.
    34th edition. Freiburg im Breisgau: Herder, 1967.
Dillon, Richard J. "Ministry: Stewardship of Tradition." *Theology Digest* 20 (1972):
    108–15.
Dulles, Avery. *Models of the Church*. Garden City, N.Y.: Doubleday, 1974.
Echlin, Edward P. *The Deacon in the Church*. Staten Island: Alba House, 1971.
Emerton, Ephraim, trans. & ed. *The Letters of St. Boniface*. New York: Columbia
    University Press, 1940.
"Eucharist and Ministry: A Lutheran-Roman Catholic Statement." *Theological
    Studies* 31 (1970): 712–34.
Freire, Paulo. *Education for Critical Consciousness*. New York: Sheed and Ward,
    1964.
———. *Pedagogy of the Oppressed*. New York: Seabury, 1970.
Freytag, Walter. *Spiritual Revolution in the East*. London: Lutterworth, 1940.
Gandhi, Mohandas K. *An Autobiography: My Experiments with Truth*. Boston:
    Beacon, 1957.
Gardiner, Anne Marie, ed. *Women and the Catholic Priesthood: An Expanded View*.
    New York: Paulist, 1977.
Gilkey, Langdon. *Message and Existence: An Introduction to Christian Theology*. New
    York: Seabury, 1979.
———. *Reaping the Whirlwind: A Christian Interpretation of History*. New York:
    Seabury, 1976.
———. *Shantung Compound: The Story of Men and Women Under Pressure*. New York
    Harper & Row, 1966.

Gill, R. "Localization Review: Sociology of Localization of the Church in Papua New Guinea." *Catalyst* 3 (1973): 37–60.

Glasner, Peter E. *The Sociology of Secularization: A Critique of a Concept.* London: Routledge & Kegan Paul, 1977.

Grant, Robert M. *Augustus to Constantine: The Thrust of the Christian Movement into the Roman World.* London: Collins, 1971.

———. *Early Christianity and Society.* New York: Harper & Row, 1977.

Gryson, Roger. *Les origines du célibat ecclésiastique.* Gembloux, Belgium: Editions J. Duculot, 1970.

Gutiérrez, Gustavo. *A Theology of Liberation: History, Politics and Salvation.* Maryknoll, N.Y.: Orbis, 1973.

———, and Shaull, Richard. *Liberation and Change.* Atlanta: John Knox Press, 1977.

Harnack, Adolf. *Monasticism: Its Ideals and History.* London: Williams and Norgate, 1913.

Hastings, Adrian. "Africa: The Church and the Ministry." *The Clergy Review* 58 (1973): 21–35; 116–29; 176–84.

———. "The Ministry in Africa Today." *African Ecclesiastical Review* 12 (1970): 3–10.

———. *Mission and Ministry.* London: Sheed & Ward, 1971.

Hinchcliff, Peter. *Cyprian of Carthage and the Unity of the Christian Church.* London: Chapman, 1974.

Hollis, Michael. *Paternalism in the Church.* London: Oxford University Press, 1962.

Janssen, Hermann. "Religion and Secularization." *Catalyst* 2 (1972): 50–68.

Kilmartin, Edward J. "Apostolic Office: Sacrament of Christ." *Theological Studies* 36 (June 1975): 243–64.

Kok, Theo. *On Ministry in an Independent Papua New Guinea: Some Tentative Outlines.* Bomana, Holy Spirit Seminary, Papua New Guinea. Privately printed, 1973.

Koyama, Kosuke. *Waterbuffalo Theology.* Maryknoll, N.Y.: Orbis, 1974.

Lemaire, André. *Les ministères aux origines de l'Église.* Paris: Editions du Cerf, 1971.

Lindbeck, George A. "The Lutheran Doctrine of the Ministry: Catholic and Reformed." *Theological Studies* 30 (1969): 588–612.

Lobinger, F. "Why We Should Ordain Proven Christians." *African Ecclesiastical Review* 17 (1975): 346–51.

Lonergan, Bernard. *Method in Theology.* New York: Herder, 1972.

———. *A Second Collection.* Philadelphia: Westminster, 1974.

Lynch, John E. "Critique of the Celibacy Law in the Catholic Church from the Period of the Reform Councils," *Concilium* 78 (1972): 57–75.

———. "Marriage and the Celibacy of the Clergy, the Discipline of the Western Church: An Historico-Canonical Synopsis," *The Jurist* 32 (1972): 14–38; 189–212.

McGregor, Don. "Basic Papua New Guinea Assumptions: Difficulties in Communicating the Christian Message in Melanesia." *Catalyst* 6 (1976): 175–213.

McKenzie, John L. *A Theology of the Old Testament.* Garden City, N.Y.: Doubleday, Image Books, 1976.

McSorley, Harry. "Some Forgotten Truths about the Petrine Ministry." *Journal of Ecumenical Studies* 11 (Spring 1974): 208–37.

Martin, David. *The Dilemmas of Contemporary Religion.* New York: St. Martin's Press, 1978.

————. *A General Theory of Secularization*. Oxford: Basil Blackwell, 1978.

————. *The Religious and the Secular*. New York: Schocken, 1969.

Meer, Haye van der. *Women Priests in the Catholic Church?* Philadelphia: Temple University Press, 1973.

Mende, Tibor. *From Aid to Recolonization: Lessons of a Failure*. New York: Pantheon, 1973.

Mercado, Leonardo N. *Elements of Filipino Philosophy*. Tacloban City, Philippines: Divine Word University, 1974.

————. *Elements of Filipino Theology*. Tacloban City, Philippines: Divine Word University, 1974.

Miguens, Manuel, *Church Ministries in New Testament Times*, Arlington Virginia: Christian Culture Press, 1976.

Metz, Johannes B. *Followers of Christ: Perspectives on the Religious Life*. New York: Paulist, 1978.

"The Ministerial Priesthood." Document of 1971 Synod of Bishops. Washington, D.C.: U.S. Catholic Conference, 1972.

Misner, Paul. "Papal Primacy in a Pluriform Polity." *Journal of Ecumenical Studies* 11 (Spring 1974): 239–61.

Mohler, James A. *The Origin and Evolution of the Priesthood*. Staten Island, N.Y.: Alba House, 1970.

Momis, John. "Values for Involvement." *Catalyst* 5 (1975): 11–18.

Nayagam, Xavier S. Thani. *The Carthaginian Clergy during the Episcopate of Saint Cyprian*. Tuticorin, S. India: Tamil Literature Society, 1950.

Nolan, Richard T., ed. *The Diaconate Now*. Washington: Corpus, 1968.

Newbigin, Lesslie. *Honest Religion for Secular Man*. London: SCM, 1966.

Nyamiti, Charles. *African Theology: Its Nature, Problems and Methods*. Kampala, Uganda: GABA Publications, 1971.

————. *The Scope of African Theology*. Kampala, Uganda: GABA Publications, 1973.

Peter, Carl J. "Dimensions of *Jus Divinum* in Catholic Theology." *Theological Studies* 34 (1973): 227–50.

Power, David N. *Ministers of Christ and His Church: The Theology of the Priesthood*. London: Chapman, 1969.

Rad, Gerhard von. *Old Testament Theology*. 2 vols. New York: Harper & Row, 1962–65.

Rahner, Karl. *Bishops: Their Status and Function*. Baltimore: Helicon, 1963.

————. "The Point of Departure in Theology for Determining the Nature of Priestly Office"; "Theological Reflections on the Priestly Image of Today and Tomorrow"; "On the Diaconate." *Theological Investigations*, vol. 12. New York: Seabury, 1974 (pp. 31–38; 39–60; 61–80).

————. "The Teaching of the Second Vatican Council on the Diaconate." *Theological Investigations*, vol. 10. New York: Herder & Herder, 1973, pp. 222–32.

————. "The Theology of the Restoration of the Diaconate." *Theological Investigations*, vol. 5. Baltimore: Helicon, 1966.

Sacred Congregation for Catholic Education. *The Theological Formation of Future Priests*. Vatican City: Polyglot Press, 1976.

Schillebeeckx, Eduard. *Celibacy*. New York: Sheed & Ward, 1968.

————. "The Catholic Understanding of Office in the Church." *Theological Studies* 30 (1969): 567–87.

Schütte, Heinz. *Amt, Ordination und Sukzession.* Düsseldorf: Patmos Verlag, 1974.

Segundo, Juan Luis. *The Liberation of Theology.* Maryknoll, N.Y.: Orbis, 1976.

―――. *A Theology for Artisans of a New Humanity.* 5 vols. Maryknoll, N.Y.: Orbis, 1973–74.

Shanks, T. Howland and Smith, Brian. "Liberation Ecclesiology: Praxis, Theory, Praxis." *Theological Studies* 38 (1977): 3–38.

Song, Choan-Seng. *Christian Mission in Reconstruction: An Asian Attempt.* Maryknoll, N.Y.: Orbis, 1977.

Stuhlmueller, Carroll, ed. *Women and the Priesthood: Future Directions.* Collegeville, Minn.: Liturgical Press, 1978.

Tillich, Paul. *The Socialist Decision.* New York: Harper & Row, 1977.

―――. *Systematic Theology.* 3 vols. Chicago: University of Chicago Press, 1951–63.

―――. *Theology of Culture.* New York: Oxford University Press, 1959.

Tracy, David. *Blessed Rage for Order: The New Pluralism in Theology.* New York: Seabury, 1975.

Troeltsch, Ernst. *The Social Teaching of the Christian Churches.* Chicago: University of Chicago Press, Midway Reprints, 1976.

Wiles, Maurice. "The Theological Legacy of St. Cyprian." *Journal of Ecclesiastical History* 14 (1962): 139–49.

Winter, Ralph D. "Protestant Mission Societies: The American Experience." *Missiology* 8 (April 1979): 139–78.

Yoder, John Howard. *The Politics of Jesus.* Grand Rapids: Eerdmans, 1973.

Zollitsch, Robert. *Amt und Funktion des Priesters.* Freiburg im Breisgau: Herder, 1974.

Index

Compiled by James Sullivan